FROM CALF FRIES TO CAVIAR

by Janel Franklin & Sue Vaughn

by
Janel Franklin
Sue Vaughn

Publishers of
CALF FRIES to CAVIAR
and
'CROSS THE BORDER

Library of Congress No. 88-091388
ISBN 0-9610956-1-X

Additional copies may be obtained at the cost of $16.95
per book, plus $3.00 postage and handling.
Texas residents add appropriate sales tax. Send to:

Jan-Su Publications
1012 North 9th
Lamesa, Texas 79331
or call:
806-872-8667

First Printing   1989
Second Printing   1990
Third Printing   1991
Fourth Printing   1993
Fifth Printing   1995
Sixth Printing   1999

Printed in the USA by

WIMMER
The Wimmer Companies
Memphis
1-800-548-2537

FOREWORD

Cooking for one's family and friends is one of the great joys of life. Good food...Good friends...Good times...there is a particular bond between family and friends who dine together. The recipes offered in this book are not just examples of good food. They are a great example of bonding. They have been enthusiastically given to us by people from all over the world. We have tried them all, liked them, and now have that special warm feeling for these people that can only be created with good food.

We have compiled this cookbook with the same guidelines that we prepared **CALF FRIES TO CAVIAR**. Simple, easy to prepare, step-by-step format. Make-ahead and microwave recipes for those people with busy lifestyles. "Oldies but goodies". Recipes you will enjoy cooking and eating.

We would like to acknowledge the people, many of whom we have never met, for sending their delicious recipes. A particularly big "Thank you," to Joe Belt, for another outstanding cover. To Sheryn Jones, our coordinator and mentor.

And finally, much love to our families for their love and support. And especially to our husbands Don and Harold Gene, who are always enthusiastically ready to taste absolutely anything at any time of the day or night.

Janel and Sue

CALF FRIES

CALF FRIES, or "Mountain Oysters", are the delicacies eaten on the working ranches of Texas. They are the part of the bull removed to make the animal a steer. After a long day of "working" cattle, the cowboys will clean the Calf Fries, leaving the membrane intact. They will throw them on the branding fire, sit back, and wait for them to pop open. (Indicating they are done.) The cowboys peel back the membrane and savor the delicious meat.

We have a little bit more sophisticated way of cooking them in our kitchens. We fry them in batters, crumbs, or cornmeal coatings. In the home or on the open range, they are DELICIOUS!!!!

CAVIAR

CAVIAR is roe of the sturgeon treated by heating, straining, and salting. The best caviar is made only in winter, and one of the causes of its high price is the great difficulty in preserving it. It should be spread on toast and flavored with a few drops of lemon squeezed over it, and is usually eaten as hors d'oeuvres.

TABLE OF CONTENTS

Party Food/Beverages

CALF FRIES KANSAS LEGION STYLE

We felt this recipe worth repeating from CALF FRIES TO CAVIAR.
It is still the best one we have run across.

Clean, skin and freeze **CALF FRIES** whole. To cook, partially thaw. They are much easier to cut into bite-size pieces before completely thawed.
Dip each piece in a mixture of . . . 1 dozen **EGGS**
　　　　　　　　　　　　　　　　　　1 quart **BUTTERMILK**
Then dip in . . . . 3 cups **CRACKER MEAL**
　　　　　　　　　　　　　　　　　　1 cup **FLOUR** seasoned with
　　　　　　　　　　　　　　　　　　　BLACK PEPPER

Deep fry in hot shortening until crisp and brown. Drain on paper towels and serve with Kansas Treat.

KANSAS TREAT: Combine 1 quart **CATSUP,** ½ jar **HORSERADISH,** 3 tablespoons **WORCESTERSHIRE SAUCE** and **HOT PEPPERS** to taste. (More horseradish, if you prefer, and the peppers are optional.)

COTTON PICKIN' DIP: Combine 1 cup **MAYONNAISE,** ½ cup (wet) **HORSERADISH,** ½ teaspoon **ACCENT,** 2 tablespoons **LEMON JUICE,** and ½ teaspoon **SALT.** Serve either hot or cold. (Adjust horseradish to your taste, but the sauce should speak with authority!)

MEXICAN QUESO: Heat until melted, 1 can **RO-TEL** (tomatoes and chopped chilies), 1 pound **VELVEETA CHEESE,** and 2 **TOMATOES,** chopped. Serve warm. This dip is especially good with leftover cold **CALF FRIES.**

CAVIAR

Serve **CAVIAR** (3 to 4 ounces), chilled and nestled in a bowl of crushed **ICE.**
Surround with tiny bowls of . . . . . 2 **EGGS,** hard boiled and
　　　　　　　　　　　　　　　　　　shredded
　　　　　　　　　　　　　　　　　1 **ONION,** minced
　　　　　　　　　　　　　　　　　　SOUR CREAM or **YOGURT**
　　　　　　　　　　　　　　　　　　SWEET BUTTER
　　　　　　　　　　　　　　　　　　LEMON WEDGES, seeded

Serve with thin-sliced **WHITE** and **BROWN PARTY BREAD, UN-SALTED CRACKERS,** and **COCKTAILS.**

CAVIAR PIE

Combine . . . . 1 package (8 oz.) **CREAM
CHEESE**
1 cup **SOUR CREAM**

Beat until smooth and divide into 2 compote dishes.
Hard-boil 2 **EGGS.** Separately chop **EGG WHITES** and **YOLKS** and
sprinkle with 2 teaspoons **LEMON JUICE.**
Layer over cream cheese . . . . 1 medium **ONION,** minced
1 jar (3½ oz.) **WHITEFISH ROE
CAVIAR EGGS**

Refrigerate. Serve with **CRACKERS.**

YIELD: 10 TO 12 SERVINGS.

RED RAIDER "TOMATERS"
Red and blacks.

Wash thoroughly . . . . 24 **CHERRY TOMATOES**

Cut a thin slice from top of each tomato and carefuly scoop out the pulp.
Discard pulp. Invert shells on paper towels to drain.
Combine and mix until
smooth . . . . 8 ounces **CREAM CHEESE,**
softened
¼ cup **MAYONNAISE**
¼ plus 2 Tbsp. chopped **GREEN
ONIONS**

Spoon or pipe mixture into the tomato shells. Top each stuffed tomato
with a small amount of well drained **BLACK CAVIAR.** Serve with remaining caviar.

YIELD: 2 DOZEN.

INTERESTING CHANGE: *For appetizers, dips and
salads, use shells of pineapple, cantalope or other melons. Can also serve as table decorations.*

9

TEXAS CAVIAR
Clara Lou Sawyer's New Years Special Dip

Rinse and drain well . . . . 1 qt. (32 oz.) **BLACK-EYED PEAS,**
cooked
Add . . . . 1 small **ONION,** minced
1 Tbsp. fresh **GREEN CHILI**
PEPPER, minced
Add . . . . 1 large clove **GARLIC,** crushed
½ cup **RED WINE VINEGAR**
⅓ cup **OIL**
½ tsp. **SALT**
½ tsp. **SUGAR**
¼ tsp. freshly ground **BLACK**
PEPPER

Mix all ingredients. Cover and refrigerate 2 days. Before serving, garnish with **PIMENTOS.** Will keep up to 2 weeks–if folks will let it last that long.

MEXICAN HOT DIP
One of those short notice "GOODIES."

Cook until browned . . . . 1 pound **GROUND BEEF,**
very lean
Add . . . . ½ cup **ONION,** chopped
Cook until tender and add . . . . 1 can (8 oz.) **TOMATO SAUCE**
¼ cup **TOMATO CATSUP**
1 package (8 oz.) **CREAM**
CHEESE
½ cup **PARMESAN CHEESE,**
grated
1 clove **GARLIC,** minced
1 tsp. **OREGANO,** (opt.)
1 tsp. **SUGAR**
SALT and **PEPPER**

Stir over low heat or microwave until cheese melts. Serve warm with **CORN CHIPS**.

YIELD: 1 QUART.

"MEXICO BAR" CHILI CON QUESO
Serve with fresh, warm salted **TOSTADA CHIPS.**

Heat in microwave until
melted, stirring at 1½ minute
intervals . . . .   1 pound **VELVEETA CHEESE,**
cubed
2 ounces **MONTEREY JACK
CHEESE,** grated
2 ounces **CHEDDAR CHEESE,**
grated
½ cup **ONION,** diced
1 **TOMATO,** finely chopped
1 clove **GARLIC,** minced
¼ bunch **CILANTRO,** chopped
1 tsp. **CHILI POWDER**
1 tsp. **CUMIN**
1 tsp. **BLACK PEPPER**
½ cup **HALF AND HALF CREAM**

Serve in chafing dish.

CHILI CON QUESO

Place in microwave-safe bowl . . .   3 Tbsp. **OIL**
½ cup **ONION,** chopped
1 clove **GARLIC,** minced
1 tsp. **CHILI POWDER**
Cook on high 3 minutes or until **ONION** is tender-crisp.
Add . . . .   1 can (14 oz.) **WHOLE
TOMATOES,** drained
and chopped
¼ tsp. **SUGAR**
1 can (4 oz.) **GREEN CHILIES,**
drained and chopped
Bring to a boil. Add . . . .   4 ounces **CHEDDAR CHEESE,**
grated
4 ounces **MONTEREY JACK
CHEESE,** grated

Heat until cheeses are melted. Serve immediately with **TORTILLA
CHIPS.**

PEQUIN SAUCE

This is our world traveler, Julie Sedberry's, favorite.

Place on cookie-sheet . . . . 1 small package **PEQUINS** (small round red peppers)

Roast in 400 degree oven for 1 minute. Stir. Roast 1 minute longer. Crush between layers of wax paper.

Blend on medium speed with . . . . 2 cans **STEWED TOMATOES**
4 chopped **GREEN ONIONS** with tops
½ tsp. **SALT**
½ tsp. **ACCENT**
GARLIC POWDER to taste

Refrigerate until ready to serve. So good with **CORN TORTILLAS.**

GOOOOOD HOT STUFF

Best when eaten on Jack Givens porch in Ruidoso!

Chop or dice . . . . 2 ripe **TOMATOES**
½ **ONION** red, if available
1 fresh **JALAPENO PEPPER**
Add to taste . . . . **LEMON JUICE**
GARLIC SALT
SEASONED SALT (just a little)

Stir together and place in the refrigerator at least 1 hour. Serve with **TORTILLA CHIPS.**

PRAIRIE FIRE

Rowena Conner often uses this as "A gift from my kitchen."

Heat together until cheese is
melted . . . . 2 cans **FRITO BEAN DIP**
¼ pound **BUTTER** (do not use margarine)
½ pound **SHARP CHEDDAR CHEESE,** grated
1 medium **ONION,** diced
1 can (4 oz.) **WHOLE CHILIES,** (chop and leave a few veins and seeds if you want it **HOT.**)
1 can (4 oz.) **WHOLE JALAPENOS,** chopped

Serve in chafing or other warming-dish with wide **CORN CHIPS** for dipping.

SCRUMPTIOUS ASPARAGUS DIP

Place in blender . . . .   1 can (14½ oz.) **ASPARAGUS,**
drained
½ cup **SOUR CREAM**
¼ tsp. **HOT SAUCE**
1 tsp. **DRIED DILL WEED**
1 tsp. **SEASONED SALT**

Whip until smooth. (Add more **SEASON** to taste.) Serve with **CORN CHIPS.**

GOURMET SHRIMP DIP
Must be prepared ahead of time.

Blend well . . . .   8 ounces **COTTAGE CHEESE,**
small curd
½ cup **MAYONNAISE**
4 to 6 ounces **FROZEN** or
FRESH SHRIMP, cooked
and chopped
1 small **ONION,** minced
⅛ tsp. **GARLIC SALT**
½ tsp. **WORCESTERSHIRE SAUCE**
¾ tsp. **PREPARED MUSTARD**
½ tsp. **CELERY SEED**

Cover and refrigerate at least 5 hours. Serve with **CRACKERS** or **CHIPS.**

GAMBLERS DIP
Betty House gave this to us in Las Vegas.

Grind in food grinder . . . .   2 pounds **VELVEETA CHEESE**
1 medium **ONION**
5 fresh **JALAPENO PEPPERS,**
(remove seeds)
Put into large bowl of mixer
Add . . . .   1 pint **MAYONNAISE,** (at room
temperature)

Now just beat thunder out of it. This makes a large batch. Keeps indefinitely in refrigerator.

GREEN ONION DIP

Cream together . . . . 1 pkg. (8 oz.) **CREAM CHEESE**
                                1 carton (8 oz.) **SOUR CREAM**
Add . . . . ½ tsp. **SALT**
                                4 pkgs. **GREEN ONION** mix

Let set 2 hours. Serve with **CORN CHIPS,** or your favorite **CRACKERS.**

AVOCADO DIP
This is excellent.

Mash and blend well . . . . 3 large **AVOCADOS**
                                3 Tbsp. **LEMON JUICE**
Add . . . . ½ **ONION,** chopped
                                1 **TOMATO,** chopped
                                1 cup **LETTUCE,** chopped
                                3 Tbsp. **PICANTE SAUCE**
Add to taste . . . . **GARLIC SALT**
                                PEPPER

Mix well and serve with **TORTILLA CHIPS.**

SEAFOOD SPREAD
Pam Guettner serves this often.

Soften and spread on plate . . . . . . 1 pkg. (8 oz.) **CREAM CHEESE**
Spread evenly with . . . . 1 small jar **RED COCKTAIL**
                                SAUCE
Drain and spread over sauce . . . . . 1 can **CRABMEAT**

Serve with assorted **CRACKERS.**

VARIATION:
Drain one can small **SHRIMP** and use to replace crabmeat.

FESTIVE SWIRLS
Make the day before. Pop in microwave for one minute before serving.

Mix together . . . . 1 can (4 oz.) **MUSHROOM PIECES AND STEMS,** drained and chopped
6 slices **BACON,** fried crisp and crumbled
½ tsp. **GARLIC POWDER**
4 Tbsp. **MAYONNAISE**

Set aside.
Have ready to spread . . . . 6 ounces **CREAM CHEESE**
Remove *2 triangles* from . . . . 1 can (8 count) **CRESCENT ROLLS**

(Put remaining **CRESCENT DOUGH** in the refrigerator to keep it from getting sticky.) Be careful not to separate. Keep pieces connected in rectangular shape. Slightly pat out the perforation. Spread a layer of cream cheese over the rectangle of dough. Then spread ¼ of the mushroom mixture over the cream cheese. Roll the dough lengthwise. Refrigerate the roll. Repeat procedure with remaining crescent dough. When all are made, carefully slice into ½-inch pieces. Place the slices on a greased cookie sheet. Brush each slice with *BEATEN EGG WHITE and sprinkle* with *POPPY SEEDS.* Bake at 375-degrees for 8 to 10 minutes or until lightly browned. Serve warm. Store leftovers in an airtight container in the refrigerator. These may be frozen. Heat the swirls for a minute or two in microwave before serving.

YIELD: 30 SWIRLS.

CHILIES RELLENOS SQUARES

Sprinkle in a greased 8-inch
square baking dish . . . . 2 cans **GREEN CHILIES,** drained and chopped
3 cups grated **MONTEREY JACK CHEESE**
Pour over cheese . . . . 4 **EGGS,** well beaten

Bake in preheated 300-degree oven until center is firm. Remove from oven. Place pan on a wire rack to cool for a few minutes. Cut into squares. (May cover tightly and refrigerate for up to 3 days. Reheat by baking in a slow oven, 300-degrees, for 15 minutes.)

YIELD: APPROXIMATELY 15 2-INCH SQUARES

MEXICAN PINWHEELS
They are wonderful...NO BAKING.

Mix well..................... 8 ounces **CHEDDAR CHEESE,**
grated
8 ounces **CREAM CHEESE,**
softened
8 ounces **SOUR CREAM**
4 ounces **RIPE OLIVES,** diced
4 ounces **GREEN CHILIES,** diced
SEASONING SALT
Have on hand .... **FLOUR TORTILLAS**

Spread mixture on tortillas. Spread very thin. Roll up like a jelly roll.
Chill. Cut into 1-inch pieces.

VARIATIONS: Add minced **JALAPENOS,** to taste.
Omit 4 Tbsp. **SOUR CREAM** and add 4 Tbsp. chunky **PICANTE.**
Dice and add 2 fresh **GREEN ONIONS,** include tops.
Create any of your own combinations of above ingredients. They are all
good.

HAWAIIAN CHEESE BALL
When in Hawaii, make with fresh PINEAPPLE.

Mix together .... 16 ounces **CREAM CHEESE,**
room temperature
1 Tbsp. **SEASONED SALT**
2 Tbsp. **ONION,** finely chopped
¼ cup **BELL PEPPER,** chopped
1 can (8½ oz.) **CRUSHED
PINEAPPLE,** drained
1 cup **PECANS,** finely chopped

Mix well. Chill. To serve, shape mixture into a ball and roll in 1 cup
finely chopped **PECANS.** Or put the mixture in a dish, chill and serve it
with a spoon or knife to spread on **CRACKERS.**

SOFT TORTILLAS: *To make tortillas more pliable,
warm in oven a few minutes. (Be careful or they will
become dry and brittle).*

16

CHUTNEY CHEESE BALL

The combination of flavors makes this recipe one of our top ten.
VERY GOOD!

Mix well...................... 24 ounces **CREAM CHEESE**
                                    1 cup **SOUR CREAM**
                                    1 cup **RAISINS,** chopped
                                    1 cup **SALTED PEANUTS,** chopped
                                    8 slices **BACON,** cook very crisp, drain well, and crumble
                                    ½ cup **GREEN ONION,** chopped, tops, also
                                    4 tsp. **CURRY POWDER,** adjust to your own taste

Shape into large balls. Wrap and refrigerate. Before serving, top with **CHUTNEY.** Sprinkle with **COCONUT** and **PARSLEY.** Serve with **UNSALTED CRACKERS.**

PEGGY SCOTT'S CHEESE BALL

Compliments of Jenny Dyer.

Use hands to blend .... 16 ounces **CREAM CHEESE,** softened
                                    1 can (8½ oz.) **CRUSHED PINEAPPLE,** drained
                                    1½ cups **PECANS,** finely chopped
                                    ¼ cup **BELL PEPPER,** finely chopped
                                    2 Tbsp. **ONION,** finely chopped
                                    SALT
                                    Pinch of **PARSLEY**

Shape into ball or log. Chill. Roll in ½ cup finely chopped **PECANS.** Decorate. Serve.

FRIED CHEESE

Cut into ¼-inch sticks........... 1 pound **MOZZARELLA CHEESE**
Dip sticks into .... ½ cup **FLOUR**
Then dip into .... 2 **EGGS,** slightly beaten
Roll in....................... 1 cup finely crushed dry **BREADCRUMBS**

Fry in ½-inch deep **OIL** on medium heat until browned on all sides. NOTE: To keep cheese from melting during frying, keep very cold in the refrigerator.

FIGGIN SCOWS
We have no idea what the name means. But we like them!

Brown lightly .... 1 pound **HOT SAUSAGE**
                              1 pound **GROUND BEEF**
Add and stir until melted ...... 1 pound grated **VELVEETA CHEESE**
                              OREGANO

Mix well and spread on **BREAD ROUNDS**. (May use regular **BREAD** and cut circles with biscuit cutter.) Place under broiler for a few minutes to brown. (If you make these ahead of time and freeze, thaw and brown under broiler. Do not brown before freezing.)

VEGETARIAN PIZZA
Tasty appetizer from the kitchen of Linda Huffaker.

Place 2 cans **CRESCENT ROLLS** on ungreased cookie sheet. Pat out the seams to make one solid crust. Prick with fork real good. Bake for 20 minutes at 375-degrees. Let completely cool.
Spread with mixture of .... 8 ounces **CREAM CHEESE,** softened
                               ½ cup **MAYONNAISE**
                               ½ cup **SOUR CREAM**
                               1 pkg. **HIDDEN VALLEY SALAD DRESSING MIX,** dry

Spread on cooked dough. Top with your favorite **RAW VEGETABLES**. (Use enough vegetables for the topping to be *very thick*.)
Our favorites:
Diced: **GREEN ONIONS,** tops also, **BROCCOLI, CARROTS, FRESH MUSHROOMS, CAULIFLOWER, YELLOW SQUASH.**

Refrigerate until time to serve. Cut into squares. This is almost a meal. In fact, this is all we have, at times.

TASTY SNACKER CRACKERS
You will want to keep these in cupboard—all the time!

Cover 2 cookie sheets with foil. Place **SALTINE CRACKERS** side-by-side on cookie sheets. (About 2½ packs.) Brush with melted **BUTTER**. Sprinkle 8 ounces **SHARP CHEDDAR CHEESE** over **CRACKERS**. Sprinkle sparingly with **CAYENNE PEPPER** and **PAPRIKA**. Place under broiler until cheese melts. Put in 180- degree oven for 5 hours. Break apart while still warm. Store in dry place.

CHEESE WAFERS

Even the little ones can help prepare these appetizers.

Blend together ....   1 cup **MARGARINE**, softened
   2 cups **SHARP CHEDDAR CHEESE**, grated
   2 cups **FLOUR**, sifted
   ⅛ tsp. **CAYENNE PEPPER**
   Dash of **SALT**
Mix well. **FOLD** in ....   2 cups **RICE KRISPIES**

Roll in balls the size of marbles. Place on ungreased cookie sheet. Mash with fork, dipped in **FLOUR.** Bake 10 minutes until lightly browned. Freezes well.

YIELD: APPROXIMATELY 120.

ARMADILLO EGGS

The most "goodest" and "funest" recipe in the cookbook.

Wash and drain ....   2 cans (11 oz. ea.) whole **MILD PICKLED JALAPENO PEPPERS**, devein and remove seeds.

Set aside.
Grate ....   1 pound **CHEDDAR CHEESE**
Stuff **PEPPERS** and add rest of
   cheese to ....   1 pound regular **PORK SAUSAGE**
   1½ cup **BISCUIT MIX**

Set aside.
Beat well ....   2 **EGGS**

Set aside. Pat about 1 Tablespoon sausage mixture in palm of hand. Lay pepper stuffed with cheese on sausage. Pat mixture around pepper. Seal dough real well so that cheese will not come out of pepper.
Dip in beaten **EGGS** and
   roll in ....   1 package **PORK SHAKE AND BAKE**

Bake for 30 to 40 mintues in preheated 350-degree oven.

Catherine Barham gave us this recipe and she prefers the plain **SHAKE AND BAKE.** We have tried it both ways and it is good either way. These freeze very well. Bake first. Reheat in microwave.

CREAM CHEESE AND MUSHROOM LOGS
Thank you, Linda Feazell, for these tasty appetizers.
They are always a hit.

Mix well...................... 1 small jar sliced **MUSHROOMS**,
diced, drained
8 ounces uncooked **PORK
SAUSAGE,** room temperature
8 ounces **CREAM CHEESE,**
softened
SAVOR SALT and **SEASON
SALT,** to taste
Separate into 8 rectangles .... 2 tubes **CRESCENT DINNER
ROLLS**

(With fingers, mash together perforations on rectangles.) Spread with **SAUSAGE MIXTURE.** Roll lengthwise. Place on dish, seam side down and refrigerate several hours. When ready to bake, brush with beaten **EGG,** and sprinkle with **POPPY SEED.** Cut each log into 6 or 8 smaller logs. Place on greased cookie sheet, seam side down. Bake in preheated 375-degree oven until golden brown. Approximately 15 to 20 minutes. (Can be made a day ahead and baked later.)

SAUSAGE BITES
Men will remember these.

Brown until crumbly .... ½ pound **HOT SAUSAGE**

Drain and set aside.
Mix .... 2 **EGGS,** slightly beaten
1 cup **COTTAGE CHEESE**
1 Tbsp. **CHOPPED CHIVES**
¼ cup grated **PARMESAN
CHEESE**
PEPPER to taste

Set aside.
Have on hand .... **BUTTERFLAKE DINNER
ROLLS** (6 count)

Divide each roll into 8 sections. (Should have 48 total). Thinly roll each section and press into greased miniature muffin tin cups. Add sausage and top with egg mixture. Bake at 350-degrees for 20 minutes or until filling is lightly brown.

YIELD: SERVES 12 TO 15 PEOPLE.

CAPT'N HOOK'S SEAFOOD MOLD

Nancy prepares this delicious recipe for all the McCord "pirates".

Grease mold with **MAYONNAISE**.
Mix together .... ⅓ cup **CATSUP**
2 tsp. **DRY MUSTARD**

Place in the bottom of the mold. Freeze.
Meanwhile, combine .... 1 can **CREAM OF MUSHROOM SOUP**
8 ounces **CREAM CHEESE**

Cook over low heat, stirring constantly, until well mixed.
Remove from heat and add ...... 1 cup **CELERY,** diced
1 cup **MAYONNAISE**
8 ounces **CRABMEAT,** canned or frozen
4 ounces small **SHRIMP,** canned or frozen
⅓ cup **ONION,** diced
Dash of **PEPPER**
Mix together. Add .... 2 Tbsp. (2 pkgs.) unflavored **GELATIN,** dissolved in ¾ cup **WATER**

Blend with soup mixture. Pour into mold. Chill overnight. To serve, unmold on **LETTUCE LEAVES.** Serve with **CRACKERS.**

21

SHRIMP WILKINS

This is the best way we know to eat fresh shrimp.
Thanks JDS!!!

You will need . . . . 2 pounds **SHRIMP IN SHELLS**
2 **STICKS BUTTER**, melted
1 **LEMON**

Various doses of the following. **SALT** and **PEPPER** (Lots), **TABASCO**, **SOY SAUCE, LEMON PEPPER, WORCESTERSHIRE SAUCE, DILL, GARLIC POWDER.**

Nestle the shrimp on their sides in a 10x20-inch flat pan. Put the butter, spices and sauces all over their little bodies. Broil 5 to 10 minutes. DO NOT OVERCOOK.

Accompany these little devils with the most absorbent **FRENCH BREAD** you can find and if all else fails, throw away the shrimp and eat the bread dipped in the sauce.

If you have not eaten shrimp this way before, you must understand that it is most important to suck the shells prior to shucking and devouring their bodies.

TURKEY YUM YUMS

Drain . . . . 1 can (8 oz.) **PINEAPPLE CHUNKS**
Cut into chunks . . . . 1 large **SWEET BELL PEPPER**
Cut into ¾-inch cubes . . . . 1 pound cooked **TURKEY BREAST**

Alternate on small skewers or toothpicks, 2 cubes of turkey with 1 pepper and 1 pineapple chunk.
Brush with . . . . **SWEET** AND **SOUR SAUCE**

Bake in 400-degree oven for about 10 minutes. Heat rest of sweet and sour sauce for dipping.

CHICKEN LIVER AND BACON ROLL-UPS

The mustard gives this appetizer that special ummmph!

Dip **CHICKEN LIVERS** in **DIJON MUSTARD**. Roll in **CORNFLAKE CRUMBS**. Wrap with ½ piece **BACON**. Place in preheated 425-degree oven for 25 minutes. Or until **BACON** is crispy.

MINI TURKEY CRESCENTS

Unroll . . . . 2 cans (8 oz. ea.) refrigerated
CRESCENT ROLL DOUGH

Cut each triangle in half to form two triangles. Roll up as directed on package to form mini-crescents. Place on ungreased baking sheet. Bake in 375-degree oven for 5 to 7 minutes. Or until brown. Cool. Slice in half lengthwise.

Combine . . . . 1 package (9 oz.) frozen, chopped
SPINACH, thaw and squeeze dry
1 cup (4 oz.) **SWISS CHEESE,** grated
⅓ cup **MAYONNAISE**
2 Tbsp. **ONION,** finely chopped
⅛ tsp. **TARRAGON**

Spread scant tablespoon on bottom of crescent halves.

Top with. . . . . ½ pound cooked **BREAST OF TURKEY** cut into eight ⅛-inch slices.

Cut the eight slices into four crosswise pieces. (32 pieces.) Top with remaining crescent half and place on baking sheet. Cover loosely with foil. Bake in 400-degree oven for 15 minutes.

YIELD: 32 APPETIZERS

TURKEY ASPARAGUS ROLL-UPS

Trim crust from . . . . 18 slices soft **BREAD**
Flatten with rolling pin and
spread with . . . . 8 ounces **CREAM CHEESE,** softened
Drain. . . . . 1 can (15 oz.) **ASPARAGUS SPEARS**
Cut into finger-size strips . . . . 1 pound **BREAST OF TURKEY,** cooked

Place 1 **ASPARAGUS SPEAR** and 1 slice **TURKEY** on **BREAD.** Roll up. Tie with strip of **CARROT.** (Use vegetable peeler to make carrot strips.)

YIELD: 18 APPETIZERS

PARTY FARE

These are fun because you can create your own favorite filling.

Beat on medium speed of mixer
until smooth . . . . 3 ounces **CREAM CHEESE,**
softened
½ cup **BUTTER** or **MARGARINE,**
softened
Add . . . . 1 cup **FLOUR**
SALT

Mix well. Divide dough into about 25 to 30 balls. Place in greased miniature muffin pans. Shape each into a shell. Prick bottom and sides of
pastry generously with fork. Bake at 400-degrees for 10 minutes or until
brown. Fill with **CHICKEN SALAD FILLING**, or with your favorite. This
will make 2 to 2½ dozen.

CHICKEN SALAD FILLING

Put into food processor or *chop*
very fine . . . . ¾ cup **CHICKEN**
¼ cup **CELERY**
2 Tbsp. **GREEN PEPPER**
2 Tbsp. **DILL PICKLE**
Add . . . . ⅓ cup **MAYONNAISE**
⅛ tsp. **WHITE PEPPER**

Stir well. Cover and chill until ready to serve. (You may fill the shells
ahead of time, cover and chill until ready to use.)

BUFFALO WINGS

These are very inexpensive to serve.

Buy approximately . . . . 3 pounds **CHICKEN WINGS**

Cut wings at joint and discard the tips.
Combine in plastic bag . . . . 1 cup **FLOUR**
1 tsp. **ONION SALT**
½ tsp. **PEPPER**
Add chicken pieces, a few at a
time, and shake to coat. Place
in a foil lined pan with . . . . ½ cup **SHORTENING,** melted

Bake 25 minutes at 400-degrees. Turn chicken wings over and bake an
additional 20 to 25 minutes, or until crisp. Drain on paper towels. Trans-
fer to serving platter. Serve with **BARBECUE SAUCE, SWEET AND
SOUR SAUCE,** or **BUTTERMILK RANCH DRESSING.**

CHICKEN NUT PUFFS

Bring to boil . . . . 1 can (10½ oz.) **CHICKEN BROTH**
½ cup **OIL**
2 tsp. **SEASONED SALT**
½ tsp. **CAYENNE PEPPER,**
optional
1 tsp. **CELERY SEED**
1 Tbsp. **PARSLEY FLAKES**
2 tsp. **WORCESTERSHIRE
SAUCE**

Remove from heat.
Add all at once . . . . 1 cup sifted **FLOUR**

Cook over low heat. Beat rapidly until mixture leaves side of pan and
Add, one at a time . . . . 4 **EGGS**

Beat after each egg until mixture shines.
Stir in . . . . 1 can (5 oz.) **BONED CHICKEN**
⅓ cup **TOASTED ALMONDS**
chopped

Drop by ½ teaspoons full on greased cookie sheets. Bake 10 to 15 minutes
at 450-degrees. Serve hot. May be cooked, frozen and reheated in slow
oven when ready to serve.

YIELD: 100 PUFFS

NO "CHICKHI" RUMAKI
For those people who dislike chicken livers.

Drain well . . . . 16 ounces **WATER CHESTNUTS**
15 ounces **PINEAPPLE CHUNKS**
Cut each slice in half of . . . . 1 pound **BACON**

Wrap bacon around 1 **WATER CHESTNUT** and 1 chunk **PINEAPPLE.**
Secure with toothpick. Heat in 8-inch square baking dish at 300-degrees
for 1 hour, or until bacon is crisp.
Mix . . . . 1 cup **CATSUP**
1 Tbsp. **TERIYAKI SAUCE**
1 cup **SUGAR**

Pour sauce over **RUMAKI**. Heat for 1 hour. Prepare ahead of time.

YIELD: 8 TO 10 SERVINGS.

ZIPPY MEATBALLS
Bake or fry these little "tasties."

In medium bowl, beat well ...... 1 **EGG**
Add......................... ¾ cup **SOFT BREAD CRUMBS**
(about 1 slice bread)
¼ cup **CHILI SAUCE**
½ tsp. **SALT**
½ tsp. **INSTANT MINCED ONION**
⅛ tsp. **GARLIC POWDER**
¾ pound **GROUND BEEF**
¼ cup **CELERY,** minced

Mix well and shape into about 30 **MEATBALLS** 1-inch in diameter. Melt 2 tablespoons **SHORTENING** in large skillet on medium heat. Add meatballs and brown on all sides. Continue cooking until done, about 12 minutes including browning. Or place in lightly oiled baking dish and cook, *uncovered* for 15 minutes at 450-degrees. Warm **BARBECUE SAUCE** while meatballs cook. Serve with wooden picks. Dip in the warmed sauce.

Uncooked **MEATBALLS** may be made a day ahead and refrigerated. Freeze for longer storage.

Cooked **MEATBALLS** may be frozen and reheated in preheated 400-degree oven for 7 minutes.

WATER CHESTNUTS HORS D'OURVES
Make-ahead goodies.

Marinate .... 1 can (8 ounce) **WATER CHESTNUTS,** drained
In........................... ¼ cup **DARK RUM**
2 Tbsp. **SOY SAUCE**

Place in refrigerator. Stir occasionally. Marinate at least 1 hour. Coat very well with **SUGAR.**
Cut in half .... 4 slices **BACON**

Then cut lengthwise again. You will have 16 pieces. Wrap the bacon strips around the water chestnuts. Secure with toothpicks. Place on cookie sheet. Bake 400-degrees for 15 to 18 minutes or until bacon is crisp. Drain on paper towels.

YIELD: 10 SERVINGS.

HEART BISCUITS

Shirley Draper served these at daughter Andria's wedding.
So clever and very good.

Combine .... 3 cups **FLOUR**
1½ Tbsp. **BAKING POWDER**
¾ tsp. **BAKING SODA**
¼ tsp. **SALT**
Cut in with pastry blender or use
    two knives.................. ½ cup **BUTTER**
When mixture resembles
    cornmeal add ....1½ cups **BUTTERMILK**

Stir gently, just enough to mix. Knead gently, on floured board, 4 or 5 times. Roll to about ½-inch thickness. Cut with biscuit cutter or heart shaped cookie cutter. Place on lightly greased cookie sheet. Bake in 450-degree oven for 10 to 12 minutes. Brush with melted **BUTTER**. Serve with **SHAVED HAM** (1½ pounds per 2½ dozen biscuits) and **MUSTARD SAUCE**.

MUSTARD SAUCE

Combine .... ½ cup **MAYONNAISE**
2 Tbsp. **DIJON MUSTARD**
2 Tbsp. **SWEET PICKLE RELISH**
2 Tbsp. **TANGY MUSTARD,** or
may use flavored **SANDWICH SPREAD**

YIELD: ABOUT 2½ DOZEN BISCUITS AND 1 CUP MUSTARD.

DRUNKEN WIENERS

Savory and good.

In large saucepan .... 1 cup **BOURBON**
1 cup **POWDERED SUGAR,** sifted
2 cups **CATSUP**
1 Tbsp. **WORCESTERSHIRE SAUCE**
Add .... 2 pounds **COCKTAIL WEINERS**

Simmer for 40 minutes. Serve in chafing dish. May be prepared ahead.

YIELD: SERVES 20.

ELEGANT AND FATTENING LITTLE MINIATURE CHEESECAKES

Eat on Holidays when calories don't count!

Cream together	24	ounces **CREAM CHEESE,** softened
	1	cup **SUGAR**
Beat in	5	**EGGS**
	1½	tsp. **VANILLA**

Pour into miniature paper muffin cups. (Approximately 24)
Bake for 40 minutes at 300-degrees. Remove from oven and cool for 5 minutes. A hole will form in the center of each cheesecake.

Blend together	8	ounces **SOUR CREAM**
	¼	cup **SUGAR**
	¼	tsp. **VANILLA**

Fill holes with **SOUR CREAM** mixture. Place a dab of **PRESERVES** in the center of the filling. Return to oven for 5 more minutes. (Use **STRAWBERRY** for Christmas, **PEACH** for Easter, etc.)

ORANGE CLUNGEES

Frequently served at Suzanne Darbys bridge table.

Crush into fine crumbs	1	box (12 oz.) **VANILLA WAFERS**
Mix with	½	cup melted **BUTTER**
	1	cup **POWDERED SUGAR**
	1	cup **PECANS,** chopped
	1	can (6 oz.) **FROZEN ORANGE JUICE,** thawed and undiluted

Blend well and chill. Form into 1-inch balls. Roll each in **POWDERED SUGAR**. Refrigerate 24 hours.

YIELD: ABOUT 30 BALLS.

THAW FROZEN ORANGE JUICE: Thaw in the container after removing the lid. At high power it will take 30 seconds for 6 ounces and 45 seconds for 12 ounces.

BOURBON BON BON BALLS

For a festive look for the holidays, serve in colorful foil cups.

Place in double boiler or
microwave . . . . 1 package (6 oz.) **SEMISWEET CHOCOLATE CHIPS**

Heat until melted. Stir occasionally. Remove from heat.
Stir in . . . . ½ cup **BOURBON**
3 Tbsp. **LIGHT CORN SYRUP**

Set aside.
Combine .2½ cups **VANILLA WAFER CRUMBS**
½ cup sifted **POWDERED SUGAR**
1 cup **PECANS,** finely chopped

Stir into chocolate mixture. Let stand 30 minutes. Shape into 1-inch balls. Roll in **SUGAR.** Store in an airtight container in refrigerator.

YIELD: 60 TO 65 BON BONS.

CANDIED STRAWBERRIES

These aren't hard to make, but time consuming.

Mix together and *refrigerate*
overnight . . . . 1 can (14 oz.) **SWEETENED CONDENSED MILK**
1 package (4 oz.) **FROZEN COCONUT**
1 cup **PECANS,** finely chopped
1 Tbsp. **SUGAR**
3 packages (3 oz. ea.) **STRAWBERRY JELLO,** dry
1 tsp. **VANILLA**

Remove about ¼ of the mixture from the refrigerator at a time and shape into small strawberries. (These are very rich.) Roll small end and sides in **RED CRYSTALS DECOR.** (Colored sugar.) Dip large end of strawberry in **GREEN CRYSTALS DECOR.** (Colored sugar.) Use **PARSLEY** for stems, or tint **SLIVERED ALMONDS** with **GREEN FOOD COLORING.** (Pour 2 tsp. into glass bowl with ½ tsp. **WATER.** Place almonds in mixture and stir until desired green color. Place on several folded paper towels. Let dry overnight. Place 1 sliver in end of strawberry for stem.)

May need to add more **SUGAR** if dough is too sticky.

PARTY MERINGUES
Wonderful make-ahead recipe.

HAVE EGGS AT ROOM TEMPERATURE!
Beat 3 **EGG *WHITES*** with ¼ teaspoon **CREAM OF TARTAR** in a small bowl at high speed of an electric mixer until foamy. Add 1 cup **SUGAR,** *1 tablespoon at a time,* beating until stiff peaks form. (Do not overbeat.) Fold in ½ teaspoon **FLAVORING.** (We use **LEMON FLAVORING** because we usually make lemon filling. Use vanilla if making chocolate or other fillings.)

Drop meringue by rounded teaspoonfuls onto a cookie sheet lined with unglazed brown paper. Make an indention in the center of each meringue with the back of a spoon. Bake at 250-degrees for 1 hour. Turn off oven. Let cool in oven for 2 additional hours. Carefully remove meringues from paper. Store in an airtight container until ready to use. Makes 45 to 50 meringues.

FILLING:

Combine . . . . 1 cup **SUGAR**
3 Tbsp. **CORNSTARCH**
1 Tbsp. plus 1 tsp. grated **LEMON RIND**
Stir well . . . . 1 cup **LEMON JUICE**
⅔ cup **WATER**

Microwave on **HIGH** for 3 minutes. (Stir after 2 minutes.)
Stir about ¼ hot mixture in . . . . . . 6 **EGG YOLKS**, slightly beaten

Add remaining hot mixture. Stir well. Return to microwave. Continue cooking for 1 minute intervals until filling is thick, stirring between each minute of cooking. Let cool. Refrigerate until ready to serve. (To cook on burner top, cook first mixture over medium heat, stirring constantly, until mixture boils. Boil for 1 minute, stirring constantly. Stir about ¼ into egg yolks, add to remaining hot mixture. Return to heat, stirring constantly, until thick. Cool and refrigerate.)

NOTE: We repeated "JANET HARRIS' WONDER RECIPE" from CALF FRIES TO CAVIAR in the pie section. Use any variation for this recipe and others in this cookbook. It is so good, we felt it worth repeating.

SNAILS

Use as a dessert or appetizer. Wonderful for a coffee or brunch.

Combine and mix well . . . . 1 pound **BUTTER** or
                                         MARGARINE, softened
                                       1 pint **SOUR CREAM**
                                       4 cups **FLOUR**

Chill mixture for at least an hour.
While dough is chilling mix . . . . . 2 cups **PECANS,** finely chopped
                                     1½ cups **SUGAR**
                                       2 Tbsp. **CINNAMON**

Form 6 balls from dough. On floured board, roll each ball thin like a pie crust. Sprinkle generously with ⅙ of the sugar mixture. Roll mixture into dough with rolling pin. Cut into 12 slices like tiny pie slices. Roll as crescent rolls. Repeat with each ball. Bake on ungreased cookie sheets at 400-degrees for 15 minutes. Frost while still warm.

FROSTING:
Combine . . . . 2 cups **CONFECTIONERS**
                                                 SUGAR, sifted
                                               ¼ tsp. **MAPLE FLAVORING**

Add enough **MILK** to make spreading consistency.

CELEBRATION PUNCH

Everyone thinks this punch has a lot of ingredients
Elizabeth Day's "secret" ingredient, is the trick.

Mix in large punch bowl . . . . 1 2-liter bottle (67.6 oz.) **7 UP** or
                                         DIET 7 UP
                                       1 can (46 oz.) **PINEAPPLE JUICE,**
                                         unsweetened
                                       2 Tbsp. **ELIZABETH'S "SECRET"**
                                         INGREDIENT, (VANILLA)

Tint with food coloring. Fill with crushed **ICE**. NOTE: Make extra and freeze in a pretty mold with **FRUIT** to use as **ICE RING** in punch bowl.

YIELD: 20 SERVINGS.

MOCK CHAMPAGNE

Mix in punch bowl . . . .   1 bottle (32 oz.) **WHITE GRAPE JUICE**
1 bottle (33.8 oz.) **GINGER ALE**

Tint any color you wish. It is very pretty to freeze part of the mixture with **FRUIT** in a mold and use as your ice ring for your punch bowl.

VARIATION:
Substitute 1 bottle (32 oz.) **7 UP** for **GINGER ALE.** Add **ALMOND FLAVORING.** (Optional.)

REIS' APPLE MINT PUNCH
A different taste. Very good!

Melt . . . .   1 jar (10 oz.) **APPLE MINT JELLY**
(cheap kind will be fine)
In . . . .   2 cups boiling **WATER**
Cool. Mix with . . . .   1 cup **ORANGE JUICE**
1 cup **PINEAPPLE JUICE**
½ cup **LEMON JUICE**
Freeze at this point if you wish. To serve, let thaw 1 hour until slushy.
Add . . . .   1 bottle **GINGER ALE**

Garnish with **MINT LEAVES.**

APRICOT SLUSH
Southern Bush says to be sure and try the variation.

Bring to boil and simmer 15   9 cups **WATER**
    minutes . . . .   2 cups **SUGAR**
Remove from heat. Cool.
Add . . . .   1 pint **APRICOT BRANDY**
1 can (12 oz.) **LEMONADE,**
undiluted
1 can (12 oz.) **ORANGE JUICE,**
undiluted

Freeze. To serve. Add 1 scoop mixture, per glass. Finish filling with **GINGER ALE.**

VARIATION: Substitute **RUM** for **BRANDY,** and increase **LEMONADE** to 24 ounces. (Omit the **ORANGE JUICE.**)

WEDDIN' PUNCH

Dissolve and set aside . . . .   1 package (6 oz.) **JELLO,** any flavor
  2 cups **HOT WATER**

Combine and cook until clear . . . .   3 cups **SUGAR**
  2 cups **WATER**
Remove from heat.
Add . . . .   1 quart **PINEAPPLE JUICE**
  ½ cup **LEMON JUICE**
  1 ounce **ALMOND FLAVORING**

Add the **JELLO** mixture, pour into quart zip lock bags. Freeze. (It is much easier to tear off the bags than to get out of containers.) To serve, add 1 quart **GINGER ALE.** (Stir until just mushy.)

This will keep in the deep freeze for a year or longer.

PINK LADY PUNCH

Combine and pour over **ICE RING** in punch bowl . . . .   1 bottle **CHAMPAGNE**
  1 bottle **SAUTERNE**
  1 can (32 oz.) **HAWAIIAN PUNCH**
  1 quart **CLUB SODA**
  1 small can **FROZEN LEMONADE,** diluted with **WATER**

YIELD: 40 SERVINGS.

"RUIDOSO DOWNS" STING

Mix in blender . . . . 1½ ounces **BANANA LIQUOR**
  ¾ ounce **RUM**
  3 ounces **STRAWBERRIES**
 1½ ounces **HALF AND HALF CREAM**
  ½ **BANANA**
  1 Tbsp. **VANILLA ICE CREAM**

This is a very rich drink. Also good for a **DESSERT.**

STONE'S EGGNOG
This will serve approximately 150 people.

Beat until very stiff . . . .   3 dozen **EGG WHITES**
Set aside.
Beat until light and fluffy . . . .   3 dozen **EGG YOLKS**
Gradually add . . . . 4½ cups **SUGAR**
Add . . . .   4 quarts **MILK**
                                            3 quarts **SOUTHERN COMFORT**
                                            1 pint **RUM**
Fold in . . . .   4 quarts **WHIPPING CREAM,**
                                            stiffly beaten

Fold in egg whites and refrigerate. Serve with **NUTMEG.**

MOCHA EGGNOG
Eggnog is one of the few native customs of the United States.
This is our favorite variation of the classic drink.

Stir together . . . .   2 cups **WHIPPING CREAM**
                                            5 Tbsp. **CHOCOLATE SYRUP**
                                            2 Tbsp. **INSTANT COFFEE**
                                            GRANULES
Set aside.
In large bowl, mix . . . .   5 **EGG YOLKS**
                                            ⅓ cup **SUGAR**
Beat until the mixture is thick
   and lemon-colored.
Stir in . . . .   ¾ cup **BOURBON**
                                            ¼ cup **BRANDY**

Add the cream mixture and chill. Just before serving, beat the **EGG WHITES** in a large bowl until soft peaks form. Fold egg whites into the cream mixture.

YIELD: THIS WILL ONLY MAKE 1½ QUARTS, SO YOU WILL PROB-ABLY WANT TO DOUBLE THE RECIPE.

HUTCH AND HADEN'S "L'PHANT EARS"

These wonderful, fattening "little goodies" are even fun to make.

Mix together . . . .   1 cup **WHITE SUGAR**
                                                 ½ cup **CINNAMON**

Spread evenly on a sheet of foil or wax paper.
Have refrigerated . . . .   1 can **CINNAMON BUNS**, found
                                                 in dairy case (8 count)

Remove buns from can one at a time and lay them on the sugar and cinnamon mixture. Using a rolling pin, roll each of the buns out very thin, turning it often so as to absorb as much sugar mixture as possible. The diameter should be about 6 to 8 inches. Place them on a foil lined cookie sheet. (You will need two cookie sheets. Each will only hold three at a time. Do not overlap.) Bake in preheated 375-degree oven on center rack. Check them often so they do not scorch and be careful not to overbake them because they are very thin. **AND THEY REALLY DO LOOK LIKE ELEPHANT EARS.**

Heloise shared this recipe with her readers. Thanks!! We have enjoyed it so much.

The little "Franklin boys" **CHOC'LIT TOAST** came from Heloises' column.

Spread slice of **BREAD** with **BUTTER** or **MARGARINE**. Sprinkle with **COCOA POWDER** and **SUGAR**. Broil until toasted. The kids like it better than cinnamon toast and so does their "H.G." (Grandfather) who is a **CHOCAHOLIC**.

MINCEMEAT SWIRLS

Our special treat on Christmas morn.

Use any basic **SWEET YEAST ROLL** recipe. Roll into rectangle. Spread with **READY MINCEMEAT PIE FILLING** and sprinkle with **CINNAMON**. Roll like a jelly roll. Slice into 1-inch slices and place in a greased pan. Let rise until double. Bake in a preheated 250-degree oven 15 to 20 minutes. When cool, spread with **POWDERED SUGAR ICING.**

NOTE: Slice raw dough with electric knife for smooth, even slices.

VARIATION:
The quick way! Use **FROZEN BREAD DOUGH.** Thaw and proceed.

FINGER CINNAMON ROLLS
These are nice for appetizers, also.

Separate into 4 rectangles .... 8 ounce can **REFRIGERATOR CRESCENT ROLLS**

Press out perforations.
Spread with................... 2 Tbsp. soft **MARGARINE**
Sprinkle with .... 2 Tbsp. **BROWN SUGAR**
1 tsp. **CINNAMON**
½ cup **RAISINS**

Start on short side, roll up and seal edge with fingers. Refrigerate 2 hours. Slice each roll into 5 equal slices. Cook on ungreased cookie sheet in preheated 375-degree oven for 17 to 22 minutes. Cool slightly and glaze.

GLAZE

Mix well...................... ½ cup **POWDERED SUGAR**
1 Tbsp. **MILK**
¼ tsp. **VANILLA**

Drizzle over rolls.

TO FREEZE; Take out of oven before browned. Cool. Add glaze. Freeze. Before serving, thaw, brown in oven and serve.

UPSIDE-DOWN ORANGE PUFFS
Let the children or grandchildren help with these

Have open and ready to use ..... 1 can (4.5 ounce) **REFRIGERATED BISCUITS**
Combine and mix well .... 2 Tbsp. **BUTTER** or **MARGARINE**, melted
¼ cup **SUGAR**
3 Tbsp. **ORANGE JUICE**
1 tsp. grated **ORANGE RIND**

Pour about 1 tablespoon orange mixture in each cup of a 6-cup muffin pan. Place 1 biscuit in each cup. Bake at 400-degrees for about 10 minutes. Invert pan on serving plate. Let set for 5 minutes before removing the pan. Serve warm.

EASY CHEESE BLINTZES

The Kennedy's served this at the girls Christenings.
Terri says these must be frozen.

Cream . . . . 1 pound **CREAM CHEESE,** softened
2 **EGG YOLKS**
½ cup **SUGAR**
Set aside. Mix . . . . 3 tsp. **CINNAMON**
½ cup **SUGAR**
Set aside. Remove 1 slice at a
time from . . . . 1 (2 pound) **LOAF SANDWICH BREAD,** thin sliced, crust removed

Roll with rolling pin until fairly flat. Spread cheese mixture over bread and roll jelly roll fashion. Dip in melted **BUTTER**, then in sugar and cinnamon mixture. Repeat with rest of bread. Place on waxed paper lined cookie sheet and freeze. Take out of freezer ½ hour before cooking. Thaw 15 minutes; then cut in half. Put on ungreased cookie sheet or wire rack and bake at 400-degrees for 15 minutes. Makes about 40.

Great for a coffee or a special breakfast.

APPLE KUCHEN

One of Shirley Carvers easy and unique goodies.

Mix together until crumbly . . . . . . 1 box **YELLOW CAKE MIX** (without pudding)
½ lb. **MARGARINE**, softened
½ cup **COCONUT**

Press into the bottom of a greased 13x9x2-inch pan, leaving edges slightly higher. Bake in 350-degree oven for 10 minutes.
Drain and arrange on top of
crust . . . . 1 can (20 oz.) **APPLE SLICES**
Mix and sprinkle over apples . . . . ½ cup **SUGAR**
1 tsp. **CINNAMON**
Mix together and drizzle over
entire mixture . . . . 1 cup **SOUR CREAM**
1 **EGG**

Continue baking in 350-degree oven for 30 minutes. This will not appear to be done but will firm up as it cools.

"EASY DOES IT" CARAMEL ROLLS

Thaw .... 2 loaves (1-pound) **FROZEN BREAD DOUGH**

Cut 1 loaf into small pieces. Place dough pieces in a greased 13x9x2-inch baking dish.

Combine .... 1 cup packed **BROWN SUGAR**
1 package (5½ oz.) **REGULAR VANILLA PUDDING** and **PIE FILLING** mix
½ cup **BUTTER** or **MARGARINE**, melted
¼ cup **MILK** or light **CREAM**

Mix well. Drizzle one-half of the sugar mixture over the dough pieces. Sprinkle with ¼ cup **NUTS** and ¼ cup **RAISINS**. Cut remaining loaf of dough into small pieces. Place dough pieces over first layer. Drizzle remaining sugar mixture over dough pieces. Sprinkle with ¼ cup **NUTS** and ¼ cup **RAISINS**. Cover and refrigerate several hours or overnight. Bake at 325-degrees for 50 to 60 minutes.

VARIATION:
Use **FROZEN ROLLS** and cut into 4 pieces each. Substitute any flavor of pudding and pie filling mix. Use any kind of nuts.

"HONEY DRIPPIN" COFFEE CAKE

Combine and set aside .... 2 cups **CORNFLAKES**
½ tsp. **CINNAMON**
Blend together .... 3 Tbsp. **HONEY** or **MAPLE SYRUP**
2 Tbsp. **MARGARINE** or **BUTTER**, melted
Open .... 1 package (10 count) **REFRIGERATED BISCUITS**.

Dip each biscuit in honey mixture, then in crumb mixture. Overlap biscuits in greased 3-cup ring mold. Sprinkle with chopped **NUTS**. Bake at 400-degrees for about 20 minutes. Turn out on serving dish and serve immediately.

COFFEE CAKE
This is a good basic SOUR CREAM sweet dough.

Dissolve in small bowl . . . . 2 envelopes **ACTIVE DRY YEAST**
¾ cup warm **WATER**
1 Tbsp. **SUGAR**

Let set 10 minutes.
Meanwhile, combine . . . . ½ cup **BUTTER** or **MARGARINE**, melted
1 cup **SOUR CREAM**
½ cup **SUGAR**
2 **EGGS,** beaten
1¼ tsp. **SALT**
½ tsp. **NUTMEG,** (opt.)
1 Tbsp. grated **ORANGE RIND**

Beat until well blended. Add 2 cups **FLOUR**. Beat until well mixed. Add yeast mixture and 2 more cups flour. Beat for 2 minutes at medium speed, scraping down side of bowl occasionally. Gradually stir in the remaining 2 cups flour to make medium-soft dough. (Dough should be softer than bread dough.) Turn out onto lightly floured surface. Knead 5 minutes until smooth. Shape dough into ball and place in oiled bowl. Turn to grease. Cover loosely with plastic wrap. Refrigerate at least 6 hours or overnight. (Can be refrigerated for up to 2 days.)

To make **COFFEE CAKES,** turn out onto lightly floured surface. Knead briefly. Divide into 6 parts. Cover. Let rest for 20 minutes. Roll out one portion at a time into a 10-inch square. Keep remaining portions covered and in refrigerator. Spread with filling. Sprinkle with **CINNAMON** and **SUGAR**. Roll up tightly as for jelly roll. Pinch long seam and ends to seal. Place on greased cookie sheet, gently flatten filled roll-up to 3-inch width. With scissors, make 1-inch diagonal cuts, 1 inch apart on both sides. (Herringbone style.) Cover and let rise until doubled. Brush with **EGG WASH**. (1 **EGG** and 1 tablespoon **WATER**, well blended.) Bake in preheated 350-degree oven for 20 to 25 minutes. Drizzle with **ICING**.

CHEESE FILLING: Mix in blender 8-ounce package **CREAM CHEESE**, ¼ cup **SUGAR**, ¾ tsp **LEMON RIND**, 1 tsp. **LEMON JUICE** and 1 **EGG YOLK**.
Optional: **RAISINS**. (Fills 2 **COFFEE CAKES**.)

APRICOT FILLING: Combine 1 cup **APRICOT PRESERVES**, ¼ cup chopped **PECANS** and ½ cup chopped pared **APPLE**. (Fills 2 **COFFEE CAKES**.)

NOTE: There is no limit to what you can create. These are just some of our favorites.

TO FREEZE: Wrap airtight and seal. Defrost roll-ups in their wrappings in refrigerator overnight or until softened enough to shape. Place on lightly greased cookie sheet. Overwrap loosely with sprayed foil, not pressing down on glazed tops. Tuck foil ends under cookie sheet. Heat cakes in 300-degree oven 10 to 15 minutes. Cool to lukewarm in foil. Remove to serving plate. (Deliver warm to a friend as if you have been baking all day.)

"EXTRA SPECIAL" FRENCH TOAST SPECIAL
This is H.G.'s Sunday morning request.

Buy   1   loaf **DAY OLD UNSLICED BREAD**

Cut 6 slices about ¾-inch thick. (We buy **TEXAS SIZE**, which is a real thick sliced white **BREAD**.) Trim and cut into two triangles.

Combine   2   cups **LIGHT CREAM**
                                            8   **EGGS**, well beaten
                                         ¼   tsp. **SALT**

Mix well. Dip triangles into mixture, letting them absorb as much as possible. Fry in ½-inch hot **VEGETABLE OIL**. (If you have an electric skillet, set at 325°.) Cook until golden brown, *turning only once*. Put triangles in shallow baking pan and bake in 400-degree oven 3 to 5 minutes, or until well puffed. Drain on paper. Sprinkle with **CONFECTIONERS' SUGAR**. Serve with all flavors of **SYRUP**.

Be sure and try Harold Gene's favorite toppings. Spread with **PEANUT BUTTER**, top with sliced **BANANAS**. Cover with **MAPLE SYRUP**, or cover with sliced **FRESH STRAWBERRIES** and **WHIPPING CREAM**.

BACON: *Try frying the entire pound at once. Freeze in small packages. Take out amount needed and thaw in oven or microwave until warm. Makes bacon much crispier and you only have to clean up once.*

STUFFED "TEXAS-STYLE" FRENCH TOAST

This was sent to us in an order for cookbooks one day.
We have lost the name, but thanks for a really good recipe.

Cream together . . . . 8 ounces **CREAM CHEESE,** softened
                 1½ tsp. **VANILLA**
Beat until fluffy. Add . . . . ½ cup **PECANS,** finely chopped

Set aside. Cut a 1 pound loaf of **FRENCH BREAD** into 10 or 12 slices about 1½-inches thick. Make a pocket in the top of each slice. Be careful not to cut all the way through. Fill each with 1½ tablespoons of the **CREAM CHEESE** mixture.

Beat together . . . . 4 **EGGS**
                 1 cup **WHIPPING CREAM**
                 ½ tsp. **VANILLA**
                 ½ tsp. **ORANGE FLAVORING**

Carefully dip the filled bread slices in the egg mixture. Be careful not to squeeze out the filling. Cook in small amount of **OIL** in skillet, (or griddle) until golden brown. Turn only once. To keep toast hot for serving, place them on a baking sheet in a warm oven. Meanwhile, heat together a 12-ounce jar of **APRICOT PRESERVES** and ½ cup **ORANGE JUICE.** Drizzle over hot toast.

BAKED PANCAKE WITH APPLE SYRUP

Melt in ovenproof skillet . . . . 2 Tbsp. **BUTTER** or **MARGARINE**
Combine in mixing bowl . . . . ⅔ cup **FLOUR**
                 ½ tsp. **BAKING POWDER**
                 ⅔ cup **MILK**
                 4 **EGGS,** beaten

Mix well. Pour into hot skillet. Bake at 400-degrees for 15 to 18 minutes or until pancake is puffy and golden. Cut into wedges. Serve with hot **APPLE SYRUP**.

SYRUP: Combine ½ cup **MAPLE SYRUP** with 2 medium **APPLES, PEELED AND THINLY SLICED.** Bring to boil, reduce heat and simmer 2 minutes.

SAUSAGE AND APPLE MOLD
This makes a pretty dish.

Combine .... 2 pounds **SAUSAGE**
2 **EGGS**, slightly beaten
½ cup **MILK**
1½ cups **CORNBREAD STUFFING**
¼ cup **ONION**, diced
1 cup **APPLES**, pared
and chopped

Mix well. Press lightly into a greased 6-cup ring mold. Turn out onto a shallow baking pan. Bake at 350-degrees for 1 hour. Drain well. For a festive way to serve, place scrambled **EGGS** in middle of ring. Garnish with **CINNAMON APPLES**. Add **BREAD**. Enjoy!

Make this the day before and partially bake for 30 minutes. Finish baking just before serving.

TACO EGGS
Tasty, colorful dish. This will serve about 10 people.

Beat just until blended .... 9 **EGGS**, slightly beaten
½ cup **MILK**
⅛ tsp. **SALT**

Pour into greased 9x13x2-inch baking dish. Bake in preheated 325-degree oven for 20 minutes or until set.
Sprinkle with .... 2 cups **CHEDDAR CHEESE**,
grated

Bake 5 more minutes, or until cheese is melted. Let stand 5 minutes before cutting into squares. Serve with a dish of **SALSA**, **CORN MUFFIN STICKS**, **SAUSAGE LINKS**, and sliced **TOMATOES** and **AVOCADOS** that you have sprinkled with **LIME JUICE**.

Boy, what an impressive **BRUNCH**. Never let your guest know how simple everything was to prepare.

COMPANY BREAKFAST CASSEROLE
To be made the night before serving.

Grease a 13x9x2-inch pan.
Place in pan .... 6 slices **BREAD**
Cook and crumble .... 1 pound **SAUSAGE**

Spoon on top of bread.
Top with...................... 1½ cups **CHEDDAR CHEESE**,
                                grated
Blend .... 8 **EGGS**
                                2 cups **MILK**
                                1 tsp. **SALT**
                                1 tsp. **DRY MUSTARD**

Pour over other ingredients. Refrigerate overnight. Bake in 350-degree oven about 35 minutes.

CHEESE-ONION-EGG SCRAMBLE
Microwave quick.

Combine .... 6 **EGGS**
                               ½ cup **MILK**
                               3 ounces **CREAM CHEESE**
                               SALT and **PEPPER**

Mix in blender until frothy. Melt 3 Tbsp. **MARGARINE** in microwave safe baking dish. Add egg mixture.
Sprinkle with .... ⅓ cup **GREEN ONIONS**, chopped
                               with tops.

Stir well. Microwave for 1 to 2 minutes. Break up set portions of eggs with fork, and stir toward center of dish. Microwave for 2 to 3 more minutes or until eggs are almost set, stirring gently at 1-minute intervals (eggs will be soft and moist). Stir gently again. Cover. Let stand 1 or 2 more minutes. Serve with good hot **BREAD**.

BAKED EGGS IN NESTS
Kids love this one.

Place ¾ cups **SOFT BREADCRUMBS** in a greased 8-inch square baking dish. Use back of spoon to make 6 nests in **CRUMBS**. Break an **EGG** into each nest.

Combine . . . . ¾ cup **MILK**
                               ½ tsp. **SALT**
                               ½ tsp. **PEPPER**

Mix well and pour over eggs and crumbs. Sprinkle with more bread-crumbs. (About ¾ cup.) Dot with **BUTTER**. Bake at 350-degrees for 15 minutes.

Sprinkle with . . . . 3 ounces **SHARP CHEDDAR CHEESE**, grated

Bake an additional 5 minutes or until eggs are to desired degree of doneness.

YIELD: 6 SERVINGS.

COMPANY OMELET
Slightly different way to do EGGS.

Melt in large skillet . . . . 3 Tbsp. **BUTTER** or **MARGARINE**

Combine and pour into skillet . . . 8 **EGGS**, beat well with fork
                               2 Tbsp. chopped **GREEN PEPPER**
                               1 Tbsp. **PIMIENTO**, diced
                               2 cups cooked **PASTA**, any kind
                               1 cup shredded **CHEDDAR CHEESE**
                               SALT and **PEPPER**

Cover and cook over medium heat 15 to 20 minutes. Or until the eggs are set. **DO NOT STIR**. Cut into wedges and remove from skillet. Serve with **FRUIT CUPS** and a basket of **MUFFINS**.

YIELD: 6 TO 8 SERVINGS.

COUNTRY GRITS AND SAUSAGE

Newlyweds? Cut recipe in half.

Brown, drain, and set aside . . . . . . 2 pounds mild **PORK SAUSAGE**, crumbled
Cook according to directions . . . . ½ cup **UNCOOKED QUICK GRITS**
Pour hot grits in large mixing
   bowl and add . . . . 4 cups **EXTRA-SHARP CHEESE**, shredded

Stir until melted. Set aside.
Combine . . . . 4 **EGGS**, beaten
                                    1 cup **MILK**
                                     ½ tsp. **DRIED WHOLE THYME**
                                     ⅛ tsp. **GARLIC SALT**

Mix well. Add a small amount of hot grits mixture to egg mixture, stirring well. Stir egg mixture into remaining grits mixture. Add cooked sausage, stirring well. Pour into a 13x9x2-inch baking dish. Cover and refrigerate overnight. Remove from refrigerator; let stand 15 minutes. Bake for 50 to 55 minutes at 350-degrees.

YIELD: 8 SERVINGS.

OVERNIGHT BREAKFAST CASSEROLE

Helen Brown's "lake house" special.

Cut crust from enough **BREAD** slices to cover a 13x9x2-inch baking dish. **BUTTER** one side of each slice. Place buttered side down in buttered baking dish.
Pour over a mixture of . . . . 12 **EGGS**, well beaten
                                     ¾ cup **MILK**
                                     1 can **MUSHROOM SOUP**, undiluted
                                     SALT and **PEPPER**
Add . . . . 1 pound **SAUSAGE**, crumbled, cooked and drained

Cover and set in refrigerator overnight. Bake uncovered in preheated 350-degree oven for 30 minutes, or until eggs are set. Sprinkle with 1 cup grated **CHEDDAR CHEESE**. Return to oven until cheese is melted.

SAUSAGE BAKE IN A SHELL
SAUSAGE and BREAD are cooked together. Yummy!

Cook until brown . . . . 1 pound **BULK PORK SAUSAGE**, crumbled
½ cup **ONION**, chopped
Drain off pan drippings. Add . . . . 1 **EGG**, beaten
2 ounces **SWISS CHEESE**, grated
1 ounce **PARMESAN CHEESE**, grated, optional
1 Tbsp. **FRESH PARSLEY**, chopped
¼ tsp. **HOT SAUCE**

Set aside.
Combine . . . . .1½ cups **BISCUIT MIX**
¾ cup **MILK**
¼ cup **MAYONNAISE**

Stir well. Spread one-half of batter in a greased 9-inch square pan. Spoon sausage mixture over batter. Spread remaining batter over sausage mixture. Combine 1 **EGG YOLK** with 2 tsp. **WATER**. Brush on batter. Bake at 400-degrees for 30 minutes. Let stand 5 minutes before serving.

YIELD: 6 SERVINGS.

SHIP WRECK
Louisiana SHRIMP and EGG scramble.

Thaw according to package . . . . . . 8 ounces **FROZEN SHRIMP** (chop into bite-size pieces if using large ones)
Set aside. Cook until crisp . . . . 3 slices **BACON**

Remove from skillet, drain.
In **BACON DRIPPINGS**, sauté . . . ¾ cup **GREEN PEPPER**, chopped
½ cup **ONION**, diced
Add . . . . ¼ tsp. **SALT**
¼ tsp. **CAYENNE**
SHRIMP
Heat. Combine . . . . 6 **EGGS**, beaten
¼ cup **HALF** and **HALF CREAM**
½ tsp. **WORCESTERSHIRE SAUCE**
BACON

Add to shrimp mixture and cook until eggs are firm. Stir occasionally.

YIELD: 6 SERVINGS.

COUNTRY BRUNCH
Tastes so good, no one will ever suspect it is so easy to prepare.

Trim crusts from . . . . 16 slices **WHITE BREAD**, cut in half

Prepare . . . . 1 pound **COOKED HAM**, cubed
1 pound **CHEDDAR CHEESE**, shredded
1 pound **MOZZARELLA CHEESE**, shredded

Cover bottom of a greased 13x9x2-inch baking dish with one-half of bread, one-half of ham, and one-half of each of the cheeses. Repeat layers.

Combine . . . . 6 **EGGS**, beaten
3 cups **MILK**
½ tsp. **DRY MUSTARD**
¼ tsp. **ONION SALT**

Pour over layers. Refrigerate overnight. Remove from refrigerator 30 minutes before baking.

Combine . . . . 3 cups **UNCRUSHED CORN FLAKES**
½ cup **BUTTER**, melted

Sprinkle over casserole. Bake at 375-degrees for 45 minutes. (Cover loosely with foil to prevent top from over-browning). Let stand 10 to 15 minutes before cutting into squares.

YIELD: 12 SERVINGS.

EASY EGGS RANCHEROS
A tasty dish for breakfast or brunch.

Lightly grease a 9-inch quiche dish.
Combine and pour into dish . . . . .   1 can (8 oz.) **TOMATO SAUCE**
                                       1 tsp. **CHILI POWDER**
                                       ½ tsp. **CUMIN**
Very carefully, break evenly over
  sauce in dish . . . .   8 **EGGS**
Sprinkle with . . . .   ¼ tsp. **FRESHLY GROUND**
                                       PEPPER
                                       ¼ tsp. **PAPRIKA**

Cover and bake at 350-degrees for 15 to 20 minutes.
Sprinkle with . . . .   1 cup **CHEDDAR CHEESE**, grated

Bake an additional 5 minutes. Spoon eggs onto **WARM TOSTADOS SHELLS**, top with dollop of **SOUR CREAM** and **JALAPENO** slices.

YIELD: 4 SERVINGS.

EARLY BIRD BURRITOS
These are just as good for "supper".

Sauté . . . .   ¼ cup **GREEN PEPPER**, chopped
                                       ¼ cup **ONION**, chopped
In . . . .   2 Tbsp. **BUTTER** or
                                       MARGARINE
Reduce heat, add . . . .   ¼ pound **VELVEETA CHEESE**,
                                       cubed
                                       6 **EGGS**, beaten

Cook slowly, stirring occasionally, until eggs are set and cheese is melted. Heat in microwave, or wrap in foil and heat in oven, 4 large (10-inch) **FLOUR TORTILLAS**. Spoon egg mixture into middle of tortilla. Fold bottom over mixture about ⅓ way up. Fold over two of the sides. Serve with **SALSA** or **PICO DE GALLO**.

VARIATION: Dice 1 medium **POTATO** and sauté with the pepper and onion.

TORTILLA SCRAMBLE
Good for Lunch, Brunch, or Supper !!!

Heat in 350-degree oven for 15 minutes about 8 **FLOUR TORTILLAS**.
While **TORTILLAS** are heating,
cook until brown . . . . ½ pound **PORK SAUSAGE**,
crumbled
3 **FRESH GREEN ONIONS**,
chopped, with tops

Remove from skillet and drain on paper towels. Set aside.
Wipe out skillet. Add . . . . 3 Tbsp. **MARGARINE**
Combine and pour in pan . . . . 4 **EGGS**
2 Tbsp. **HEAVY CREAM**
SALT and **PEPPER**

Cook over medium heat, stirring often, until eggs are firm but still moist.
Add sausage mixture. Spoon an equal amount of sausage-egg mixture
into center of each warm tortilla. Sprinkle with grated **SHARP CHED-
DAR CHEESE**. Serve immediately with **PICANTE SAUCE**.

SOUTHERN STYLE CASSEROLE
We used RICE this time in place of the GRITS.

Combine . . . . 4 **EGGS**, beaten
1 cup cooked **RICE**
½ cup **MILK**
¼ cup **MUSHROOMS**, chopped
SALT and **PEPPER**

Pour into a buttered 8x8x2-inch baking dish. Bake at 350-degrees for 25
to 30 minutes or until set. Cut into 4 squares, and serve hot with **CHEESE
SAUCE**. (Make **SAUCE** while egg mixture is baking.)

CHEESE SAUCE:
In small saucepan, melt . . . . 1 Tbsp. **MARGARINE**
Add . . . . 1 Tbsp. **FLOUR**
Stir until smooth. Gradually
add . . . . ¾ cup **MILK**,

Cook over medium heat until thickened and bubbly. Stir constantly.
(Add more **MILK** if mixture becomes too thick.)
Add . . . . ½ cup **CHEESE**
SALT and **PEPPER**

Stir until cheese melts. Pour over egg squares.

HUEVOS POBLANOS

Ideal for brunch, late night supper, and after skiing.

Whirl in blender . . . .   1 can (4 oz.) **GREEN CHILIES**, chopped, do NOT drain
1½ cups **LIGHT CREAM**
SALT

Pour into buttered baking dish. Carefully break 6 **EGGS** on top of cream and chile mixture.

Sprinkle with . . . .   ½ cup **SWISS CHEESE** grated

Bake at 350-degrees until eggs are set. Serve with warm **TORTILLAS**, **HOT BISCUITS** or **TOASTED ENGLISH MUFFINS**.

YIELD: 3 TO 6 SERVINGS.

MINI McMUFFINS A LA JAN-SU

These are easy and good.

Split and toast . . . .   3 **ENGLISH MUFFINS**
Combine . . . .   ¼ pound cubed **VELVEETA CHEESE**
¼ cup **MILK**
2 Tbsp. **GREEN ONION**, sliced

Stir over low heat until cheese is melted. For each serving, top muffin half with 1 slice **HAM** and 1 slice **TOMATO**. Broil until hot. Top with cheese sauce.

YIELD: 6 SERVINGS

THE BREAKFAST "PATTIE-MELT"

Sandwiches for breakfast? Why not?

Toast . . . .   4 **FROZEN WAFFLES**
Cover each waffle with . . . .   1 slice **VELVEETA CHEESE**
2 **BACON** slices, crisply cooked
1 **APPLE** ring, cored

Add second Velveeta slice to each waffle. Broil until cheese is melted.

51

"PAPPYS" GRIT PATTIES
These are a good substitute for bread.

Cook according to directions . . . . ⅓ cup uncooked **REGULAR GRITS**
Stir in . . . . 2 Tbsp. **SELF RISING FLOUR**
¼ tsp. **SALT**
⅛ tsp. **PEPPER**
1 **EGG**, slightly beaten

Mix well. Drop mixture by tablespoonfuls into **HOT OIL**. Gently flatten with spatula. Brown on both sides; drain on paper towels. Serve patties immediately. (Try to turn only once.)

YIELD: 8 SERVINGS.

BERRIES IN A GIANT PUFF
Bakes in a different shape every time you make it.

Place in a 9-inch pie plate . . . . 3 Tbsp. **MARGARINE**

Place in preheated 475-degree oven to melt margarine and heat plate. In medium mixing bowl whisk
together . . . . 2 **EGGS**
½ cup **MILK**
½ cup **FLOUR**
½ tsp. **GRATED ORANGE PEEL**

Remove pie plate from oven. Pour in egg mixture. Immediately return to oven. Bake 10 to 12 minutes or until very puffy and golden. Remove from oven. Leave puff in pie plate.
Fill with . . . . ¾ cup **BLUEBERRIES**
¾ cup **RASPBERRIES**
¾ cup **STRAWBERRIES**

Top with . . . . **WHIPPED TOPPING** or **SOUR CREAM**

Cut into wedges and serve.

YIELD: 4 SERVINGS

VARIATION: Use only 2 ½ cups **STRAWBERRIES**.

CHEESE AND CHILI PUFF
For extra zip, serve with SALSA.

Combine . . . . 1 pound **CHEDDAR CHEESE**,
coarsely grated
1 pound **MONTEREY JACK
CHEESE**, coarsely grated
4 ounces **CHOPPED GREEN
CHILIES**, more if you like it hot

Spread evenly in a buttered baking dish.
Mix . . . . 1 cup **SOUR CREAM**
3 **EGGS**, slightly beaten
1 tsp. **SALT**
⅛ tsp. **PEPPER**

Pour over cheese mixture. Bake uncovered 45 to 50 minutes at 350-degrees. Serve immediately.

YIELD: 8 TO 10 SERVINGS.

EGG McMUFFINS A LA JAN-SU
Soooo, everybody has their version.

Toast and keep warm . . . . 4 **ENGLISH MUFFINS**, split
Separate **YOLKS** from
 WHITES of . . . . 8 hard boiled **EGGS**

Chop **EGG WHITES**. Finely grate **EGG YOLKS**. Set aside.
Melt in heavy saucepan . . . . 6 Tbsp. **BUTTER** or
MARGARINE
Gradually add . . . . 6 Tbsp. **FLOUR**

Cook about 1 minute, stirring constantly.
Gradually stir in . . . . 4 cups **MILK**

Cook over medium heat, stirring constantly, until thickened and bubbly.
(May need to add more **MILK** if mixture becomes too thick to pour.)
Remove from heat, add . . . . ¾ tsp. **SALT**
¾ tsp. **PAPRIKA**
¼ tsp. **PEPPER**
2 cups **COOKED HAM**, diced

Gently fold in egg whites. Pour ham mixture over toasted English Muffin half. Sprinkle egg yolk over each serving.

EARLY MORNING EYE-OPENERS

DICK PIRTLES' FRENCH TOAST:

Slice dry **BREAD** ¾-inch thick. Then halve into triangles. Trim crust. Combine 2 beaten **EGGS**, ½ cup **CREAM**, and dash of **SALT**. Soak **BREAD**. Fry **BREAD** in **OIL** until golden brown. Drain. Place toast on a baking sheet. Bake in a 400-degree oven until it puffs up (about 3 to 5 minutes.) Sprinkle with **POWDERED SUGAR** and serve with **APPLE-SAUCE, HONEY, MAPLE SYRUP**, or **JAM**.

CROISSANT BENEDICT:
Make **HOLLANDAISE SAUCE** day ahead.

Top bottom half of split **CROISSANT** with warm thinly sliced cooked **HAM**, then a poached **EGG**. Cover with **CROISSANT** top. Spoon on **HOLLANDAISE SAUCE**.

CHEESY CROISSANT: "Brown-bag" this one if a microwave is available.

Mix equal amounts of soft or softened **CREAM CHEESE** and shredded **CHEDDAR**. Spread on bottom half of **CROISSANT**. Sprinkle with chopped **WALNUTS**. Set top half in place. Brush with melted **BUTTER** or **MARGARINE** and sprinkle with grated **PARMESAN CHEESE**. Bake in preheated 350-degree oven until hot, about 10 minutes or heat in microwave.

QUICKIE COFFEE CAKE RING: Allow 30 minutes baking time.

Butter an 8-inch ring mold. Pour 2 to 3 Tbsp. **HONEY** on the bottom of the pan. Chop finely about ½ cup **NUTS**. Open 2 cans **REFRIGERATED BISCUITS**. Roll each biscuit in chopped nuts. Place them into the mold, slightly overlapping. Pour ¼ cup honey over the top. Bake about 30 minutes in a 375-degree oven.

FLAVORFUL WAFFLES: Add chopped pecans, crumbled bacon or grated cheese.

Breads

CANNING JAR BREAD

Bruce and Jayme gave these to the children's nursery school teachers for Christmas. They received many requests for the recipe.

Wash and dry 8 pint size (wide-mouth) canning jars. *Grease well.* Preheat oven to 325-degrees.

Cream . . . . ⅔ cup **SHORTENING**
2⅔ cups **SUGAR**
Add . . . . 4 **EGGS**
⅔ cup **WATER**
Beat well and add . . . . 2 cups **PUMPKIN**
ADD WITH SPOON . . . . 3⅓ cups **FLOUR**
½ tsp. **BAKING POWDER**
2 tsp. **SODA**
1½ tsp. **SALT**
1 tsp. each **CINNAMON** and **CLOVES**
1 cup **PECANS**, chopped (opt.)

Fill jars ½ full. Bake in preheated oven for 45 to 55 minutes. When done, remove one *at a time* from oven. Put scalded lid on and seal. For gifts, tie ribbon around lid. Hot glue appropriate ornament.

VARIATION: Omit the **PUMPKIN** and substitute any of the following:

2 cups **APPLESAUCE**
1 can **WHOLE CRANBERRY SAUCE**
2 cups shredded **APPLES**
2 cups shredded **CARROTS**

2 cups shredded **ZUCCHINI**
2 cups mashed **BANANAS**
1 cup shredded **APPLES**, plus 1 cup shredded **CARROTS**.

CINNAMON BREAKFAST BISCUITS

· *For people on the run.*

Melt in small bowl . . . . ½ cup **MARGARINE**
Mix separately . . . . ½ cup **SUGAR**
2 tsp. **CINNAMON**
Separate . . . . 2 cans **BISCUITS**

Dip each biscuit in margarine, then in cinnamon and sugar. Overlap 15 biscuits around outer rim of greased 9-inch pan. Overlapping remaining 5 in center. Sprinkle with remaining sugar and cinnamon. Bake in 425-degree oven for 15 minutes.

VARIATION: Just before browned, cover with **PRESERVES** of your choice. Return to oven and finish cooking.

WALLACE'S APRICOT NUT BREAD
This is a third generation recipe.

Place in medium bowl, cover, and let set on cabinet overnight, 1 can (6 oz.) thawed frozen **ORANGE JUICE** and 2 packages (6 oz. ea.) chopped **DRIED APRICOTS**.

Cream in large bowl . . . . 2 cups **SUGAR**
                                           4 Tbsp. **MARGARINE**
                                           2 **EGGS**, beaten

Drain juice and reserve. Set aside apricots. Add to juice enough **WATER** to make 1¼ cups liquid.

Add alternately with . . . . 4 cups **FLOUR**
                                              4 tsp. **BAKING POWDER**
                                              ½ tsp. **SODA**
                                              1 tsp. **SALT**

When well mixed, add apricots and 2 to 3 cups **PECANS**. Pour into 2 loaf pans, (or 4 individual pans) lined with wax paper. Set on counter top for 30 minutes to rise. Bake in preheated 325-degree oven for 45 to 55 minutes, until toothpick inserted in center comes out clean. Keep refrigerated. Wrap well for freezer. These will keep indefinitely.

BISCUIT MONKEY BREAD
EASY-DO

Sprinkle evenly in bottom of
  well-greased bundt pan . . . . ½ cup **PECANS**, chopped
Combine . . . . ½ cup **SUGAR**
                                                   1 tsp. **CINNAMON**
Cut into quarters . . . . 3 cans (10 oz.) refrigerated
                                               BUTTERMILK BISCUITS
Dip into sugar mixture and layer in pan.
Combine . . . . : . . . . 1 cup firmly packed **BROWN SUGAR**
                                                   ½ cup **MARGARINE**, melted

Pour over dough. Bake at 350-degrees for 30 to 40 minutes. Cool about 10 minutes, invert onto serving plate.

CRUNCHY STRAWBERRY MUFFINS
Always a favorite.

Mix in medium bowl . . . .   1 cup **FLOUR**
                                        1 tsp. **BAKING POWDER**
                                        ¼ tsp. **SALT**
                                        4 Tbsp. **SUGAR**
                                        ½ tsp. **CINNAMON**
Cut in with pastry blender . . . .   4 Tbsp. **MARGARINE**
Mix together   2   **EGGS**
                                        4 Tbsp. **MILK**
Stir into flour mixture. Do not overmix.
Stir in . . . .   1 cup fresh **STRAWBERRIES**,
                                        sliced.

Pour into well greased muffin tins. Top with **STREUSEL**.

STREUSEL

Mix in small bowl . . . .   4 Tbsp. **FLOUR**
                                        4 Tbsp. **SUGAR**
                                        1 tsp. **CINNAMON**
                                        2 Tbsp. **MARGARINE**, softened

Mix together and top each muffin with mixture. Bake at 350-degrees for
20 to 25 minutes or until golden. Serve warm.

RASPBERRY BREAD
Great holiday gift for family and neighbors.

Mix together in large mixing
   bowl . . . .   3 cups **FLOUR**
                                      2 cups **SUGAR**
                                        3 tsp. **CINNAMON**
                                        1 tsp. **SODA**
                                        1 tsp. **SALT**
Mash and mix separately . . . .   1 pkg. (20 oz.) frozen
                                        RASPBERRIES, thawed and
                                        juice reserved
Add . . . .   4 **EGGS**, beaten
                                        1 cup **VEGETABLE OIL**

Mix well. If batter is too thick, add some of the reserved juice. Pour into 2 greased and floured 9x5x3-inch loaf pans. Bake in preheated 350-degree oven for 1 hour. May also use for miniature muffins for a party.

YIELD: 2 LOAVES.

VARIATION: **STRAWBERRIES** may be substituted.

MULTI GRAIN PEAR MUFFINS
These are good and healthy.

Mix in bowl. . . . . .1½ cups **PEARS**, chopped
                                    ½ cup **MILK**
                                    ⅓ cup **VEGETABLE OIL**
                                    1 **EGG**
In separate bowl mix. . . . .   ¾ cup **FLOUR**
                                    ¾ cup **CORNMEAL**
                                    ½ cup **WHOLE WHEAT FLOUR**
                                    ½ cup **OLD-FASHIONED**
                                    ROLLED OATS
                                    ½ cup **SUGAR**
                                    2 tsp. **BAKING POWDER**
                                    ½ tsp. **SALT**
                                    ¼ cup **RAISINS**

Combine ingredients. Stir just until blended. Bake in ¾-inch muffin cups. Bake 375-degrees for 35 minutes or until browned.

YIELD: 12 MUFFINS.

CINNAMON BITS
A make ahead and freeze.

Cut crust off and flatten with
  rolling pin . . . . 1 loaf thin white **SANDWICH BREAD**
Spread each piece with a thin
  layer of . . . . 1 pkg. (8 oz.) **CREAM CHEESE**
Mix in small bowl . . . . 1 cup **SUGAR** and 3 tsp. **CINNAMON**
Roll slices of bread tightly and cut into quarters.
Dip in . . . . **MARGARINE**, melted

Then dip each roll in sugar mixture. Place on cookie sheet and freeze. After frozen, store in plastic bag. When ready to serve, place on cookie sheet and bake at 350-degrees until rolls are bubbly and puffy. Serve with **SOUR CREAM** and **STRAWBERRY PRESERVES** for dipping.

BANANA MUFFINS

Combine and beat until fluffy . . . . ½ cup **MARGARINE**, softened
                                     1 cup **SUGAR**
Add and beat well . . . . 2 **EGGS**
Stir in . . . . 3 ripe **BANANAS**, mashed
Add . . . . .1¼ cups **FLOUR**
                                     ½ tsp. **SODA**

Stir just enough to moisten all ingredients. Fill muffin pans two-thirds full. Bake at 350-degrees for 25 minutes or until done.

YIELD: 12 TO 15 MUFFINS

VARIATION: May add ½ cup chopped **PECANS**.

MUFFIN BATTER: Stir only enough to moisten. Batter will appear lumpy.

EVER-READY REFRIGERATOR MUFFINS
Made with 100% Bran.

Heat to boiling .... 2 cups **WATER**
Pour over .... 2 cups 100% **BRAN CEREAL**
Set aside.
Cream together .... 2½ cups **SUGAR**
                                  1 cup plus 3 Tbsp. **SHORTENING**
Add and beat well .... 4 **EGGS**
Stir in .... 2 tsp. **SALT**
                                  5 tsp. **SODA**
                                  4 cups **BUTTERMILK**
Add first mixture. Combine and
   add .... 4 cups 40% **BRAN FLAKES CEREAL**
                                  6 cups **FLOUR**

Mix well, cover and store in refrigerator until ready to use. Will keep 5 or 6 weeks. When ready to bake, spoon batter into greased muffin tins, filling cups ⅔ full. Bake in preheated 400-degree oven for 20 minutes.

YIELD: FULL RECIPE 5 TO 6 DOZEN.

EFFIE'S BUNS
I always looked forward to my Aunt Effie's rolls.

Mix together in large mixing
   bowl .... 2 pkg. **YEAST**
In .... 3 cups warm **WATER**
When yeast has dissolved add ... ½ cup **SUGAR**
                                  1 Tbsp. **SALT**, rounded
                                  2 Tbsp. **SHORTENING**
Add part of .... 7 or more cups **FLOUR**

Add enough to make the consistency of pancake batter. Beat with electric mixer for 10 minutes. Then add the remainder of flour to make a stiff dough. Place in a large greased bowl. Cover and let rise in warm place, free from drafts. When it has doubled in size, punch down with fingers. Do this 2 to 3 times. Make into 2 loaves or make into rolls. Place in greased pans. Bake loaves at 350-degrees for 45 to 50 minutes or until loaves sound hollow when tapped. Bake rolls until brown. When baked, brush tops with **MARGARINE**.

EARTH BREAD
A truly different bread from the kitchen of Barbara White.

In large mixing bowl mix	2 cups hot **WATER**
	1 cup **OATS**
	½ cup **BROWN SUGAR**
	1 Tbsp. **SALT**
	2 Tbsp. **SHORTENING**, melted
Set aside. Cool to lukewarm.	
Dissolve	1 pkg. **YEAST**
In	¼ cup lukewarm **WATER**
Add to first mixture.	
Add to make stiff dough	2¼ cups **WHOLE WHEAT FLOUR**
	3¼ cups regular **FLOUR**

Let rise in same bowl 1½ hours or until doubled. Knead without flour. Just dust hands with flour. Grease 2 to 3 loaf pans and dust with powdered sugar. Divide dough evenly in pans. Let rise in warm place for about 1 hour. Bake in preheated oven at 325-degrees for 30 to 45 minutes until brown.

BOBBIES QUICK "ALMOST" YEAST ROLLS

Melt in 13x9x2-inch pan	¼ cup **MARGARINE**
Mix in bowl	2 cups **SELF-RISING FLOUR**
	2 Tbsp. **SUGAR**
Add and stir together to make soft dough	1 cup **MILK**

Turn out on floured surface, knead 5 to 6 times. Roll out and cut into squares or use biscuit cutter. Place in pan and turn in margarine. Bake at 450-degrees for 10 to 15 minutes or until brown. Will be very buttery.

TO FREEZE UNBAKED YEAST ROLLS: Freeze individually on cookie sheet. Package frozen dough in plastic bags and freeze. When ready to use, remove and allow dough to rise in a pan and bake.

YEAST ROLLS

Easy rolls for a beginning cook.

Heat to lukewarm . . . .   2 cups **WATER**
Add to water and stir
    until dissolved . . . .   2 packages **DRY YEAST**
                                           1 cup **SUGAR**
                                           1 Tbsp. **SALT**
Add . . . .   1 cup **OIL**
                                           7 cups **FLOUR**, one cup at a time

This is a very stiff dough. Knead on a lightly floured board until smooth. Put dough in a large greased bowl, cover with a cloth and let rise at room temperature until double in size. Punch down. Roll out, cut and place in greased pan. Place in draft-free place until double in size (about 1 to 1½ hours). Bake in a preheated oven at 400-degrees for 12 to 15 minutes.

YIELD: 3 TO 4 DOZEN ROLLS.

CHEESE ROLLS

Mix all together in large
    mixing bowl . . . .   2 cups warm **WATER**
Add and let dissolve . . . .   1 pkg. dry **YEAST**
Add . . . .   ½ cup **SUGAR**
                                           1 tsp. **SALT**
                                           5 Tbsp. **SHORTENING**
                                           5 cups **FLOUR**
Cover and let rise in warm draft-free place.
Mix into dough . . . .   2 cups **CHEDDAR CHEESE**,
                                           grated

Make into rolls. Let rise again until double. Bake at 425-degrees for 10 to 15 minutes, until brown.

LIGHT BREAD
This is a Fortner family tradition.

PART I

Scald........................	2 cups **MILK** (may use powdered milk)
Add.........................	3 Tbsp. **SUGAR**
Then add	1 cup **COLD WATER**

Set aside.

Dissolve	2 packages **DRY YEAST**
In..........................	¼ cup **LUKEWARM WATER**

Add to milk mixture when it is slightly cool.

Then add	4 cups **FLOUR**

PART II

Mix together in separate mixing bowl	¾ cup **SUGAR**
	1 cup **SHORTENING**, melted
	1 tsp. **SALT**
	2 **EGGS**, well beaten
	1 tsp. **ALMOND FLAVORING**

Add Part II to Part I

Slowly add	4 cups **FLOUR**

Knead until satiny feeling. (May use electric mixer with dough hooks). May need to add a little more flour. Let rise 1 hour or until double in size. Divide in 4 parts, knead lightly on floured board. Put in greased bread pans. Let rise until double in size again. Bake at 350-degrees approximately 40 minutes, or until golden brown. Should sound hollow when tapped on top.

YIELD: 4 LOAVES.

VARIATION: May substitute 2 cups **WHOLE WHEAT FLOUR** or **BUTTER FLAVORED SHORTENING**. Make into rolls or make **CINNAMON** rolls with the dough.

SOFT CRUST: When bread is baking a small dish of water in the oven will help to keep the crust from getting hard.

QUICK CHEESE BREAD

Mix together . . . .   3 cups **BISCUIT MIX**
   2 cups **CHEDDAR CHEESE**,
   grated
   1 cup **MILK**
   2 **EGGS**
   ½ cup **OIL**
   1 Tbsp. **POPPY SEED**
   2 Tbsp. **INSTANT ONION**

Mix and pour into a greased 2-quart baking dish. Bake in a preheated 350-degree oven for 30 to 35 minutes.

YIELD: 6 SERVINGS

SPUDS MACKENZIE'S MUFFINS
Spuds suggests using 2 cans of beer. (One to drink.)

Mix . . . .   3 cups **SELF-RISING FLOUR**
   3 Tbsp. **SUGAR**
   2 cups **BEER** (room temperature)
   1 **EGG**

May roll and cut with biscuit cutter or fill muffin tins ⅔ full. Bake in preheated 350-degree oven for 15 to 20 minutes.

VARIATION:
May add ¼ cup grated **ONION** or ½ cup grated **CHEESE** or both.

YEAST BISCUITS
These are quick and easy.

Dissolve together . . . .   1 pkg. **DRY YEAST**
   1 cup **WATER**, lukewarm
Add . . . .   ½ tsp. **SALT**
   3 Tbsp. **SHORTENING**
   2 Tbsp. **SUGAR**
   2½ cups **FLOUR**

Mix well. Knead 2 to 3 minutes. Roll dough to ½-inch thickness. Cut with biscuit cutter. Let rise 35 to 45 minutes or until doubled in size. Place on slightly greased cookie sheet. Bake in preheated oven at 375-degrees 10 to 15 minutes or until brown.

CORNMEAL BISCUITS
A good taste treat.

Combine	2 cups **FLOUR**
	¾ cups **CORNMEAL**, coarse ground
	1 Tbsp. **SUGAR**
	1 Tbsp. **BAKING POWDER**
	½ tsp. **SODA**
	½ tsp. **SALT**
Cut in with pastry blender or two knives, using scissor motion ...	½ cup **MARGARINE**
Add and stir until all ingredients are moistened	1 cup **BUTTERMILK**

On floured surface knead 4 to 5 times. Roll to ½-inch thickness, cut with 2½ inch biscuit cutter. Bake on greased baking sheet 10 to 12 minutes at 425-degrees until browned.

YIELD: 18 BISCUITS.

HIGH-RISE DINNER BISCUITS

Scald and cool to lukewarm	4 cups **MILK**
Add and dissolve..............	3 pkgs. **YEAST**
Add.........................	¾ cup **SUGAR**
	1 cup **SHORTENING**
Add and mix..................	3½ cups **FLOUR**
Let rise two hours in a very large bowl.	
Add.........................	2 tsp. **SALT**
	2 Tbsp. **BAKING POWDER**
	1 tsp. **SODA**
	4½ cups **FLOUR**

Mix, roll out and cut with biscuit cutter. Place on **OILED** cookie sheet. Freeze. Remove frozen biscuits and store in plastic bags. Keep frozen until ready to bake. *Do not thaw* before baking. Do not grease pan. Preheat oven to 450-degrees. Bake 10 to 12 minutes.

YIELD: 50 to 60 BISCUITS.

BUTTERMILK BISCUITS

Sift together into a bowl	2 cups **FLOUR**
	½ tsp. **SALT**
	2 tsp. **BAKING POWDER**
	½ tsp. **SODA**
Cut into dry ingredients with pastry blender, or two knives using scissor motion	6 Tbsp. **SHORTENING**
Quickly stir in	¾ cup **BUTTERMILK**

Turn onto slightly floured board or waxed paper and knead about 6 times. Roll or pat to desired thickness, and cut with biscuit cutter. Place on a lightly oiled baking sheet. Bake in a preheated 475-degree oven for 10 to 12 minutes.

YIELD: 12 MEDIUM BISCUITS.

CHEESY SAUSAGE BISCUITS

Crumble into a large skillet	1 pound mild **SAUSAGE**
Add	1 small **ONION**, finely chopped
Cook until sausage is browned. Drain well on paper towels.	
Combine	1 can (11 oz.) **CHEDDAR CHEESE SOUP**, undiluted
	½ cup **WATER**
	3 cups **BISCUIT MIX**

Mix together and drop by heaping tablespoonfuls about 2 inches apart on lightly greased baking sheets. Bake at 425-degrees for 15 minutes or until lightly browned.

MAYONNAISE BISCUITS

Combine and mix well	1 cup **SELF-RISING FLOUR**
	½ cup **BUTTERMILK**
	2 Tbsp. **MAYONNAISE**

Drop by teaspoonfuls onto a lightly greased cookie sheet. Bake in a preheated 425-degree oven for 10 to 12 minutes.

YIELD: 8 TO 10 ROLLS.

ANGEL FLAKE BISCUITS
A biscuit and roll combination.

Mix in a medium bowl .... 5 cups **FLOUR**
4 Tbsp. **SUGAR**
1 tsp. **SALT**
3 Tbsp. **BAKING POWDER**
1 tsp. **SODA**

Cut in with a pastry blender, or
two knives, using scissor
motion .... 1 cup **SHORTENING**
Dissolve in a separate bowl, and
add to dry mixture............ 1 package **DRY YEAST**
2 Tbsp. **WATER**, warm
Add .... 2 cups **BUTTERMILK**

Mix well. Store in the refrigerator, in an air-tight container. Will keep up to 5 days. To bake, put dough on lightly floured board or waxed paper, and roll to desired thickness. Cut and put on a greased cookie sheet. Bake in a preheated 400-degree oven for 12 to 15 minutes. These rolls should be allowed to rise about 20 minutes before baking.

YIELD: 4 DOZEN.

WHOLE WHEAT BISCUITS
A real eye opener.

Combine in a medium bowl ..... 1¼ cups **FLOUR**
¾ cup **WHOLE WHEAT FLOUR**
2 Tbsp. **SUGAR**
1 tsp. **BAKING POWDER**
½ tsp. **SODA**
½ tsp. **SALT**

Cut in with pastry blender or
knives, using a scissor
motion .... 3 Tbsp. **MARGARINE**
Dissolve .... 1 pkg. **DRY YEAST**
In .... ¼ cup **WARM WATER**
When dissolved, add .... ⅔ cup **BUTTERMILK**

Stir into flour mixture until moistened. Cover and refrigerate overnight.

Turn out onto floured board, knead 1 minute. Roll ½-inch thick. Cut with biscuit cutter. Bake in pan sprayed with **COOKING SPRAY**, 12 minutes at 425-degrees until golden. May keep refrigerated 3 to 4 days.

YIELD: 15 BISCUITS.

BACON BISCUITS

Combine	2	cups **BUTTERMILK BAKING MIX**
Cook crisp, crumble and add	8	slices **BACON**
Mix	¾	cup **MILK**
	1	**EGG**
Add to top mixture along with . . .	1	cup **CHEDDAR CHEESE**, grated
	2	Tbsp. **ONION**, finely chopped
	1	jar (2 oz.) **PIMENTOS**, chopped drained

Stir just to mix. Fill greased muffin pans two-thirds full. Bake in a 400-degree oven 25 to 30 minutes. Serve warm.

YIELD: 2 BISCUITS.

BROCCOLI CORNBREAD
This is one of Thelma Scott's GOODIES.

Mix together	5	**EGGS**
	1	pkg. (10 oz.) chopped **BROCCOLI**, uncooked
	1	medium **ONION**, chopped
	¾	cup **MARGARINE**
	2	pkgs. (6 oz. ea.) **CORNBREAD MIX**, dry
	2	cups **COTTAGE CHEESE**
	1	tsp. **SALT**

Bake in a 13x9x2-inch pan that has been sprayed with **COOKING SPRAY.** Bake at 350-degrees for approximately 1 hour or until real brown on top. Soooo Good !!

VARIATION:
Try adding ½ small can chopped **JALAPENOS**.

BACON TRICK: Coat bacon with flour to keep from curling.

PICANTE CORNBREAD
For that South of the Border flavor.

Combine in a medium bowl . . . . .   1 cup **FLOUR**
¾ cup **CORNMEAL**
1½ tsp. **BAKING POWDER**
½ tsp. **SODA**
½ tsp. **SALT**
Add and slightly stir . . . .   1 cup **BUTTERMILK**
2 **EGGS**
4 Tbsp. **MARGARINE**, melted
6 Tbsp. **PICANTE SAUCE**

Heat large iron skillet or 8x8x2-inch pan that has 3 or 4 tablespoons of **BACON GREASE** and sprinkled with **CORNMEAL** and a little **SALT**. When cornmeal is light brown, add cornbread mixture. Bake at 425-degrees for 35 minutes or until golden brown.

YIELD: 6 TO 8 SERVINGS.

CORNBREAD STICKS

Mix in a medium bowl . . . .   1 cup **CORNMEAL**, yellow
stone ground
⅓ cup **FLOUR**
⅓ tsp. **SODA**
2 tsp. **BAKING POWDER**
1 tsp. **SALT**
1 tsp. **SUGAR**
Add all at one time . . . .   1 cup **BUTTERMILK**
1 **EGG**
¼ cup **OIL**

Mix well. Spoon into 2 hot greased cornbread stick pans. Bake in a preheated 450-degree oven 15 to 20 minutes until brown. Turn out of pans and serve immediately.

CHILI-CHEESE CORNBREAD

Combine in large bowl . . . . 3 **EGGS**, slightly beaten
1 can (17 oz.) **CREAM-STYLE CORN**
1 can (4 oz.) chopped **GREEN CHILIES**, drained
½ cup **MAYONNAISE**
¾ cup **ONION**, diced
2 cups **CHEDDAR CHEESE**, grated
2 cups **BUTTERMILK**
Stir to blend, add . . . . 3 cups self-rising **CORNMEAL MIX**

Stir just until moistened. Pour into greased 13x9x2-inch pan. Bake at 375-degrees for 40 to 45 minutes or until golden brown.

YIELD: 16 TO 18 SERVINGS.

WAFFLE BAKE CORNBREAD
A nice change from ordinary cornbread.

Mix together . . . . 1½ cups **CORNMEAL**
¾ cup **FLOUR**
2½ tsp. **BAKING POWDER**
½ tsp. **SODA**
2 Tbsp. **SUGAR**
½ tsp. **SALT**
Beat together . . . . 2 **EGGS**
1¼ cups **BUTTERMILK**
Mix both together, then add . . . . . . 6 Tbsp. **BACON DRIPPINGS** or **OIL**

Heat waffle baker and bake batter until steam no longer rises from sides of waffle baker (4 to 5 minutes). These may be frozen and reheated by dropping into the electric toaster.

YIELD: 8 WAFFLES.

INSTANT HUSH PUPPIES

Combine .... 2 cups **SELF-RISING CORNMEAL**
1 small **ONION**, chopped
¾ cup **MILK**
1 **EGG**, slightly beaten

Drop by tablespoonfuls into ..... **HOT OIL**

Cook only a few at a time, turning once. Fry until golden brown. Drain on paper towels.

YIELD: ABOUT 24 PUPPIES.

HOT WATER CORNBREAD PONES
May bake or fry these "goodies".

Measure into a small bowl .... 1 cup **CORNMEAL**
¾ tsp. **SALT**

Pour enough **BOILING WATER** into meal to make a stiff paste.

TO FRY: Heat enough **SHORTENING** in heavy skillet to be about 1-inch deep. With wet hands, shape dough into 2-inch long and ¼-inch thick oval pones. Or you may prefer dropping by teaspoonfuls into the hot shortening. Fry until golden brown.

TO BAKE: Heat oven to 475-degrees. With wet hands, make oval pones, 3-inches long and ½-inch thick. Put into a hot skillet with a small amount of melted **SHORTENING**. Bake until golden brown. Serve with lots of **BUTTER**.

FLUFFY BISCUITS: Kneading the dough for a half minute after mixing improves the texture of baking powder biscuits.

COWBOY CORNBREAD
Different and good.

In medium bowl, mix with
whisk . . . . .1½ cups **CORNMEAL**
           ½ cup **FLOUR**
           ½ tsp. **SODA**
           ½ tsp. **SALT**
Add and stir well . . . . 1 cup **MILK**
           2 **EGGS**
           2 Tbsp. **VEGETABLE OIL**
Fold in . . . . 2 cups **CHEDDAR CHEESE**,
           grated
           1 can (10.5 oz.) **CREAM STYLE CORN**
           1 **ONION**, chopped
          10 to 13 slices **BACON,** cooked
           and crumbled
           2 Tbsp. **PIMENTO**, chopped

Mix well and pour into a greased iron skillet or baking dish. Bake in a preheated oven at 350-degrees for 40 to 45 minutes.

YIELD: 8 TO 10 SERVINGS.

BAR-B-QUE BREAD
Hayes Stripling Sr's specialty.

Mix ½ cup **BAR-B-QUE SAUCE** with ½ cup **BUTTER** and 2 tablespoons **WORCESTERSHIRE SAUCE**. Spread generously on **BREAD**. Toast on grill, or put under broiler. Serve with **STEAK** cooked on grill.

EASY BREAD
"A real treat."

Combine . . . . ¼ cup **MARGARINE**, melted
           ½ tsp. **PARSLEY FLAKES**
           ¼ tsp. **GARLIC POWDER**
Brush on . . . . 2 (3 oz. ea.) **FRENCH ROLLS**, cut
           in half horizontally
Sprinkle with . . . . 2 Tbsp. **PARMESAN CHEESE**,
           grated
           ½ tsp. **POPPY SEEDS**

Place on baking sheet and broil until golden brown. Cut bread halves into 2 pieces.

YIELD: 4 SERVINGS.

GARLIC BUBBLE BREAD

Combine and mix . . . . ¼ cup **MARGARINE**, melted
1 **EGG**, beaten
1 tsp. **DRIED PARSLEY**
¼ tsp. **SALT**
½ tsp. **GARLIC POWDER**
Pinch off nugget size pieces of . . . 1 loaf frozen **BREAD DOUGH**, thawed

Dip in butter mixture and place in a well-greased loaf pan. Let rise until double. Bake at 375-degrees for 30 minutes. Cool for 10 minutes before removing from pan.

BREAKAWAY BUNDT BREAD
Has a tasty vegetable filling.

Cut into quarters . . . . 3 cans (10 oz. ea.) **BISCUITS** (not buttermilk or flakey)
Sauté together . . . . 1 cup **CELERY**, chopped
1 cup **GREEN BELL PEPPERS**, chopped
1 cup **GREEN ONION**, chopped
In . . . . ¼ cup **MARGARINE**
Melt separately . . . . ¾ cup **MARGARINE**
Mix with . . . . 6 slices **BACON**, cooked and crumbled
1 cup **CHEDDAR CHEESE**, grated

Add sautéed vegetables, pour over biscuit pieces and toss to coat well. Pour into greased and floured bundt pan. Bake at 350-degrees for 45 minutes. Cool in pan. A great addition to **SALADS**.

"TEXANS" FRENCH ONION SOUP
A cold winters delight.

Sauté in heavy saucepan until tender	4 large **ONIONS,** thinly sliced and separated into rings
In	½ cup **MARGARINE,** melted
Blend in and stir until smooth . . .	1 Tbsp. **FLOUR**
Gradually add	1 can (10½ oz.) **CHICKEN BROTH,** undiluted
	1 can (10½ oz.) **BEEF BROTH,** undiluted
	2 cups **WATER**
	¼ tsp. **PEPPER**

Simmer about 15 minutes. Place 8 ovenproof servings bowls on a baking sheet.

Place in each bowl	1 slice (¾-inch-thick) **FRENCH BREAD**

Pour soup over bread.

Top with	1 slice **MOZZARELLA CHEESE**
Sprinkle each with	2 tsp. **PARMESAN CHEESE**

Broil until cheese melts.

YEILD: 8 BOWLS.

15 MINUTE CHEESE SOUP

Blend in medium saucepan	1 jar (16 oz.) **CHEESE WHIZ**
	1 can (14½ oz.) **CHICKEN BROTH**
	1 cup **MILK**
	1 tsp. **TABASCO SAUCE**
	2 tsp. **WORCESTERSHIRE SAUCE**

Heat until almost boiling, stirring constantly.

Add	2 Tbsp. **CORNSTARCH**
Dissolved in	¼ cup **WATER**
Add to soup. Then add	1 Tbsp. **MARGARINE**

Heat until thickness you want.

VARIATION:
Add **BROCCOLI** pieces or **BACON** crumbled to first step.

CREAMY TOMATO SOUP

Combine in medium saucepan . . .   1 can (10¾ oz.) **TOMATO SOUP,** undiluted

                                   1 can (12 oz.) **EVAPORATED MILK**

When blended and warm add . . . .   1 can (14½ oz.) **STEWED TOMATOES,** undrained

                                   ½ cup **CHEDDAR CHEESE,** grated

Heat until soup is hot and cheese is melted.

Cook and crumble . . . .   6 slices **BACON**

Ladle into bowls and sprinkle top with bacon.

YIELD: 4 SERVINGS.

NEW ENGLAND CLAM CHOWDER
Very thick and creamy.

In a large saucepan brown . . . .   4 slices **BACON,** chopped

                                     1 small **ONION,** chopped

Drain and add liquid of . . . .   2 cans (6½ oz. ea.) **MINCED CLAMS**

                                   4 medium **POTATOES,** finely diced

                                   1 tsp. **SALT**

                                   ½ tsp. **PEPPER**

Cover and simmer until potatoes are tender.

Combine and add to above mixture . . . .   2 Tbsp. **CORNSTARCH**

                                   ¼ cup **MILK**

Then add . . . .   2 Tbsp. **MARGARINE**

                                  3¾ cups **MILK**

Add clams.

Cover and cook over medium heat, stirring constantly, until thickened. (Do not boil).

YIELD: ABOUT 8 CUPS.

SHERRY MEAD'S "CHEDDAR CHOWDER"

VEGGIES:

Bring to boil	2 cups **WATER**
Add	2 cups **POTATOES,** diced
	½ cup **CARROTS,** sliced
	½ cup **CELERY,** sliced
	¼ cup **ONION,** chopped
	1½ tsp. **SALT**
	¼ tsp. **PEPPER**

Cover and simmer 10 minutes. DO NOT DRAIN.

WHITE SAUCE:

Melt in saucepan	¼ cup **BUTTER** or **MARGARINE**
Add	¼ cup **FLOUR**
Add, stirring constantly	2 cups **MILK**
Add	4 ounces **CHEDDAR CHEESE,** cubed
	4 ounces **VELVEETA CHEESE,** cubed

Stir until cheese is melted.

Add	1 cup cooked **HAM**
	1 can **WHOLE KERNEL CORN,** drained

Add undrained vegetables. Heat but do not boil. Freezes well.

VARIATION:
Substitute 8 strips crisply-fried **BACON** for ham. Or sliced **WEINERS** for ham.

CORN-TOMATO CHOWDER

Cook until crisp	4 slices **BACON,** cut in small pieces

Drain bacon and reserve 2 tablespoons grease.

Add and cook for 5 minutes	½ cup **ONION,** chopped
	⅓ cup **GREEN PEPPER,** chopped
Add	1 can (17 oz.) **CREAM-STYLE CORN**
	1 can (16 oz.) **TOMATOES**
	1 cup **WATER**
	¾ tsp. **SALT**
	¼ tsp. **CHILI POWDER**
	¼ tsp. **PEPPER**

Add bacon. Cover and simmer for 20 minutes.

YIELD: 6 CUPS.

E-Z CHEESY-BROCCOLI SOUP
This is easy and very delicious.

Cook according to package
   directions . . . .   1 pkg. (10 oz.) frozen **CHOPPED BROCCOLI**
Drain well.
Sauté . . . .   ½ cup **ONION,** chopped
   ¼ cup **GREEN PEPPER,** chopped
In . . . .   2 Tbsp. **MARGARINE**
Add broccoli and . . . .   1 can (10¾ oz.) **CREAM OF CHICKEN SOUP**
   1½ cups **MILK**
   1 cup **WATER**
   ¾ pound **AMERICAN CHEESE,** cubed

Cook over medium heat until cheese is melted, stirring often.

YIELD: 5½ CUPS.

MICROWAVE BROCCOLI SOUP

In a 2-quart bowl combine . . . .   2 cups fresh **BROCCOLI** pieces
   3 cups **WATER**
   3 **CHICKEN** flavored **BOUILLON CUBES**
   ½ tsp. **SALT**
   ½ tsp. **PEPPER**
   ½ tsp. **ROSEMARY,** crushed (optional)
Cover, microwave on **HIGH** 10 minutes. Process in blender.
Beat in small bowl . . . .   1 **EGG**

Add small amount of soup to egg and stir. Add mixture to soup. Microwave on **HIGH** for 1½ minutes or until egg thickens soup.

YIELD: 1 QUART.

VARIATION:
¼ cup grated **CHEESE** may be added.

POPS SOUP
A good quick meal-in-one pan.

Brown in large saucepan . . . . 1 pound **GROUND BEEF**
Stirring to crumble.
Add . . . . 1 pkg. (16 oz.) **FROZEN** mixed
    VEGETABLES
  2 cups **TOMATO JUICE**
  2 cups **BEEF BROTH**
  2 cups **POTATOES,** cubed
  ½ tsp. **SALT**
  ½ tsp. **PEPPER**

Simmer 25 to 30 minutes until potatoes are tender. So good served with
CORNBREAD.

YIELD: 4 SERVINGS.

VARIATION:
ONIONS or other kinds of **VEGETABLES** may be added.

WEST TEXAS SOUP
This has just a hint of Mexican flavor.

Heat in skillet . . . . 2 Tbsp. **OIL**
Add and brown . . . . 2 pounds **BEEF STEW MEAT,**
  trimmed & cut in chunks
Place in slow cooker.
Add . . . . ¾ cup **ONION,** chopped
  2 cloves **GARLIC,** minced
  2 cans (14½ ozs. ea.)
    TOMATOES
  1 can (10¾ oz.) **TOMATO SOUP**
  1 can (10½ oz.) **BEEF BROTH**
  1 can (10½ oz.) **CHICKEN**
    BROTH
  ¼ cup **WATER**
  1 tsp. ground **CUMIN**
  1 tsp. **CHILI POWDER**
  1 tsp. **SALT**
  ½ tsp. **LEMON PEPPER**
  2 tsp. **WORCESTERSHIRE**
    SAUCE
  ⅓ cup mild **PICANTE SAUCE**

Cook on low for at least 10 hours. When serving place enough **TOR-
TILLA** quarters in bottom of each bowl to cover. Pour soup over tortilla
pieces: sprinkle with grated **CHEDDAR CHEESE.**

YIELD: 10 TO 12 SERVINGS.

SOMBRERO STEW
A meal in itself!

Brown in dutch oven	3	pounds lean boneless **BEEF,** cut into 1-inch cubes
	1	cup **ONIONS,** chopped
In	3	Tbsp. **BACON DRIPPINGS**
Add	1	can (28 oz.) **TOMATOES,** undrained and chopped
	1	can (4 oz.) **WHOLE GREEN CHILIES,** drained
	½	cup **BEEF BROTH**
	½	cup **CHICKEN BROTH**
	2	tsp. **GARLIC SALT**
	2	tsp. **PEPPER**
	1	tsp. ground **CUMIN**
Cover and simmer for 1 hour.		
Add	4	**POTATOES,** sliced

Cover and simmer another 30 minutes or until potatoes are tender.

YIELD: ABOUT 3½ QUARTS.

TEXICAN STEW
So simple you will make it again.

Brown on all sides	1½	pounds **STEW MEAT,** cut in 1-inch cubes
In	4	tsp. **OIL**
Add	1	**ONION,** chopped
	1	**GREEN PEPPER,** chopped
	1	clove **GARLIC,** minced
Cook a few minutes and add	2	Tbsp. **CHILI POWDER**
Stir to coat then add	1	can (16 oz.) **TOMATOES,** drained
	1	tsp. **SALT**
	¼	tsp. **PEPPER**
	1	can (16 oz.) **KIDNEY BEANS**
	1	can (8¾ oz.) **WHOLE KERNEL CORN**
	2	cups **WATER**

Simmer for 1 hour or until meat is fully cooked.

YIELD: 6 TO 8 SERVINGS.

LONE STAR STEW
A hearty stew for hungry cowboys.

Fry in a large stew pot	3	slices **BACON**
Remove bacon. Set aside.		
Add and sear..................	2	pounds **STEW MEAT**
Lower heat and add............	1	can (16 oz.) **TOMATOES**
	2	cups **BEEF BROTH**
	2	cups **WATER**
	2	ribs **CELERY,** sliced
	2	**ONIONS,** chopped
	2	cloves **GARLIC,** minced
	1	ounce **WORCESTERSHIRE SAUCE**
	1	tsp. **CHILI POWDER**
Cover and simmer 2 hours.		
Add to taste...................		**SALT, PEPPER** and **SEASONED SALT**
Add........................	4	**CARROTS,** sliced
	4	medium **POTATOES,** chunked
Cook about 1 hour or until vegetables are tender but not falling apart.		
Add........................	1	can (8 oz.) **WHOLE KERNEL CORN**

Add crumbled **BACON** and cook another 5 minutes. Serve in large bowls with plenty of **CRACKERS** or **CORNBREAD.**

VARIATION:
Stew should vary according to the **LEFTOVERS** in the refrigerator. That makes it interesting.

COWBOY STEW

*A special treat for the Franklin children, when "Daddy Mc"
would cook Cowboy Stew in an iron skillet on an open fire
on the Mescalero Indian reservation.*

Cook 6 slices **BACON** until crisp. Drain on paper towels and crumble.
Set aside.
Sauté in bacon drippings . . . . 1 cup **ONIONS,** sliced
½ cup **GREEN PEPPER,** diced
1 clove **GARLIC,** minced
Add . . . . .1½ pounds lean **GROUND BEEF**
Crumble and cook until brown.
Add . . . . 2 cans (1 lb. 13 oz. ea.)
TOMATOES
1 Tbsp. **CHILI POWDER**
SALT and **PEPPER**
Simmer 30 minutes. Add . . . . 1 can (12 oz.) **WHOLE KERNEL
CORN,** drained
1 can (16 oz.) **RED KIDNEY
BEANS**
2 cups **POTATOES,** diced

Simmer 15 more minutes. Sprinkle with crumbled **BACON** before serving. Serve with hot **CORNBREAD** and a **SALAD.** NOTE: Easy to prepare
for an outdoor cookout. Have veggies chopped and in baggies. Only need
one pan.

TACO SOUP

Connie Harris shared this winner with us.

Brown together in a large pot . . . . 2 lbs. **GROUND BEEF,** lean
1 **ONION,** chopped
Season meat with . . . . 2 tsp. **SEASONING SALT**
Then add, including juice . . . . 1 can (15 oz.) **KIDNEY BEANS**
1 can (15 oz.) **PINTO BEANS**
2 cans (16 oz. ea.) **STEWED
TOMATOES**
1 can (15½ oz.) **HOMINY**
1 can (15½ oz.) **TOMATO JUICE**
1 can (4 oz.) **DICED GREEN
CHILIES**
Stir and add . . . . 1 pkg. **TACO SEASONING,** dry
Optional. . . . . 1 pkg. **RANCH DRESSING,** dry

Simmer for about 45 minutes. This can either be served with **CRACKERS**
or is delicious served over **CORN CHIPS.** This is great for serving the
multitudes. This may also be frozen.

NINE BEAN SOUP MIX
Excellent for gifts.

Combine .... 1 lb. **DRIED YELLOW SPLIT PEAS**
1 lb. **DRIED BLACK BEANS**
1 lb. **RED BEANS**
1 lb. **DRIED PINTO BEANS**
1 lb. **DRIED NAVY BEANS**
1 lb. **DRIED GREAT NORTHERN BEANS**
1 lb. **DRIED RED LENTILS**
1 lb. **DRIED GREEN SPLIT PEAS**
1 lb. **DRIED BLACK-EYED PEAS**
1 lb. **DRIED PEARLED BARLEY**

Mix well and divide into 10 two-cup portions. Bag or put in fruit jars with bows and give to friends. Attach following instructions:

NINE BEAN SOUP

Wash and place in large pot.
Add water until it is 2 inches
above the level of .... 2 cups **NINE BEAN SOUP MIX**
Cover and let soak overnight.
Drain and add .... 2 qts. **WATER**
1 lb. **HAM,** diced
1 large **ONION,** chopped
1 clove **GARLIC,** minced
½ tsp. **SALT**
Cover and bring to boil. Reduce heat.
Simmer 1½ hours, or until beans are tender.
Add .... 1 can (16 oz.) **CHOPPED TOMATOES,** undrained
1 can (10 oz.) **CHOPPED TOMATOES** with **GREEN CHILIES,** undrained

Simmer 30 minutes stirring occasionally. Makes 2 quarts of soup.

TASTIER HOMEMADE SOUP: Add bouillon cubes.

HAMBONE SOUP

Barbara White prepares this on cold winter nights.

Combine in a large pan . . . . 1 **HAMBONE** with **MEAT** or ½
pound diced **HAM**
Add . . . . 2 quarts **WATER**
Bring to a boil and simmer about 20 minutes.
Then add . . . . 1 cup **ONIONS,** diced
1 cup **CELERY,** diced
1½ **TOMATOES,** peeled and diced
1½ cups **GREEN BEANS**
½ cup **WHOLE KERNEL CORN**
1 cup **TURNIPS**
1 cup **BLACKEYED PEAS**
2 cups **POTATOES,** diced
1 tsp. **SUGAR**
Add to taste . . . . **SALT & PEPPER**
½ tsp. **SEASONED SALT**

Simmer about 20 minutes or until vegetables are tender.

TAILGATE CHILI

Every one has their own version of chili.

In a large heavy pan, cook until
grey in color . . . . 2 pounds **GROUND BEEF,** lean
2 cloves **GARLIC,** finely chopped
2 medium **ONIONS,** chopped
Add . . . . 2 cans (16 oz. ea.) **WHOLE
TOMATOES**
3 tsp. **CHILI POWDER**
1 tsp. **SALT**
¼ tsp. **CAYENNE PEPPER**
¼ tsp. **PAPRIKA**
1 tsp. ground **CUMIN** seed
When bubbly, reduce heat to low. Cover and simmer for 2 hours, stirring
occasionally.
Then add . . . . 2 cans (15 oz. ea.) **PINTO
BEANS**, drained

Simmer for 15 minutes longer. Serve hot with plenty of **CATSUP** and
CRACKERS.

CAMP FIRE CHILI
An oldie and a goodie.

Brown in large heavy pot	2	pounds **CHILI GROUND BEEF**
	1	pound **GROUND BEEF**
After meat looses its color and is grey, add to cover meat		**HOT WATER**
Add	3	large **ONIONS,** chopped
	3	cloves **GARLIC,** chopped
	4	heaping Tbsp. **CHILI POWDER**
	2	tsp. **CAYENNE PEPPER**
	3	tsp. **SALT**
	1	can (8 oz.) **TOMATO SAUCE**
	1	cup **KETCHUP**

Simmer for 2 hours, stirring often. Fifteen minutes before removing from heat, sprinkle 3 Tbsp. **MASA HARINA FLOUR** over chili to thicken or add 6 **CRACKERS,** finely crushed. Serve big steaming bowls to hungry people.

SUPER BOWL CHILI
A Texas cookbook has to have chili recipes.

Fry in large heavy saucepan until grey in color. NO GREASE	2	pounds **CHILI MEAT,** very lean
Add	1	large **ONION,** chopped
	1	Tbsp. **GARLIC,** minced
	1	Tbsp. **SALT**
	3½	Tbsp. **CHILI POWDER**
	1	tsp. **GROUND CUMIN**
	3	cups hot **WATER**
	2	small cans **SNAPPY TOM**

Cook slowly for 3 hours.

DEVILED HAM SANDWICHES

Chop fine and mix	1	medium **ONION**
	¼	cup **GREEN PEPPER**
	½	cup **CELERY**
	¼	cup **STUFFED OLIVES**
Add	2	cans **DEVILED HAM**
Add until spreading consistency		**MIRACLE WHIP SALAD DRESSING**

Mix well and serve on **TOAST** or plain **SANDWICH BREAD.** Can make ahead and refrigerate until ready to serve.

STUFFINGS FOR CROISSANT SANDWICHES
Croissants make them special.

Split croissants and fill with your favorite filling. They may first be spread with melted **MARGARINE, MAYONNAISE, MUSTARD,** or your favorite **SALAD DRESSING.** Let your taste buds be your guide on this one.

BEEF au jus: Fill croissants with thinly sliced, **HOT ROAST BEEF** and sautéed, sliced **MUSHROMS.** Close croissant and top with **SOUR CREAM** mixed with prepared white **HORSERADISH** to taste.

HOT TURKEY: Spread bottom croissant half with **CRANBERRY SAUCE:** top with sliced **ROAST TURKEY.** Close croissant and spoon hot **TURKEY GRAVY** over it.

FIESTA: On bottom croissant half, spoon **CHILI;** sprinkle with chopped **ONION.** Top with sliced **MONTEREY JACK CHEESE** and bake in preheated oven until cheese melts. Serve with **JALAPENOS.**

TUNA-CHEESE: Fill with **TUNA SALAD** and top with **LETTUCE** and **CHEESE** slices.

HAM AND CHEESE: Fill with thinly sliced **HAM** and **AMERICAN CHEESE** slices.

SMOKY ROAST: Thinly sliced **ROAST** or **PORK** with smoke-flavored **CHEESE.**

CHICKEN OR TURKEY-CHEESE: Thin slices of **ROAST CHICKEN** or **TURKEY** and **PINEAPPLE-CHEESE** spread.

BLACK OLIVE SANDWICH SPREAD

Mix together . . . .   1 can (4¼ oz.) **BLACK OLIVES,** chopped
¼ cup **GREEN ONIONS & TOPS,** chopped
¾ cup **AMERICAN CHEESE,** grated
¼ cup **MAYONNAISE**

Mix and serve as desired.

PUFFED TOPLESS SANDWICHES

Combine in bowl . . . . 1⅔ cups cooked **CHICKEN,**
finely chopped
½ cup **CELERY,** diced
⅓ cup **MAYONNAISE**
1½ Tbsp. **LEMON JUICE**
¼ cup **SWEET RELISH**
Add to taste . . . .   **SALT & PEPPER**
Toast one side of . . . . 6 slices **WHOLE WHEAT BREAD**
Lightly butter untoasted side of bread. Spread with chicken mixture.
Beat into stiff peaks . . . . 3 **EGG WHITES**
Fold in . . . . ¾ cup **CHEDDAR CHEESE,** grated

Spread over chicken mixture. Bake at 450-degrees for 10 minutes or until golden brown. Serve.

YIELD: 6 SERVINGS.

BUNBURGERS

Cook until lightly browned . . . . . . 1 pound **GROUND BEEF**
Add and simmer 10 minutes . . . . . ½ cup **CELERY,** finely chopped
1 small **ONION**
½ cup **CATSUP**
1 Tbsp. **WORCESTERSHIRE SAUCE**
½ tsp. **SALT**
½ tsp. **PEPPER**
Stir in . . . . 1 cup **CHEDDAR CHEESE,** grated
Spoon mixture on bottoms of . . . . 4 **HAMBURGER BUNS**
Spread top half with . . . . **MAYONNAISE**

Place halves together. Wrap in aluminum foil and bake at 400-degrees for 20 minutes.

YIELD: 4 SERVINGS.

ONION ROLLS: Try the bakery ones for hamburger buns...soooo good.

RANCH BURGERS
May keep your Stetson hat on while eating these.

Brown in medium skillet . . . . 1 pound **GROUND BEEF**
With . . . . ½ cup **ONIONS**, chopped
                                  ½ tsp. **SEASONED SALT**
Add . . . . 1 cup **CHILI SAUCE**
                                  1 can (15 oz.) **RANCH-STYLE BEANS**
Simmer for 15 minutes. Spoon
  mixture on top of ½ of . . . . 6 **HAMBURGER BUNS**
Sprinkle with . . . . 1 cup **CHEESE**, grated

Top with the other half of hamburger buns. Serve with **PICKLE** and **CHIPS**.

YIELD: 6 SERVINGS.

PIZZABURGER

Combine . . . . .1½ pounds **GROUND BEEF**
                                  ½ tsp. **GARLIC SALT**
                                  ½ tsp. **PEPPER**
Shape into patties. Broil or grill to desired doneness.
Heat together. . . . . 1 can (16 oz.) **TOMATOES**,
                                  drained and chopped
                                  1 can (8 oz.) **TOMATO SAUCE**
                                  1 jar (2½ oz.) **MUSHROOMS**, drained
                                  1 tsp. **OREGANO LEAVES**
Simmer for 15 minutes.
Have ready . . . . 3 individual **FRENCH BREAD LOAVES**, baked and split
Place meat pattie on top of each half. Spread with sauce.
Top with. 1 pkg. (8 oz.) **MOZZARELLA CHEESE**, sliced
Then top with . . . . 2 cups **ONION**, cut in rings

Top with extra sauce; broil until cheese melts. Makes a nice meal.

YIELD: 6 OPENED FACE SANDWICHES.

BEANY BEEFBURGERS

Combine . . . . 2 pounds **GROUND BEEF**
2 tsp. **SALT**
¼ tsp. **PEPPER**
Shape into patties. Place in skillet and cook on both sides until done.
Set aside.
Combine . . . . ½ cup **CATSUP**
1 tsp. **CHILI POWDER**
1 can (16 oz.) **PINTO BEANS,** drained
4 Tbsp. **ONION,** chopped
2 Tbsp. **GREEN PEPPER,** finely chopped
Simmer in small saucepan 5 to 10 minutes, stirring occasionally.
Place beef patty on bottom
half of . . . . 6 **HAMBURGER BUNS**

Top patty with 3 or 4 tablespoons **HOT BEAN SAUCE.** Cover with bun tops.

YIELD: 6 SERVINGS.

DOG WRAPS
Let the kids do this one.

Slit down the center . . . . **BEEF HOT DOG WEINERS**
Insert with . . . . **AMERICAN CHEESE,** slices
Separate . . . . 1 can **CRESCENT ROLLS**

Place hot dog on shortest side of crescent roll. Roll up in dough. Place on cookie sheet with cheese side facing up. Bake at 375-degrees for 12 to 15 minutes or until golden brown.

BACON AND CHEESE DOGS
An old tradition revised.

Split lengthwise . . . . **FRANKFURTERS**
Insert with . . . . **CHEESE**
Wrap and secure with
toothpicks . . . . **BACON**

Place on broiler pan and broil for 5 minutes or until cheese is melted and bacon is crisp. Remove toothpick and drain. Serve on **HOT DOG BUNS.**

BAKED HOTDOGS
The all American food.

Blend together .... 6 Tbsp. **VINEGAR**
3 Tbsp. **FLOUR**
2 **ONIONS,** chopped
4½ Tbsp. **WORCESTERSHIRE SAUCE**
1 tsp. **SALT**
⅛ tsp. **CAYENNE PEPPER**
1 Tbsp. **PAPRIKA**
¾ tsp. **PEPPER**
1 Tbsp. **CHILI POWDER**
1½ cups **CATSUP**
2 Tbsp. **BROWN SUGAR**
6 Tbsp. **HOT WATER**
Pierce 5 to 6 times with a fork.... 20 **FRANKFURTERS**

Dip in sauce and arrange in a 13x9x2-inch baking dish. Pour remaining sauce over top. Cover and bake at 350-degrees for 1 hour. Serve on **HOT DOG BUNS**. May be prepared ahead.

CHEESEBURGER TURNOVERS

Combine .... ½ pound **GROUND BEEF**
3 Tbsp. **ONION,** chopped
½ tsp. **SALT**
¼ tsp. **PEPPER**
Cook until meat is lightly browned.
Roll into 5-inch circles on lightly
floured board .... 1 can (8 oz.) **REFRIGERATED BISCUITS**

Place 3 tablespoons meat mixture
on each circle. Cover with ..... 1 slice **AMERICAN CHEESE**

Moisten edges with **WATER** and place another circle over mixture. Seal edges by mashing along edges with a fork. Prick top with fork. Place turnovers on a greased cookie sheet. Bake at 425-degrees for 8 to 10 minutes.

YIELD: 5 SERVINGS.

HOT CRAB MUFFIN-WICHES
Try these for a quickie.

In small bowl blend	1 can (6 oz.) **CRABMEAT,** drained
	1 pkg. (4 oz.) **CREAM CHEESE,** softened
	1 tsp. **ONION,** minced
	2 Tbsp. **MAYONNAISE**
	2 Tbsp. **CATSUP**
	½ Tbsp. **WORCESTERSHIRE SAUCE**
Toast on cookie sheet	2 **ENGLISH MUFFINS,** halved
Spread with crab mixture.	
Top with.....................	**TOMATOES,** sliced
Top each half with	**OLD ENGLISH CHEESE,** slices

Bake at 350-degrees for 20 minutes.

YIELD: 4 SERVINGS.

HELOISE'S CHEESE SPREAD
We didn't think Heloise would mind.

Mix in medium bowl	1 pound **AMERICAN CHEESE,** coarsely grated
	1 cup **MAYONNAISE**
	½ cup **SWEET PICKLES,** finely chopped
	1 jar (2 ozs.) **PIMENTOS,** chopped and drained

If you want a thinner spread add a little liquid from the jar of pimentos. Keep refrigerated in jars with lid. Makes a quick sandwich, or good to stuff **CELERY** with mixture.

VARIATION:
To vary flavor add **CHOPPED SALAD OLIVES,** or **CHOPPED ONIONS.**

GREEN ONIONS: *Use all of it to the end; adds more flavor and color.*

ALL-PURPOSE SPREAD
Finger sandwiches, canapes, etc.

Blend together .... 6 ounces **CREAM CHEESE,** room
temperature
½ cup **MAYONNAISE** (do not
substitute)
Add and blend well .... ½ cup **PECANS,** chopped
1 cup **SALAD OLIVES,** chopped
2 Tbsp. **OLIVE JUICE**
DASH OF PEPPER

Will be slightly mushy. Refrigerate in covered container. Spread will become firm enough to spread. Delicious for finger sandwiches, or spread
on very thin **TOAST** and cover with shredded **LETTUCE.** Keeps well in
refrigerator.

MONTE CRISTO AU GRATIN
These are wonderful hot sandwiches.

Make sandwiches with .... 6 slices **BREAD**
And .... 12 slices **TURKEY, HAM** or both
Beat together .... 3 **EGGS,** slightly beaten
2 Tbsp. **WATER**
Dip sandwiches in egg and fry on
both sides in .... 2 Tbsp. **OIL**
Place in baking dish.
Mix in saucepan .... 1½ cups **SWISS CHEESE,** grated
½ cup **MILK**
½ cup **MAYONNAISE**
⅛ tsp. **GARLIC SALT**
⅛ tsp. **NUTMEG**

When cheese is melted and smooth, pour sauce over sandwiches and
broil 3 to 5 mintues. Serve while hot.

YIELD: 3 SERVINGS.

SLOPPY JOE POCKET SANDWICHES

Combine in skillet	1 pound **GROUND BEEF**
	1 **ONION,** chopped
Cook until browned	½ cup **CELERY,** chopped
Add	1 cup **TOMATO SAUCE**
	½ cup **CATSUP**
	1 Tbsp. **BROWN SUGAR**
	1 Tbsp. **VINEGAR**
	1 Tbsp. **WORCESTERSHIRE SAUCE**
	1 tsp. **DRY MUSTARD**
	¼ tsp. **SALT**
	¼ tsp. **PEPPER**

Bring to boil and then simmer 15 to 20 minutes. Cut 4 **POCKET BREAD ROUNDS** in half. Fill each with ⅓ cup meat sauce.

YIELD: 8 SANDWICHES.

MINI PIZZAS
Let the kids have a party and create their own.

For each person split	1 **ENGLISH MUFFIN**
Spread with	4 Tbsp. **PIZZA SAUCE,** canned or bottled
Top with	4 Tbsp. **GROUND BEEF,** cooked
	1 Tbsp. **ONION,** chopped
	6 Tbsp. **MOZZARELLA CHEESE,** grated

Place under broiler until cheese is melted and begins to bubble. May also microwave just until warm.

VARIATION:
Use any of the following. Try different combinations. Sliced **SALAMI** or **PEPPERONI, CHEDDAR CHEESE,** sliced **PEPPERS,** chopped **BLACK OLIVES** or cooked **GREEN PEPPERS.**

SHRIMP SANDWICH FILLING
Another one of Charlotte's "goodies."

Mix together	1 can (4½ oz.) **SHRIMP**, drained
	2 Tbsp. **LEMON JUICE**
	1 boiled **EGG,** chopped
	2 **GREEN ONIONS,** chopped
	¼ cup **CELERY,** minced
	4 **STUFFED OLIVES,** chopped
	¼ cup **MAYONNAISE**
	¼ tsp. **SALT**
	¼ tsp. **PEPPER**

Spread on sandwich **BREAD.**

VARIATION:
Fresh or frozen shrimp may be used.

REUBEN SANDWICHES
Easy to make!

For each sandwich use	2 slices **RYE BREAD**
Spread each slice with	1 Tbsp. **THOUSAND ISLAND SALAD DRESSING**
Arrange on one side	1 slice **SWISS CHEESE**
	3 slices **CORN BEEF,** thinly sliced
	2 tsp. canned **SAUERKRAUT,** drained

Place top on sandwich and butter outside of bread. Place in skillet and brown until golden and cheese is melted. Turn and toast other side. Serve warm. Add a **DILL PICKLE** for the perfect taste.

STALE CHIPS? Refresh stale potato chips, crackers or cereal by microwaving for 30 to 45 seconds, then let stand for 1 minute.

ROUNDUP SHREDDED BARBECUED BEEF
A real man pleaser.

Combine in a heavy oven-proof
pot . . . .   5 pounds **CHUCK ROAST**
  ½ cup **BROWN SUGAR**
  ¼ cup **APPLE CIDER VINEGAR**
  2 cups **WATER**
Bake in 375-degree oven for 3 hours. Remove from oven. Cool. Remove
all fat and any bones. Shred beef; return to pot.
Add . . . . .2¾ cups **CATSUP**
  1 Tbsp. **DRY MUSTARD**
  1 large **ONION,** chopped
  2 cloves **GARLIC**, minced

Stir to blend. Reduce temperature to 300-degrees and cook, covered, for
up to 4 hours. Stir every 30 minutes, adding more water and catsup to
keep well moistened. Serve on **BUNS** with **ONION, CHEESE,** and
PICKLES.

YIELD: 12 TO 14 SERVINGS.

MONTE CHRISTO SANDWICHES

Combine . . . .   ¼ cup **MAYONNAISE**
  2 tsp. **MUSTARD**
Spread on each side of . . . .   8 slices **WHITE BREAD**
Place one slice on each of 4 slices
of bread . . . .   4 slices cooked **TURKEY**
  4 slices fully-cooked **HAM**
  4 slices **SWISS CHEESE**
Top with remaining bread. Cut in half diagonally, secure with toothpick.
Beat together . . . .   3 **EGGS**
  ½ cup **SOUR CREAM**
  2 Tbsp. **MILK**
Beat until stiff and fold in . . . .   2 **EGG WHITES**
Dip sandwich halves in batter.
Cover with . . . .   1 cup fine dry **BREADCRUMBS.**

Fry in deep hot oil until golden brown. Drain and dust with **POWDERED
SUGAR.**

FRESH PINEAPPLE BOATS
Cool, refreshing, and a little bit fancy.

POPPY SEED DRESSING:

Combine in blender . . . . ⅔ cup **OIL**
    8 or 9 Tbsp. **SUGAR**
    4 Tbsp. **VINEGAR**
    3 tsp. **POPPY SEEDS**
    1 tsp. **SALT** and prepared **MUSTARD**

Process in microwave on **HIGH** speed 30 seconds.

PINEAPPLE BOATS:

Cut 2 **FRESH PINEAPPLE** in half lengthwise. (1 pineapple for every two people). Scoop out pulp, leaving shells ¼ to ½-inch thick. Set aside.

Cut into bite-size pieces . . . . **PINEAPPLE PULP** from 2 pineapples
    2 medium **RED APPLES,** unpeeled and cored
    2 cups **FRESH STRAWBERRIES,** stemmed and halved
    1 cup **SEEDLESS RED GRAPES,** halved

Spoon fruit into pineapple shells. Sprinkle with **COCONUT** and chopped **PECANS.** Serve with poppy seed dressing.

VARIATION: Add 2 cups cooked **CHUNKED CHICKEN** to fruit and serve as a main dish.

AMBROSIA
All the old timers know about this dish.

Mix in large bowl . . . . 1 can (20 oz.) chunk **PINEAPPLE,** drained
    1 can **MANDARIN ORANGES,** drained
    1½ cup seedless **GRAPES**
    1 cup miniature **MARSHMALLOWS**
    1 cup flaked **COCONUT**
    ½ cup **PECANS,** chopped

Mix and chill. Fold in . . . . ¾ cup **WHIPPED TOPPING** or **WHIPPED CREAM**
    1 Tbsp. **SUGAR**

Fold into fruit and chill.

JUBILEE FRUIT BOWL

Prepare according to directions .. 1 envelope (1.25 ozs.) **WHIPPED TOPPING MIX**

Combine in large bowl . . . . 1 can (16 oz.) **FRUIT COCKTAIL,** drained

1 can (11 oz.) **MANDARIN ORANGES,** drained

1 can (16 oz.) **PEAR HALVES,** drained and chopped

1 jar (10 oz.) **MARASCHINO CHERRIES,** drained and chopped

1 can (3½ oz.) **FLAKED COCONUT**

Fold in whipped topping, cover salad and chill.

YIELD: 10 TO 12 SERVINGS.

BLUEBERRY SALAD
A "special" salad for "special" guests.

Drain and set aside juice . . . . 1 can (5¼ oz.) crushed **PINEAPPLE**

1 can **WILD BLUEBERRIES**

Bring the fruit juices and 1⅔ cups **WATER** to a boil.

Dissolve in hot liquid . . . . 1 package (6 oz.) **CHERRY JELLO**

Cool and add berries and pineapple. Place in refrigerator. Congeal.

Meanwhile, Beat until fluffy . . . . . 8 ounces **CREAM CHEESE,** softened

1 cup **SOUR CREAM**

½ cup **SUGAR**

1 tsp. **VANILLA**

Spread over congealed mixture. Sprinkle with ½ cup chopped **NUTS.**

THAW WHIPPED TOPPING: A 4½ ounce carton will thaw in 1 minute on the defrost setting. Whipped topping should be slightly firm in the center but it will blend well when stirred. Do not overthaw!

APRICOT DELIGHT SALAD

Combine in saucepan . . . .   1 can (12 oz.) **APRICOT NECTAR**
                        ½ cup **WATER**
Bring to a boil and add . . . .   1 pkg. (6 oz.) **LEMON JELLO**
Drain and reserve juice of . . . .   1 can (15½ oz.) **CRUSHED PINEAPPLE**

Add to jello.

Fold in . . . .   1 cup miniature **MARSHMALLOWS**
                        2 large **BANANAS,** sliced

Pour into a square dish. Chill until firm.

TOPPING:
Mix in saucepan. . . . .   3 Tbsp. **FLOUR**
                        ½ cup **SUGAR**
                        1 **EGG,** beaten

Add reserved **PINEAPPLE JUICE.** Mix well and bring to a boil over low heat. Stir constantly, cooking until smooth and thick. Remove from heat and beat in 1 package (3 oz.) **CREAM CHEESE.** When smooth and cool, spread over gelatin mixture. Refrigerate several hours.

OLD FASHIONED FRUIT SALAD
A must at the Vaughn's Christmas dinners.

Place in large mixing bowl . . . . . .   3 **BANANAS,** chopped
                        2 **APPLES,** chopped
                        2 **ORANGES,** chopped
                        1 can (15½ ozs.) **PINEAPPLE** tidbits

After 15 minutes drain juice from fruit.
Add . . . .   1 jar (8 ozs.) **MARASCHINO CHERRIES**
                        1 cup **COCONUT**
                        3 Tbsp. **SUGAR**
Whip in separate bowl . . . .   1 cup **WHIPPING CREAM**
Add . . . .   2 Tbsp. **SUGAR**
                        ½ tsp. **VANILLA**

When this reaches stiff peak stage fold into fruit.

VARIATION: Add ½ cup **PECANS.**

GOOD SALAD
This one explains itself.

Stir together . . . . 1 can **CHERRY PIE FILLING**
1 box **(3½ oz.) instant VANILLA PUDDING & PIE MIX,** dry
1 can (15¼ oz.) **PINEAPPLE TIDBITS,** with juice
1 **BANANA,** diced
½ cup **PINEAPPLE JUICE,** or any other fruit juice

This makes a very sweet salad and can be used for dessert.

YIELD: 8 TO 10 SERVINGS.

VARIATION: You may use any combination of fruits or melons with this.

CHAMPAGNE SALAD
Must mean it's the best!

Mix together . . . . 1 pkg. (8 oz.) **CREAM CHEESE,** softened
¾ cup **SUGAR**
Drain well and add . . . . 2 cans (18 oz. ea.) **CHUNKED PINEAPPLE**
1 pkg. (10 oz.) frozen **STRAWBERRIES**
2 **BANANAS,** sliced
½ cup **PECANS,** chopped
Fold in . . . . 1 carton (9 oz.) **WHIPPED TOPPING**

Place in pretty bowl and chill.

FOR A QUICK FRUIT DIP: Whip together 16 ounces CREAM CHEESE and 1 pint MARSHMALLOW WHIP CREAM. Add ½ cup BROWN SUGAR and whip until smooth.

PEANUT-APPLE SALAD
Good to serve when fruits are not at their best.

Combine	3 cups unpeeled **APPLES,** chopped
	1 cup **CELERY,** chopped
Sprinkle with	1 tsp. **LEMON JUICE**
Mix together	1 Tbsp. **SUGAR**
	2 Tbsp. **MAYONNAISE**
	½ cup plain **YOGURT**
Fold into apple mixture.	
Add and toss	½ cup **PEANUTS,** coarsely chopped

Chill.

YIELD: 4 TO 5 SERVINGS.

WINTER TIME SALAD

Slice	4 tart **APPLES**
Sprinkle with	2 Tbsp. **LEMON JUICE**
Add	1 cup seedless **GRAPES**
	1 cup **MINIATURE MARSHMALLOWS**
	1 cup **CELERY,** diced
	½ cup **PECANS,** chopped
Whip	1 cup **WHIPPING CREAM**
With	3 Tbsp. **SUGAR**
Add	¼ cup **MAYONNAISE**

Mix together. Serve chilled on **LETTUCE LEAVES.**

LUNCHEON FRUIT SALAD

Slice in bowl	4 **BANANAS**
Add	2 Tbsp. frozen **ORANGE JUICE,** concentrate
Stir to coat bananas.	
Add	3 red delicious **APPLES,** diced
	¼ cup **PEANUTS**
	½ cup **RAISINS**

Mix and let chill for 1 hour. Serve on **LETTUCE LEAVES.**

FROZEN FRUIT SALAD
So handy to have in the freezer–especially during the holidays.

Combine in small saucepan . . . . . 2 **EGGS**, beaten
2 Tbsp. **VINEGAR**
¼ cup **SUGAR**
2 Tbsp. **MARGARINE**
Cook and stir until thickened. Set aside to cool.
Drain and save juice . . . . 1 can (15¼ oz.) **PINEAPPLE CHUNKS**
Slice in juice . . . . 2 **BANANAS**
Toss and drain.
Combine fruits with . . . . 1 can (11 oz.) **MANDARIN ORANGES**, drained
1 can (16 oz.) sliced **PEACHES**, drained
1 jar (6 oz.) **MARASCHINO CHERRIES**, drained
1 pkg. (7 oz.) miniature **MARSHMALLOWS**
Add egg mixture. Stir gently.
Whip and fold in . . . . 1 cup **WHIPPING CREAM**

Pour into a lightly greased 10-inch tube pan; cover and freeze until firm.
Let set at room temperature 20 minutes before slicing.

YIELD: 15 SERVINGS.

APPLE SALAD

Chill . . . . 4 small **APPLES**, or 2 large ones, chopped
1 can (15½ oz.) **PINEAPPLE TIDBITS**, reserve juice
2 cups chopped **PECANS**

While fruit is chilling, mix **DRESSING**.
Cook until thick . . . . 1 Tbsp. **FLOUR**
3 Tbsp. **SUGAR**
1 Tbsp. **WATER**
6 Tbsp. **PINEAPPLE JUICE**
Dash of **NUTMEG**

Chill. To serve, pour dressing over fruit. Spoon onto **LETTUCE LEAVES**.

MELODISE'S FROZEN CRANBERRY SALAD
Sure to please all.

Mix all together . . . . 1 can (16 ozs.) **JELLIED CRANBERRY SAUCE**
3 **BANANAS,** mashed
1 can (15½ oz.) **CRUSHED PINEAPPLE**, drained
Fold in . . . . 1 carton (8 oz.) **FROZEN WHIPPED TOPPING**

Freeze in 13x9x2-inch dish or in individual bowls. Will keep several weeks.

FRUIT COMPOTE

Mix in fruit bowl, your choice
of . . . . 6 cups mixed fresh **FRUIT, PEACHES, GRAPES, MELON, STRAWBERRIES, PEARS, PLUMS** or **APRICOTS**
Sprinkle with . . . . 3 tsp. **LEMON JUICE**
Whip . . . . 1 cup **WHIPPING CREAM**
Add . . . . 3 Tbsp. **SUGAR**
1 tsp. **VANILLA**
Fold together with . . . . 1 cup **MAYONNAISE**
2 Tbsp. **LEMON JUICE**
1 tsp. **LEMON RIND**
1 tsp. **ALLSPICE**

Serve fruit on a **LETTUCE LEAF** and spoon dressing over each individual serving.

CREAMY BANANA MOLD

Cream together . . . . 1 pkg. (8 oz.) **CREAM CHEESE**
2 Tbsp. **SALAD DRESSING**
2 tsp. **LEMON JUICE**
Add . . . . ½ cup **CRUSHED PINEAPPLE**
½ cup **MARASCHINO CHERRIES**
3 **BANANAS,** diced
½ cup **PECANS,** chopped
Beat according to directions . . . . . 1 pkg. **DREAM WHIP**

Fold together and chill overnight.

CHURCH SALAD
This salad has been blessed many times.

Drain juice into a saucepan
  from . . . . 8 ounces **CRUSHED PINEAPPLE**
Heat with . . . . 2 cups **MARSHMALLOWS**
Melt and cool.
Add . . . . **PINEAPPLE**
                         10 ounces **FROZEN STRAWBERRIES**
                         ½ cup **PECANS,** chopped
                         2 **BANANAS,** mashed
                         ½ cup **COCONUT**
Whip . . . . 1 cup **WHIPPING CREAM**
With . . . . 3 Tbsp. **SUGAR**

Fold in and freeze in paper muffin liners inside muffin pans. Keep in the freezer until ready to serve.

YIELD: 1½ DOZEN.

SUMMER FRUIT BOWL SALAD

In a large bowl combine . . . . 3 **BANANAS,** thickly sliced
                         3 cups **STRAWBERRIES,** sliced
                         1½ cups **RED GRAPES,** halved and seeded
Drain and reserve juice.
Add . . . . 1 can (20 oz.) **CHUNK PINEAPPLE**
Reserve juice . . . . 1 can (11 oz.) **MANDARIN ORANGES**
To reserved juices add . . . . 1 pkg. (3½ oz.) instant **FRENCH VANILLA PUDDING AND PIE MIX**

Stir until thickened. Gently mix into fruits. Refrigerate.

YIELD: 12 TO 16 SERVINGS.

DISSOLVE GELATIN IN THE MICROWAVE: Measure liquid in a measuring cup, add jello and heat. There will be less stirring to dissolve the gelatin.

DREAMY APRICOT SALAD
Lois Baker shared this with us.

Combine in a medium saucepan and heat to a boil stirring to dissolve.
Mix . . . .   1 pkg. (6 oz.) **APRICOT JELLO**
With . . . .   ⅔ cup **SUGAR**
2 cups **WATER**
Remove from heat. Add . . . .   2 jars (4¾ oz. each) **APRICOT BABY FOOD**
1 can (20 oz.) **CRUSHED PINEAPPLE** with **JUICE**
Combine . . . .   1 can (14 oz.) **SWEETENED CONDENSED MILK**
1 pkg. (8 oz.) **CREAM CHEESE**
Stir into jello mixture and add . . .   1 cup **PECANS,** chopped

Chill until firm.

BLUEBERRY SALAD
Company for the weekend? Prepare ahead!

Drain and reserve juice from . . . . .   1 can (15 ozs.) **BLUEBERRIES**
1 can (8¼ ozs.) **CRUSHED PINEAPPLE**
Dissolve in medium saucepan . . .   2 pkgs. (3 oz. ea.) **BLACK-BERRY JELLO**
In . . . .   2 cups boiling **WATER**
Add reserved juice and water to
make . . . .   1 cup liquid
Stir in reserved fruit. Pour into a 2 quart flat dish. Cover and chill until firm.
Combine . . . .   1 pkg. (8 oz.) **CREAM CHEESE,** softened
½ cup **SUGAR**
1 cup **SOUR CREAM**
½ tsp. **VANILLA**

When creamy spread over congealed salad.
Sprinkle with . . . .   ½ cup **PECANS,** chopped

YIELD: 10 TO 12 SERVINGS.

LAYERED CONGEALED SALAD
A good Bridge luncheon dish.

Drain and reserve juice from . . . . . 1 can (20 oz.) crushed
PINEAPPLE
1 can (17 oz.) **APRICOT** halves

Combine juices and water to make 2 cups liquid. Mash apricots and combine with the pineapple. Set aside.
Combine . . . . 1 pkg. (6 oz.) **ORANGE** flavored
GELATIN
With . . . . 2 cups **BOILING WATER**
Stir in 1 cup reserved juice. Add apricot mixture. Pour into a 13x9x2-inch dish.
Sprinkle with . . . . .1½ cups miniature
MARSHMALLOWS
Chill until firm.
Combine in saucepan 1 cup
   reserved juice and . . . . ½ cup **SUGAR**
2 Tbsp. **CORNSTARCH**
1 **EGG,** beaten well
Cook over low heat stirring constantly until thickened.
Add and stir until melted . . . . 2 Tbsp. **MARGARINE**
Let cool about 2 hours. Fold in . . . 1 carton (8 oz.) **WHIPPED
TOPPING**

Spread over salad and chill.

YIELD: 12 SERVINGS.

PEACH APRICOT SALAD

Dissolve . . . . 2 pkgs. (3 oz. ea.) **PEACH JELLO**
In . . . . 1 cup **HOT WATER**
Add and stir in . . . . 1 pkg. (8 oz.) **CREAM CHEESE**
Let cool and add . . . . 2 small jars **APRICOT BABY
FOOD**
2 cans (8¼ ea.) **CRUSHED
PINEAPPLE** with **JUICE**
Fold in . . . . ½ cup **PECANS**
1 carton (12 oz.) **WHIPPED
TOPPING**

Refrigerate until set.

LAYERED STRAWBERRY SALAD
Pretty to look at, good to eat.

Dissolve	3 pkgs. (3 oz. ea.) **STRAWBERRY JELLO**
In	1 cup **BOILING WATER**
Stir in	1 pkg. (10 oz.) frozen sliced **STRAWBERRIES,** partially thawed
	1 can (15¼ oz.) crushed **PINEAPPLE**
	3 **BANANAS,** mashed
	½ cup **PECANS,** chopped

Pour half of mixture into a lightly oiled 13x9x2-inch dish. Chill until firm. Keep remainder at room temperature.
Spread over congealed

mixture	1 carton (8 oz.) **SOUR CREAM**

Spoon remainder of gelatin over sour cream, cover and chill until firm. Cut into squares and serve on **LETTUCE LEAF.**

CONGEALED CHERRY SALAD
A luncheon delight.

Drain and reserve juice	1 can (16½ oz.) pitted, **DARK SWEET CHERRIES**
	1 can (11 oz.) **MANDARIN ORANGES**
	1 can (8 oz.) crushed **PINEAPPLE**
Dissolve	1 pkg. (6 oz.) **CHERRY GELATIN**
In	1 cup **BOILING WATER**

Stir well and add juice. Chill to consistency of unbeaten egg whites.

Fold in fruit and	½ cup **PECANS,** chopped

Pour into bowl, or mold, and chill until firm. Serve on **LETTUCE LEAVES.**

YIELD: 10 TO 12 SERVINGS.

INGREDIENTS ADDED TO GELATIN: Allow to stand until the consistency of unbeaten egg whites.

SUE'S STRAWBERRY SALAD
Cathy always requests this one.

Combine	1	pkg. (6 oz.) **STRAWBERRY JELLO**
With	2	cups **BOILING WATER**

Stir until dissolved.

Add and stir until melted	1	pkg. (10 oz.) **FROZEN STRAWBERRIES**
Add	¾	cup **COLD WATER**

Congeal in square bowl.

Whip	1	cup **WHIPPING CREAM**
With	3	Tbsp. **SUGAR**
	½	tsp. **VANILLA**

Whip cream until stiff. Cut Jello into 1-inch squares. Gently fold in whipping cream. Serve in pretty glass bowl.

ORANGE PINEAPPLE DELIGHT
A delightful combination.

Combine	1	carton (8 oz.) **COTTAGE CHEESE**, small curd
	1	pkg. (3 oz.) **ORANGE GELATIN**, dry
Add and fold in	1	carton (8 oz.) **WHIPPED TOPPING**, thawed
Fold in	1	can (8 oz.) crushed **PINEAPPLE**, drained
	1	can (8 oz.) **MANDARIN ORANGES**, drained

Blend well. Chill and serve.

VERA'S LIME JELLO

Bring to a boil	1 cup **WATER**
Add	1 pkg. (3 oz.) **LIME JELLO**
Dissolve well. Add	1 cup cold water or **PINEAPPLE JUICE**
Let set in refrigerator until congealed. Whip with electric mixer until fluffy and add	1 can (15½ oz.) **CRUSHED PINEAPPLE,** drained
	1 cup **PECANS,** chopped
	1 cup **COCONUT**
Whip	1 cup **WHIPPING CREAM**
Add	3 Tbsp. **SUGAR**

Fold together and serve.

HOT TURKEY SALAD
Can serve as a main dish.

Combine	2 cups cooked **TURKEY,** chopped
	2 cups **CELERY,** chopped
	½ cup **MAYONNAISE**
	½ cup **ALMONDS**
	2 Tbsp. **ONION,** minced

Mix and pour into a greased casserole. Cover and bake at 350-degrees for 15 minutes.

Sprinkle with	½ cup **CHEDDAR CHEESE,** grated
and	½ cup crushed **POTATO CHIPS**

Bake 5 more minutes.

YIELD: 4 SERVINGS.

HAM SALAD

Mix together	1 can **TENDER CHUNK HAM,** flake with a fork
	1½ cups **CARROTS,** grated
	1½ cups **CELERY,** sliced
	⅓ cup **ONION,** minced
	1 cup **SALAD DRESSING**
Just before serving add	1 can (4 oz.) **SHOESTRING POTATOES**

Serve in **LETTUCE** lined bowl.

MEAL-IN-ONE SALAD

Layer in 3-quart salad bowl . . . . . .   8 cups **ICEBERG LETTUCE,** torn
1 cup **CARROTS,** shredded
3 cups **HAM,** cubed
½ cup **GREEN PEPPER,** chopped
2 large **TOMATOES,** chopped

Spread dressing over top of salad, sealing to edge of bowl. Cover and chill. Sprinkle with **CROUTONS** before serving.

DRESSING:
Combine . . . .   1 pkg. (8 oz.) **CREAM CHEESE**
¾ cup **CHEDDAR CHEESE,** grated
½ cup **MAYONNAISE**
¼ cup **MILK**
1 Tbsp. **ONIONS,** finely chopped
2 tsp. **LEMON JUICE**

YIELD: 6 SERVINGS.

VARIATION: May use chopped **ONIONS,** sliced **MUSHROOMS, WATER CHESTNUTS, JICAMA** and **RADISHES.** Let your taste be your guide on this one. For the dressing you may also use **BLUE CHEESE** instead of cheddar. Very pretty served in a clear glass bowl.

SPECIAL CHICKEN SALAD

In large mixing bowl combine . . .   4 cups cooked **CHICKEN,** diced
1 can **MANDARIN ORANGES,** drained
1 can (8 oz.) **PINEAPPLE CHUNKS,** drained
1 cup **CELERY,** chopped
1 cup seedless **GREEN GRAPES**
½ cup slivered **ALMONDS,** toasted
Mix together . . . .   1 cup **MIRACLE WHIP SALAD DRESSING**
¼ cup **LEMON JUICE**
1 tsp. **SALT**
½ tsp. **PEPPER**

Pour over salad. Mix lightly. Chill before serving.

YIELD: 4 TO 6 SERVINGS.

SOUTHWESTERN CHICKEN SALAD

Cook . . . . ½ pkg. (12 oz.) **SHELL MACARONI**

Mix well . . . . 2 cups cooked **CHICKEN,** chopped
3 Tbsp. **GREEN BELL PEPPER,** chopped
2 Tbsp. **PINEAPPLE,** crushed
3 Tbsp. **ONION,** chopped
1 cup **PECANS,** chopped
2 Tbsp. **SOY SAUCE**
¼ tsp. **GINGER**
¼ tsp. **PEPPER**
½ tsp. **SALT**
½ tsp. **SEASONED SALT**

Mix with enough **MAYONNAISE** to make it moist. Serve on **LETTUCE LEAVES.**

YIELD: 4 TO 6 SERVINGS.

VARIATION: May add ½ cup cubed **CHEDDAR CHEESE** and ¼ cup chopped **CELERY.**

CHICKEN SALAD BALLS

Combine and mix well . . . . 1 cup cooked **CHICKEN,** chopped
1 Tbsp. **ONION,** chopped
2 Tbsp. **PIMENTO,** chopped
dash of **HOT SAUCE**
SALT & PEPPER
½ cup **SALAD DRESSING**
1 cup **PECANS,** chopped

Chill 3 to 4 hours and shape into 1-inch balls.

YIELD: 2 DOZEN.

RICE-A-RONI CHICKEN SALAD
An unusual combination.

Cook according to package directions	1	pkg. **CHICKEN FLAVORED**
Mix		**RICE-A-RONI**
	¾	cup **MAYONNAISE**
Add to rice. Then add	½	tsp. **CURRY POWDER**
	1	**GREEN PEPPER,** chopped
	1	cup **MUSHROOMS,** sliced
	4	**GREEN ONIONS,** sliced
	2	cups **CHICKEN,** chopped
	⅓	cup **GREEN OLIVES,** sliced
	1	can **ARTICHOKE HEARTS,** chopped

Mix together carefully. Marinate 1 to 2 days before serving.

HOT CHICKEN SALAD

Mix in large mixing bowl	4	cups cooked **CHICKEN,** cubed
	1	**GREEN BELL PEPPER,** chopped
	¼	cup **RIPE OLIVES,** sliced
	1	can (4 oz.) **MUSHROOMS,** drained
	1	jar (2 oz.) **PIMENTOS**
	1	can (8 oz.) **WATER CHESTNUTS,** sliced
Mix and add	¾	cup **MIRACLE WHIP**
	1	tsp. **SALT**
	1	tsp. **PEPPER**
	⅛	cup **LEMON JUICE**
Pour into a casserole.		
Top with	1	can **CHINESE NOODLES**

Bake at 375-degrees for 20 minutes, covered. Uncover and bake another 5 minutes. Serve hot. This makes a good dish for a luncheon.

TUNA-EGG SALAD
Hearty enough to be the main meal.

Chop . . . . 3 hard-cooked **EGGS**
Add . . . . 1 can (9¼ oz.) **TUNA,** drained
                                  and flaked
                                  1 cup **CELERY,** sliced
                                  ¼ cup **GREEN ONIONS,** chopped
                                  ¼ cup **SWEET PICKLE RELISH**
                                  ¼ cup **MAYONNAISE**
                                  ¼ tsp. **LEMON-PEPPER**
                                  ¼ tsp. **SALT**
                                  3 drops **HOT SAUCE**
Stir well and chill.
Garnish with . . . . 1 hard-cooked **EGG,** sliced

YIELD: 4 TO 6 SERVINGS.

TOSSED SHRIMP-EGG SALAD

Combine in large bowl . . . . 1 large head **LETTUCE**
                                  6 hard-cooked **EGGS,** quartered
                                  2 cups **SHRIMP,** cooked
                                  3 **TOMATOES,** chopped
                                  1 cup **CELERY,** chopped
                                  ¼ cup **PARSLEY,** minced
Mix together.
Mix . . . . .1½ cups **MAYONNAISE**
                                  ½ cup **CHILI SAUCE**

Serve over chilled salad.

YIELD: 6 SERVINGS.

SHRIMP SALAD
Sonny Heaton uses fresh shrimp from the Texas Coast.

Mix in large mixing bowl . . . . ¾ head of **LETTUCE,** chopped
                                  1½ pounds boiled **SHRIMP**
                                  4 **GREEN ONIONS,** chopped
                                  with **TOPS**
                                  3 stalks **CELERY,** diced
                                  SALT and **PEPPER** to taste

Add enough **MAYONNAISE** to moisten. Chill for at least 4 hours. Before serving, add 2 chopped **TOMATOES.** (Optional: chopped **JALAPENOS.**)

VARIATION: May substitute **CRAB MEAT** for **SHRIMP** or add both to salad.

CORNED BEEF SALAD

Dissolve . . . . 1 pkg. (3 oz.) **LEMON JELLO**
                         1¾ cups **HOT WATER**
Add . . . . 2 Tbsp. **VINEGAR**
                         ½ cup **MAYONNAISE**
Heat in oven or microwave . . . . . . 1 can **CORNED BEEF**
Drain grease and blot with paper
  towels. Mash and add to jello
  mixture. Then add . . . . 1 small jar **PIMENTOS**
                         ½ cup **ONION,** chopped
                         ½ cup **CELERY,** chopped
                         ¼ cup **BELL PEPPER,** chopped

Refrigerate. When congealed, cut into squares and serve on **LETTUCE LEAVES** with **CRACKERS.**

CABBAGE SLAW

Mix together . . . . 1 large **CABBAGE,** shredded
                         1 medium **SWEET PEPPER,**
                         chopped (optional)
                         1 large **ONION,** chopped
                         8 stuffed **GREEN OLIVES,** sliced
Mix in saucepan . . . . 1 cup **OIL**
                         1 cup **VINEGAR**
                         1 cup **SUGAR**
                         2 tsp. **SALT**
                         2 tsp. **CELERY SEED**
                         1 tsp. **GROUND MUSTARD**
                         ½ tsp. **PEPPER**

Bring to boiling point, stirring to dissolve sugar. Pour over vegetables while still hot. Let set in refrigerator several hours before serving.

CUCUMBER AND ONION
Great for Summer.

Peel and slice into thin rings . . . . . 1 medium **ONION**
                         1 medium **CUCUMBER**
Mix together . . . . 1 cup **SOUR CREAM**
                         ⅓ cup **VINEGAR**
                         ½ tsp. **SUGAR**
                         ¼ tsp. **SALT**
Add to taste . . . . **GARLIC SALT**

May add a little **MILK** to thin. Mix all together and chill.

CRUNCHY CUCUMBERS
These will stay good for months.

Combine . . . . 7 cups **CUCUMBERS,** thinly
sliced
1 large **ONION,** thinly sliced
1 **GREEN PEPPER,** sliced
1½ cups **SUGAR**
1 cup **WHITE VINEGAR**
1 tsp. **SALT**
1 tsp. **CELERY SEED**
1 tsp. **MUSTARD SEED**

Store in covered jar in refrigerator.

YIELD: 2 QUARTS.

TOMATO ASPIC
A colorful addition to any meal.

Sprinkle . . . . 3 envelopes **UNFLAVORED
GELATIN**
Over . . . . 1 can (46 oz.) **TOMATO JUICE**
Cook over medium heat to   2 Tbsp. **ONION,** grated
dissolve gelatin. Add . . . . ½ tsp. **SALT**
Chill to a thick consistency.
Fold in . . . . 1 cup **GREEN PEPPER,** chopped
1 cup **CELERY,** chopped
Spoon into a lightly greased mold. Cover and chill until firm. Unmold
on **LETTUCE** lined plate.
Combine . . . . 1 pkg. (3 oz.) **CREAM CHEESE**
Beat until smooth with . . . . ¼ cup **MILK**
Add . . . . 1 pkg. (4 oz.) **BLUE CHEESE**

Blend and spoon into center of mold.

YIELD: 12 SERVINGS.

WHEN UNMOLDING GELATIN: Moisten the serving plate with cold water. This makes it easier to position the gelatin.

CARROT-RAISIN SALAD
As pretty as it is healthy.

Combine in a bowl . . . .   ¾ pound **CARROTS**, scraped and grated
  ¼ cup **RAISINS**
  ¼ cup **PECANS,** chopped
Combine separately . . . .   ½ cup **MAYONNAISE**
  1½ Tbsp. **CIDER VINEGAR**
  1 Tbsp. **SUGAR**
  ⅛ tsp. **LEMON JUICE**

Stir well and pour over salad. Toss.

YIELD: 4 SERVINGS.

STACKED POTATO SALAD
Charlotte, thanks!!

Slice very thin . . . .   12 **NEW POTATOES,** boiled in jackets
  4 **EGGS,** boiled
Chop . . . .   1 medium **ONION**
Have ready . . . .   1 cup **MAYONNAISE**
  ½ cup **DILL PICKLES**
  ½ cup **SWEET PICKLES**
  ½ cup **SOUR PICKLES**
Season to taste with . . . .   **SAVOR SALT**
  SALT
  PEPPER

Make layers in large bowl starting with potatoes spread with mayonnaise then other ingredients. Continue layering until all ingredients are used.

ITALIAN SALAD

Combine in salad bowl . . . .   6 **TOMATOES,** peeled and sliced
  1 **ONION,** sliced
  2 **CUCUMBERS,** sliced
Add . . . .   ¼ cup **ITALIAN DRESSING**

Refrigerate until time to serve.

YIELD: 6 SERVINGS.

BACON-LETTUCE-TOMATO SALAD
The B-L-T's of salads.

Combine in large bowl .... 6 cups torn **LETTUCE**
3 **TOMATOES,** wedged pieces
1 pound **BACON,** cooked crisp
and crumbled
2 **GREEN ONIONS,** sliced

Cover and refrigerate. Serve
with .... **AVOCADO DRESSING**

AVOCADO DRESSING:
Beat on low speed with mixer
until smooth .... 2 large **AVOCADOS,** peeled and
mashed
½ cup **SOUR CREAM**
¼ cup **MILK**
¼ cup **MAYONNAISE** or **SALAD
DRESSING**
1 Tbsp. **LEMON JUICE**
½ tsp. **SALT**
3 drops **HOT PEPPER SAUCE,**
(optional)

Cover and chill several hours.

YIELD: 6 TO 8 SERVINGS.

NUTTY GREEN SALAD

Combine in large bowl .... 6 cups torn, mixed **SALAD
GREENS**
1 medium **ZUCCHINI,** sliced
1 medium **CARROT,** scraped and
diced
½ cup **PEANUTS**
⅓ cup **ITALIAN SALAD
DRESSING**

Toss. Salad can be made ahead, stored in an airtight bowl. Add salad
dressing before serving.

A DIFFERENT SEVEN LAYER SALAD

Many variations possible. Use your imagination.
Prepare a day in advance.

Layer in large salad bowl . . . .
1 small head **LETTUCE,** thinly sliced
¾ cup **CELERY,** finely sliced
⅓ cup **GREEN PEPPER,** chopped
8 **WATER CHESTNUTS,** sliced
¼ cup **RED ONION,** chopped
2 cups **CHICKEN,** cooked & chopped
1 pkg. frozen **GREEN PEAS,** uncooked

Combine separately in bowl . . . . .
2 cups **MAYONNAISE**
1 Tbsp. **SUGAR**

Spread over vegetables.
Sprinkle with . . . . 1½ cups grated **ROMANO CHEESE**
Cover tightly with plastic wrap. Chill overnight.
Garnish with . . . .
½ pound **BACON,** cooked & crumbled
1 hard cooked **EGG,** cut in wedges
1 **TOMATO** cut in wedges

Do not toss.

YIELD: 10 TO 12 SERVINGS.

VARIATION: Add **TUNA** to replace chicken. SUBSTITUTE **CHEDDAR, SWISS** or **PARMESAN CHEESE** for **ROMANO.**

HARD-COOKED EGGS: Quickly heat eggs in water until almost boiling, remove from heat and let stand 15 to 17 minutes.

SWEET AND SOUR MARINATED SALAD
This will keep for days.

Combine in large bowl . . . . 1 can (15 oz.) **LeSUEUR SHOE PEG CORN,** drained
1 can (15 oz.) **LeSUEUR ENGLISH PEAS,** drained
1 can (15 oz.) cut **GREEN BEANS,** drained
1 cup **CELERY,** diced
1 **BELL PEPPER,** diced
1 small jar chopped **PIMENTO**
1 cup **ONION,** chopped
Mix separately . . . . 1 cup **SUGAR**
½ cup **OIL**
½ cup **VINEGAR**
Add to taste . . . . **SALT & PEPPER**

Pour over vegetables. Better if stored overnight.

FRESH BROCCOLI SALAD
L. Tkacs version.

Make dressing of . . . . ½ cup **MAYONNAISE**
¼ cup **SUGAR**
1½ Tbsp. **VINEGAR**
Chill until ready to serve.
Wash and cut into flowerets . . . . . 1 bunch **FRESH BROCCOLI**
Add . . . . 4 **SCALLIONS,** sliced (may use fresh **GREEN ONIONS** with tops)
1 cup **SHARP CHEDDAR CHEESE,** grated
Cook until crisp . . . . 8 slices **BACON,** crumbled

Place vegetables in salad bowl. Pour dressing over **BROCCOLI.** Add crumbled **BACON** last.

YIELD: 8 SERVINGS.

SUPER BROCCOLI SALAD
Almost a meal.

Wash a large bunch of **BROCCOLI.** Cut into flowerets and place in a large bowl.
Add . . . . 7 **GREEN ONIONS,** chopped
                  1 cup **CHEDDAR CHEESE,** grated
Fry, crumble and add . . . . 10 slices **BACON**
Toss together.
Make dressing of . . . . ½ cup **MAYONNAISE**
                  1½ Tbsp. **VINEGAR**
                  ¼ cup **SUGAR**

Stir well. Pour over broccoli mixture, toss gently. Cover and refrigerate at least 3 hours.

YIELD: 6 SERVINGS.

VARIATIONS: ¼ cup **RAISINS** and ¼ cup **PECANS** may be added.

BERTHA'S BROCCOLI AND CAULIFLOWER SALAD
This is a wonderful salad and is also "Low Cal."

Chop together . . . . 1 head **CAULIFLOWER**
                  1 head **BROCCOLI**
                  10 **GREEN ONIONS,** including tops
Make sauce of . . . . ½ cup **LIGHT MAYONNAISE**
                  ⅓ cup **VINEGAR**
                  ½ tsp. **SALT**
                  ¼ cup **BACON BITS,** in jar
                  ¼ tsp. **BLACK PEPPER**
                  5 to 10 tsp. **SUGAR SUBSTITUTE**

Mix well. Pour over vegetables. Let set in refrigerator 24 hours. Stir twice.

MARINATED BROCCOLI SALAD

Mix together . . . . 4 cups **BROCCOLI** (1 big bunch)
½ cup unsalted **DRY ROASTED PEANUTS**
¼ cup **GREEN ONIONS,** chopped
½ cup **RAISINS**
Toss together and add dressing.
Mix . . . . 1 cup **MAYONNAISE**
¼ cup **SUGAR**

Marinate at least 4 hours.

RICE SALAD
Serves a crowd.

Bring to a boil . . . . 3 cups **CHICKEN BROTH**
Add . . . . .1¼ cups **REGULAR RICE,** uncooked
Reduce heat. Cook covered 25 minutes or until rice is tender and broth is absorbed.
Combine in large bowl . . . . 1 cup **OIL**
2 Tbsp. **VINEGAR**
1 tsp. **SALT**
¼ tsp. **PEPPER**
⅛ tsp. **RED PEPPER**
Add rice and let cool. Add . . . . 1 cup **RIPE OLIVES,** chopped
2 hard-cooked **EGGS,** chopped
1½ cups **CELERY,** chopped
¼ cup **DILL PICKLE,** chopped
1 small **ONION,** chopped
1 jar (2 oz.) **PIMENTO,** chopped
½ **GREEN PEPPER,** chopped
½ cup **MAYONNAISE**
2 Tbsp. prepared **MUSTARD**

Mix well and chill overnight.

YIELD: 10 SERVINGS.

POLYNESIAN SALAD
This will keep for several days.

Drain and place on paper towels
to drain thoroughly . . . . 1 can (8½ oz.) **PEAS**
1 can (17 oz.) **WHITE KERNEL
CORN**
1 jar (2 oz.) **PIMENTOS**
1 can (15 oz.) french style **GREEN
BEANS**

Mix all together in bowl.
Add . . . . 1 cup **CELERY,** chopped
½ cup **ONIONS,** chopped

Mix together in small bowl . . . . . . 1 cup **SUGAR**
1 cup **VINEGAR**
⅓ cup **OIL**

Stir until dissolved. Pour over vegetables. Refrigerate several hours or
overnight.

MAMMY'S MACARONI SALAD

Combine . . . . 2 cups **ELBOW MACARONI,**
cooked and drained
8 ounces **SHARP CHEDDAR
CHEESE,** cubed
1 cup **CELERY,** chopped
¼ cup **PIMENTO,** chopped
2 Tbsp. **GREEN PEPPER,**
chopped
¼ cup **ONION,** finely chopped

Add to taste . . . . **SALT & PEPPER**
1 cup **SALAD DRESSING**

Toss lightly and serve in **LETTUCE** lined bowl.

YIELD: 6 TO 8 SERVINGS.

CORNBREAD SALAD
Cathy prepares this for Bruce, Charlie and J.D.

Mix according to directions on
    package. Bake in long pan . . . . .   1 pkg. (6 oz.) **CORNBREAD MIX**
                                    1 pkg. (6 oz.) **JALAPENO CORNBREAD MIX**

Crumble in very large bowl.
Add . . . .   1 pound **BACON,** cooked and
                                       crumbled
                                        2 bunches **GREEN ONIONS,** chopped with tops
                                        1 **TOMATO,** chopped
                                        1 **BELL PEPPER,** chopped
Toss together and mix with . . . . . .   1 cup **MAYONNAISE**

YIELD: 8 TO 10 SERVINGS.

VARIATIONS: Any of these items may be added, 1 small can **GREEN CHILLIES,** chopped–3 stalks **CELERY,** chopped–¾ cup **CHEDDAR** or **AMERICAN,** grated–1 small can chopped **BLACK OLIVES**–more **TOMATOES.**

CHEESY FRITO SALAD

Mix in salad bowl . . . .   ¾ head **LETTUCE,** torn into bite size pieces
                                        2 **TOMATOES,** chopped
                                        2 **AVOCADO,** chopped
                                        4 **GREEN ONIONS,** chopped
In saucepan melt . . . .   1 cup **VELVEETA CHEESE,** cut in chunks
In . . . .   1 can (5 oz.) **EVAPORATED MILK**
When ready to serve add . . . .   2 **JALAPENOS,** chopped
                                            FRITOS

Pour hot cheese sauce over salad, toss and serve immediately.

COTTAGE CHEESE SALAD
Bet you didn't know cottage cheese could be this good!

Combine in bowl . . . . 2 cups **COTTAGE CHEESE**
½ cup **TOMATO,** diced
¼ cup **RADISH,** chopped
¼ cup **GREEN BELL PEPPER,** chopped
¼ cup **ONION,** chopped
1 tsp. **PARSLEY FLAKES**
¼ tsp. **SALT**
¼ tsp. **PEPPER**
½ tsp. **SEASONED SALT**

Mix and chill before serving.

HEAVENLY FRUIT SPREAD
Serve over fruit or as a spread.

Combine in saucepan . . . . ½ cup **SUGAR**
4 tsp. **CORNSTARCH**
Add . . . . 2 **EGG YOLKS,** beaten
1 Tbsp. **VINEGAR**
1 can (12 oz.) **UNSWEETENED PINEAPPLE JUICE**
Cook over low heat stirring constantly until thickened.
Add, stir until melted . . . . 10 large **MARSHMALLOWS**

Chill thoroughly. Pour over fruit for a salad or as a dip for fruit.

YIELD: 2 CUPS.

CREAMY FRUIT DRESSING
Try this on strawberries.

Mix together until creamy . . . . ½ cup **SOUR CREAM**
1 Tbsp. **LEMON JUICE**
1 Tbsp. **HONEY**
4 Tbsp. **FLAKED COCONUT**

Chill. Serve over **FRESH FRUITS** or **MELON BALLS.**

FAMOUS KING'S INN RESTAURANT'S
BOMBAY SALAD DRESSING

*There isn't a ready-made dressing
that will even compare with this.*

Pit and peel . . . . 1 large ripe **AVOCADO,** cut into
cubes

Place in blender. Add . . . . 2 cups **SOUR CREAM**
1 envelope **FRENCH ONION
SOUP MIX**
2 large cloves of **GARLIC,** minced
1 Tbsp. **CURRY POWDER**
Juice of one **LEMON**

Blend on high speed until smooth. Pour into glass container and refrigerate. Serve over **LETTUCE** and diced **TOMATOES.** Garnish with sliced **TOMATOES** and **AVOCADOS.**

YIELD: 2 CUPS.

CHART HOUSE DRESSING

Becky acquired this from a famous restaurant in Lake Tahoe.

Combine in blender. . . . . 1 quart **WHOLE EGG
MAYONNAISE,** *DO NOT
SUBSTITUTE*
1 cup **CATSUP**

Set aside.
Chop very fine . . . . ½ medium **RED ONION**
4 stalks **CELERY**
4 **SWEET PICKLES**
½ **SWEET GREEN PEPPER**
1½ sprigs **PARSLEY**
2 tsp. **PIMENTO** or canned **RED
PEPPERS**
2 **EGGS,** hard-boiled

Add to mayonnaise-catsup mixture. Blend just enough to mix. Refrigerate. Will keep several weeks.

Main Dishes

CHARCOALED QUAIL

We have a lot of hunters in our families,
so we are always looking for new ways to cook game.

Clean and wash **QUAIL**. Wrap each with a slice of **BACON** and secure
it with a toothpick.

Combine .... 1 cup **OIL**
1 cup **VINEGAR**
½ cup **SOY SAUCE**
½ cup **LEMON JUICE**
½ tsp. **GARLIC SALT**

Marinate quail in sauce for at least 2 hours. Cook over charcoal 5 minutes
on one side. Turn, baste and cook 5 minutes on the other side. Repeat
process so that meat cooks a total of 10 minutes on each side. Prepare at
least 2 quail per person.

BRUCE'S BEER FRIED VENISON

Best eaten right in deer camp.

Tenderize with mallet ....1½ pounds **VENISON**, cut into
¼-inch thick steaks

Mix together .... 1 **EGG**, beaten
1 cup **BEER**

Dip each steak in **FLOUR**, then in egg mixture and again in flour. Fry in
hot **SHORTENING** until done and browned on both sides. **SALT** and
PEPPER to taste. (It will toughten the meat to salt and pepper it first.)

TURKEY FRIES

Just as good as the Calf Fries.

Clean and rinse the **TURKEY FRIES**. Dry on paper towels.

Make a batter of .... 2 cups **BISCUIT MIX**
¾ cup **MILK**
¾ cup **CLUB SODA**
2 **EGGS**, slightly beaten

Mix until batter is fairly smooth. If batter does not adhere to meat good,
add more biscuit mix. Fry in hot **OIL** until golden brown. This may be
used for a batter on any kind of **FISH**, **CHICKEN**, **BEEF**, etc.

FRIED FROG LEGS
The meat is as tender and good as CHICKEN. HONEST!!

Wash **FROG LEGS** and pat dry with paper towel. Sprinkle with **SALT** and **PEPPER**. Dip in beaten **EGGS** and then in **CRACKER CRUMBS**. Fry approximately 1½ minutes on each side as you turn them. When legs curl, remove from heat and serve. Make a big bowl of **CREAM GRAVY** and cook a batch of **HOT BISCUITS**. YUMMM, GOOD!!

JERKY
Pat Swinney's contribution to our "snicking and snacking" in the Colorado mountains every summer.

Ask butcher to trim and *slice for JERKY*, 1 medium size **BRISKET**. (He will know to slice very thin with the grain.)
Place in shallow baking dish.
Combine .... 1 tsp. SEASONED SALT
1 tsp. GARLIC POWDER
1 tsp. PEPPER
2 tsp. MONOSODIUM GLUTAMATE
2 tsp. ONION POWDER
½ cup WORCESTERSHIRE SAUCE
½ cup SOY SAUCE
4 Tbsp. LIQUID SMOKE, (opt.)

Pour over meat. Marinate overnight. Preheat oven to 125-degrees. Lay strips of the marinated meat in single layer on oven rack. Place a baking sheet or foil underneath to catch drippings. Leave oven door open a crack and bake 8 to 12 hours, or until meat is chewy. Test by tasting occasionally. Store in airtight container on pantry shelf. Will keep for a long time.

"WHITE CITY" BRISKET
Jack White Jr., grandson of the founder of Carlsbad Caverns, gave us this Blue Ribbon winner.

Generously sprinkle both sides of any size **BRISKET** with **SEASONED SALT, GARLIC POWDER** and **COARSE GROUND PEPPER**. Sprinkle with **WORCESTERSHIRE SAUCE** and rub into the seasonings on the brisket until you have made a paste. Place in an **OVEN COOKING BAG**. (Turkey size). Sprinkle 1 package dry **ONION SOUP MIX** and ¼ to ½ cup **SOY SAUCE** over top. Fasten bag with tie. Punch holes in top of bag. Bake for 1 hour in 350-degree oven. Reduce heat to 250-degrees and cook 1 hour *per pound* of meat.

ROLLED BRISKET
"Nice to slice" for sandwiches.

Ask butcher to roll your **BRISKET** just like he rolls roast. This needs to be trimmed just a little. Season generously with **SEASONED SALT** or **BRISKET MARINADE MIX**. Place in pan and cook according to directions. Good to place in cooking bag (like turkey bag) and cook slowly according to instructions.

Try the **BRISKET MARINADE** in **CALF FRIES TO CAVIAR I** or "White City" **BRISKET MARINADE** recipe in this cookbook.

BEEF TENDERLOIN
Terry McCord prepared about ¼ pound per person.

Trim membrane from **TENDERLOIN**. Sprinkle with **GARIC SALT, COARSE GROUND BLACK PEPPER, SEASON SALT** and **PEPPER**. (**PEPPER** heavily.) Marinate 10 to 15 minutes. Pour **WORCESTERSHIRE SAUCE** in dish. Marinate **TENDERLOIN** in **WORCESTERSHIRE** for 1 hour on each side. Remove and wrap in **BACON STRIPS**. Secure with toothpicks. Place on grill. Sear all sides. Turn every 8 to 10 minutes. Cook 45 minutes to 1 hour. Serve with mixture of **BUTTER** and **WORCESTERSHIRE SAUCE**.

OVEN-SMOTHERED STEAK

Pat dry	1½	pounds **ROUND STEAK**
Sprinkle on both sides and pound in with a mallet or edge of saucer	3	Tbsp. **FLOUR**
	¾	tsp. **SALT**
	½	tsp. **PEPPER**
Brown in oven-safe pan	3	Tbsp. **SHORTENING**
When brown cover with	1½	cups canned **STEWED TOMATOES**
	¾	cup **WATER**
	1	**ONION**, sliced
Sprinkle generously with		**SEASONING SALT**

Cover with lid and place in preheated 325-degree oven for two hours.

YIELD: 4 SERVINGS.

SHANGHAI BEEF
A touch of the Orient.

Brown in large skillet . . . . 1 pound **ROUND STEAK**, cut
into thin strips
2 Tbsp. **OIL**
Add and stir until blended . . . . . . 2 Tbsp. **CORNSTARCH**
Stir in . . . . 1½ cups **BEEF BROTH**
1 can (8 oz.) sliced **WATER
CHESTNUTS**, drained
1 medium **RED PEPPER**, diced
6 **GREEN ONIONS**, chopped
3 Tbsp. **SOY SAUCE**
¼ tsp. **PEPPER** and **SALT**
Bring to boil, stirring frequently.
Stir in . . . . 1½ cups uncooked **INSTANT RICE**

Cover and remove from heat. Let stand 5 minutes. Fluff with fork.

YIELD: 4 SERVINGS.

OVEN SWISS STEAK
A hearty, man-pleasing dish.

Cut into serving portions . . . . 2 pounds **ROUND STEAK**
Mix together and pound into
meat with edge of saucer . . . . . . 6 Tbsp. **FLOUR**
1 tsp. **SALT**
½ tsp. **PEPPER**
In a skillet brown meat in . . . . ¼ cup **OIL**
Place browned meat in baking dish. Set aside. Blend remaining flour
mixture with drippings in skillet.
Add . . . . 1 can (8 oz.) **STEWED
TOMATOES**
½ cup each chopped **CELERY,
CARROTS, ONIONS**
1 tsp. **WORCESTERSHIRE
SAUCE**
½ tsp. **PEPPER** and **SEASONED
SALT**
1 cup **WATER**

Bring to a boil, stirring constantly. Pour over steak in baking dish. Cover
and bake in 325-degree oven for 2 hours until steak and vegetables are
tender. Sprinkle with ¼ cup grated **AMERICAN CHEESE**.

YIELD: 4 SERVINGS.

BEEF AND VEGETABLE STIR FRY
Prepare veggies early. Have a meal in minutes

Partially freeze . . . .   1 pound boneless **ROUND STEAK**

Slice across grain into 3-inch long and ¼-inch wide strips. Set aside.

Rinse and dry . . . .   ¾ pound fresh **MUSHROOMS**, sliced

   1 small bunch **BROCCOLI FLOWERETS**

Peel . . . .   2 **ONIONS**, coarsely chopped

   4 to 5 **CARROTS**, sliced diagonally

Preheat wok. Add 2 Tbsp. **OIL**. Heat to medium heat and add steak strips. Stir fry until browned. Add the vegetables and cook on low 10 minutes.

Add . . . . 1½ cups **BEEF BROTH**

Cook about 10 minutes until the vegetables are crisp-tender.

Add . . . .   ¼ cup **SOY SAUCE**

   2 Tbsp. **CORNSTARCH**

   ½ tsp. **SUGAR**

     SALT and **PEPPER**

Cook until thickened. Serve over **RICE**.

YIELD: 6 SERVINGS.

VARIATION:
Three boneless **CHICKEN BREASTS** may be substituted for the steak strips.

STEAK ON A STICK
Cook these on the grill.

Combine in a shallow bowl . . . . . . ¼ cup **SHERRY**
           1 Tbsp. **SOY SAUCE**
           1½ tsp. **WINE VINEGAR**
           2 tsp. **CATSUP**
           2 tsp. **HONEY**
           ¼ tsp. **GARLIC SALT**
Add . . . . 1 pound boneless **SIRLOIN STEAK**, cut into 1-inch cubes
Let marinate at least 2 hours in refrigerator, turning occasionally. Thread steak on skewers
  alternately with . . . . 2 large **ONIONS**, cut in chunks
           ½ pound fresh **MUSHROOMS**
           1 large **GREEN PEPPER,** cut in 1-inch pieces
Cook over medium coals for 5 to 10 minutes or until they reach the desired doneness. Baste with marinade as they cook.

YIELD: 4 SERVINGS.

VARIATION:
PINEAPPLE CHUNKS, **CHERRY TOMATOES** and **RED PEPPER** may also be used.

PINEAPPLE RIGHT-SIDE-UP BAKE

Opened *refrigerated* can of **HASH** (**ROAST BEEF** or **CORNED BEEF**) at both ends. Remove hash, using lid as pusher. Slice into 3 patties. Fry until golden brown. Remove to foil-lined baking dish. In same skillet fry 6 slices of **BACON**. Drain on paper towel. Top each hash pattie with a **PINEAPPLE** slice and 2 **BACON** strips. Place under broiler for a few minutes. Serve on **LETTUCE LEAVES**.

VARIATION:
Place a slice of **CHEESE** on each one before placing under the broiler.

BARBECUE SAUCE
Try it on our favorite, BEEF RIBS.

Combine .... 5 ounces **SOY SAUCE**
½ cup **BROWN SUGAR**
1 Tbsp. **LEMON JUICE**
½ cup **BOURBON**
1 tsp. **WORCESTERSHIRE SAUCE**
1 cup **WATER**
1 small **ONION**, grated

Pour over meat in glass dish and cover tightly with foil. Refrigerate at least 24 hours. (2 to 3 pounds **BEEF, CHUCK ROAST, EYE OF ROUND, RUMP, STEAK,** or **BEEF RIBS.**) Place meat on grill and cook over low coals until done. Sauce may be divided in half and 1 part used to baste meat as it is cooked. Remaining half can be heated to a boil and thickened with **CORNSTARCH** to serve over grilled meat.

12 HOUR ROAST
Don't let this interfere with your nap, it can cook longer!

Place in a large pan .... 3-4 pound **ROAST**
Place on top of roast .... 2 cups **PINTO BEANS**, uncooked
1 can **GREEN CHILIES**, chopped
1 can **TOMATOES**
1 **ONION**, chopped
1 can **TOMATO SAUCE**

Cover entire contents with **WATER**. Place in 250-degree oven covered with lid. Cook at least 12 hours. (May need to cook longer). Season with **SALT** and **PEPPER**. Serve with **SALAD, CORNBREAD,** and a **DESSERT** for a complete meal.

QUICK STEPPIN' TEXAN
The casserole for busy people.

Brown in medium skillet .... 1½ pounds **GROUND BEEF**
1 large **ONION**, chopped
Add and mix .... 2 cans (4 oz. each) **GREEN CHILIES**, chopped
1 can (10 ozs.) **TOMATOES AND CHILIES**
1 cup **CHEESE**, grated

Crush **BAR-B-QUED CORN CHIPS** to cover bottom of 13x9x2-inch pan. Pour ingredients over chips. Cover with additional chips. Cook in 350-degree oven for 30 minutes.

ELEGANT MEAT LOAF

Beef

SAUCE:
Combine and set aside . . . . 6 Tbsp. **BROWN SUGAR**
½ cup **CATSUP**
½ tsp. **NUTMEG**
1½ tsp. **DRY MUSTARD**

LOAF:
Soak a few minutes . . . . ½ cup **OATMEAL**
1 cup **MILK**
Add . . . . .1½ pounds lean **GROUND CHUCK**
2 **EGGS**, beaten
⅓ cup **ONION**, minced
1 tsp. **SALT**
⅛ tsp. **PEPPER**
⅛ tsp. **SAGE**

Mix well. Form into individual loaves and place in baking dish. Make slight indention in top of loaves. Pour sauce into indentions. Bake in 350-degree oven for 45 minutes. (Make 1 loaf, if you prefer, but increase cooking time to 1 hour.)

NICE N' EASY MEAT LOAF
"Ole" inexpensive standby.

Mix lightly but thoroughly . . . . . . 2 pounds **GROUND BEEF**
1 cup **TOMATO SAUCE**
1 **EGG**
1 Tbsp. **WORCESTERSHIRE SAUCE**
⅓ cup **GREEN PEPPER**, chopped
2 medium **ONIONS**, chopped
1 tsp. **SALT**
¼ tsp. **PEPPER**
¾ cup **CRACKER CRUMBS**

Shape meat mixture into a 9x4x3-inch loaf pan. Gently turn out onto a rack in an open roasting pan. Bake in a 350-degree oven for 1 hour and 15 minutes. Pour ¼ cup **CATSUP** over top of loaf and continue baking 10 more minutes or until done.

YIELD: 6 SERVINGS.

TEXAS SCRAMBLE

In skillet, brown . . . .   1 pound **GROUND BEEF**
                                           ½ cup **ONION**, chopped
Add . . . .   1 can (1 lb. 12 oz.) **PORK AND BEANS**
                                           ¼ tsp. **TABASCO SAUCE**
                                           ½ cup **CATSUP**
                                           1 Tbsp. **WORCESTERSHIRE SAUCE**
                                           2 Tbsp. **VINEGAR**

Bake in a 1½-quart casserole at 350-degrees for 30 minutes.

YIELD: 6 SERVINGS.

MAKE-AHEAD LASAGNE
So easy. You don't even cook the lasagne before mixing!

Have ready to use . . . .   8 ounces uncooked **LASAGNE NOODLES**
                                           8 ounces **MOZZARELLA CHEESE**, grated
                                           10 ounces **COTTAGE CHEESE**
                                           3 ounces **PARMESAN CHEESE**, grated

SAUCE:
In large skillet, brown . . . .   1 pound **GROUND BEEF**
Drain fat. Add . . . .   1 package (3 oz.) **SPAGHETTI SAUCE MIX**
                                           6 ounces **TOMATO PASTE**
                                           2½ cups **WATER**, may need more
Simmer for 10 minutes.

Oil a 13x9x2-inch baking dish. Spread 1½ cups sauce in dish. Arrange layer of uncooked lasagne noodles on sauce. Top with more sauce, and some of each of the cheeses in layer. Repeat, making sure noodles are immersed in sauce. *Refrigerate several hours or overnight.* (This must be allowed to set several hours.) Bake in 350-degree oven for 45 minutes or until bubbly. Cut into squares to serve. May also be frozen, then baked.

ITALIAN LASAGNA
Ruth Polston's specialty.

Brown...................... 1 pound lean **GROUND MEAT**
1 medium **ONION**, chopped
1 clove **GARLIC**, minced
Add........................ 6 ounces **TOMATO PASTE**
12 ounces **WATER**
2 crushed **BAY LEAVES**
2 Tbsp. **PARMESAN CHEESE**
SALT and **PEPPER**

Let simmer 1 hour. Stir often. It burns easily.
Cook according to directions
on package.................. 1 pound **LASAGNA**
Drain and wash. Grease a 13x9x2-inch baking dish. Layer alternate layers of **LASAGNA** and **SAUCE**.
Sprinkle with .... 12 ounces grated **MONTEREY JACK CHEESE**
Dot with .... 1 cup **RICOTTA** or **COTTAGE CHEESE**

Bake at 350-degrees for 20 minutes or until heated through. Ideal for large groups. Can be prepared a day ahead. Just cover well, refrigerate and cook just before serving.

NOTE: For a final touch, sprinkle with **PARMESAN CHEESE**.

YIELD: 8 TO 10 SERVINGS.

HOUSECLEANING SPAGHETTI
Novis Curry says she triples the recipe and
freezes in serving size portions.

Saute until brown .... 1½ pounds **GROUND MEAT**
1 **ONION**, chopped
Add........................ 1 **GREEN PEPPER**, chopped
1 stalk **CELERY**, chopped
2 cans,(3 oz. each) **TOMATO PASTE**
SALT

Let simmer at least 2 hours. Or place in dutch oven and bake in 250-degree oven 2 or 3 hours. (Or until housecleaning is finished.) Stir often Add **WATER** or **TOMATO JUICE** if sauce becomes too dry. Serve over cooked **SPAGHETTI**.

YIELD: 6 SERVINGS.

TEXAS HASH

In a large skillet, cook until meat
   is brown and vegetables are
    tender crisp . . . .   1 pound **GROUND BEEF**
                                          2 large **ONIONS**, chopped
                                          1 large **GREEN PEPPER**, chopped
Drain off fat and stir in . . . .   1 can (16 oz.) **TOMATOES**
                                         ½ cup regular **RICE**, uncooked
Add . . . .   2 tsp. **SALT**
                                          2 tsp. **SEASONED SALT**
                                         ½ tsp. **PEPPER**
                                          2 tsp. **CHILI POWDER**
                                         ½ cup **WATER**

Heat and pour into a slightly greased 2-quart casserole. Cover and bake in 350-degree oven for 55 to 60 minutes. Serve with **SALAD** and **DESSERT** and you have a complete meal. Also good wrapped in a warm **FLOUR TORTILLA** with **HOT SAUCE**.

YIELD: 6 TO 8 SERVINGS.

HUNGRY MAN'S FAVORITE
This is a real rainy-night supper dish.

Bake favorite **CORNBREAD** recipe. Bake in deep pan so it will be thick.
Boil in **SALTY WATER** until
   almost done . . . .   1 medium **CABBAGE**, cored and
                                               cut into wedges
Mash into chunks . . . .   1 can **CORNED BEEF**
Add to . . . .   1 can **CREAM OF MUSHROOM
                                             SOUP**, dilute only slightly

Heat. Add **DRAINED** cabbage. Place thick slices of hot cornbread into individual soup plates and cover with the cabbage-beef mixture. Serve with rest of **CORNBREAD** and lots of **BUTTER**. Pop a **DESSERT** in the oven and this would be a natural for company.

NO CANNED TOMATOES? Try substituting 1 can tomato paste plus 1 cup water. Makes very little difference.

REVIS' CASSEROLE

Passed around at the beauty salon, like all good recipes.

Have on hand . . . . 1 package (8 oz.) **NOODLES**, uncooked
Brown in medium skillet . . . . 2 pounds lean **GROUND BEEF**
Stir . . . . 1 can (15 oz.) **TOMATO SAUCE**
                                               1 Tbsp. **SUGAR**
                                                 1 tsp. **GARLIC POWDER**
                                                 1 tsp. **SALT**
                                                 ½ tsp. **PEPPER**
Set aside. Combine . . . . 1 cup **COTTAGE CHEESE**
                                                 1 cup **SOUR CREAM**
                                                 8 ounces **CREAM CHEESE**, softened
                                                 1 **SWEET PEPPER**, chopped
                                                 1 bunch **FRESH GREEN ONIONS**, chopped with tops

Grease well a 13x9x2-inch baking dish. Place ½ of the uncooked noodles in dish. Put ½ of meat sauce, next. Then add all the cheese mixture. Add rest of noodles, meat sauce and sprinkle with grated **PARMESAN CHEESE**. Cover with foil, bake in preheated oven for 45 minutes at 350 degrees. Can be frozen.

NOTE: This may be made in two smaller casseroles.

YIELD: 6 TO 8 SERVINGS.

BEEF JALAPENO CORNBREAD PIE

This dish is very popular with the Arlys Askew grandchildren.

Make **CORNBREAD** first by
  combining . . . . 1 cup plus 2 tablespoons **YELLOW CORNMEAL**
Add . . . . 2 **EGGS**
                                                 1 tsp. **BAKING SODA**
                                                 ¾ tsp. **SALT**
                                                 1 cup **MILK**
                                                 ¼ cup **BACON DRIPPINGS** or **OIL**
                                                 1 can (17 oz.) **CREAM CORN**
Mix well and set aside.
Brown . . . . .1½ pounds **GROUND MEAT**
Grate . . . . ¾ pound **CHEDDAR CHEESE**
Chop . . . . 1 large **ONION**
Open . . . . 2 cans **CHOPPED CHILIES**

Grease a 13x9x2-inch baking dish. Pour ½ the cornbread mixture into dish. Add, meat, onions, peppers, cheese and rest of cornbread. Bake for 50 minutes at 350-degrees

CHEESEBURGER PIE

Grease a 10-inch pie plate with **BUTTER** or **MARGARINE**. Put 2 cups of **VEGETABLES** of your choice in the bottom of the plate.

Brown together . . . .   1 pound **GROUND BEEF**
                                                    1 **ONION**, chopped

Pour meat mixture over vegetables in plate.

Cover with . . . .   ¾ cup **AMERICAN CHEESE**,
                                                    grated
Make mixture of . . . .   ¾ cup **BISCUIT MIX**
                                                    3 **EGGS**
                                                    1½ cups **MILK**

Pour over mixtures in pie plate. Sprinkle with ¼ cup grated **CHEESE**. Bake at 400-degrees for 30 minutes. Cut in squares.

YIELD: 4 SERVINGS.

BAR-B-QUE CUPS
These are fun to do. Children love them.

In a large skillet brown . . . .   1 pound **GROUND BEEF**
                                                    ¼ cup **ONION**, chopped
Drain, and stir in . . . .   ½ cup **BARBECUE SAUCE**
                                                    2 Tbsp. **BROWN SUGAR**
Heat until very hot. Set aside.
Separate . . . .   1 can (10 oz.) **BISCUITS**

Place each biscuit in ungreased muffin cup. Press dough to cover bottom and sides of cup. Spoon meat mixture into cups. Sprinkle with ½ cup grated **CHEDDAR CHEESE**. Bake at 400-degrees for 10 to 15 minutes or until golden brown.

VARIATION:
PIZZA CUPS: USE **PIZZA SAUCE** IN PLACE OF **BARBECUE SAUCE** AND TOP WITH **MOZZARELLI CHEESE**.

A CLEAN MEASURE: Dip the spoon in hot water to measure shortening, butter, etc., and the fat will slip out more easily.

SKILLET SUPPER
Not fancy but fine.

Brown in a large skillet . . . . 1½ pounds **GROUND MEAT**, lean
1 large **ONION**, chopped
Season with . . . . 1 tsp. **SEASONED SALT**
½ tsp. **SALT**
½ tsp. **PEPPER**
Add . . . . 1 can **ROTEL TOMATOES AND GREEN CHILIES**
Stir and cover with . . . . ½ **CABBAGE**, chopped

Cover with a tight fitting lid and cook on low heat until cabbage is tender. May season with **SOY SAUCE**. Serve this with a **SALAD** and don't forget the **CORNBREAD**.

FRIDAY NIGHT SPECIAL
A good meal stretcher for leftovers.

Combine . . . . 2 cups cooked **TURKEY** or **CHICKEN**, diced
3 cups cooked **RICE**
1 cup cooked mixed **VEGETABLES**
1 cup **ONIONS**, chopped
1 can (10¾ oz.) **CREAM OF CHICKEN SOUP**, condensed
1 tsp. **POULTRY SEASONING**
1 tsp. **CELERY SALT**
¼ tsp. **PEPPER**
½ cup **CHICKEN BROTH**

Pour into a buttered shallow 2-quart casserole. Bake at 350-degrees for 20 minutes. Sprinkle with 1 cup grated **CHEESE** and bake 5 minutes longer.
YIELD: 6 SERVINGS.

FRENCH FRIED LIVER
Even "I hate liver" people will love it!

Cut into strips the size of french
  fries . . . . 1 pound fresh **LIVER** (beef or
                                             pork)
Soak in **HOT WATER** to tenderize. Set aside.
Mix . . . . 1 cup **CORNMEAL**
                                             1 cup fine **CRACKER CRUMBS**
                                              SALT and **PEPPER**

Drain well. Place liver in bag and shake to coat evenly. Fry strips in deep hot **OIL**. They will fry quickly. Watch closely. Drain on paper towels.

NOTE: Use kitchen shears or very sharp knife to cut up strips.

HONEY-PEPPER PORK LOIN
WITH BAKED APPLES
*Requires little effort to prepare,
yet looks and tastes like labors of love.*

PORK LOIN ROAST: Trim fat to even thickness on a 2½ to 3 pound **CENTER-CUT PORK LOIN ROAST**. Set roast, bones down, in a 13x9x2-inch pan. Mix 3 tablespoons **HONEY** with 1 tablespoon **COARSELY GROUND BLACK PEPPER**. Rub ⅔ of the mixture evenly over the fat on roast. Bake on the middle rack of a 350-degree oven for 1½ hours. (155 degrees on meat thermometer.)

BAKED APPLES: While **PORK ROAST** is baking, rinse and core 4 **RED APPLES**. (Winesap or Rome Beauty.) Spread *remaining* **HONEY** mixture evenly over tops of apples. After roast has cooked about 45 minutes, set apples, honey side up, in the pan alongside the roast. Bake apples until tender when pierced, about 45 minutes, or until roast is done. Add **SALT** to taste.

To serve: place pork roast and apples on platter along with **BAKED POTATO WEDGES**.

YIELD: 4 SERVINGS.

PORK DIPPERS

We have chicken and steak strips. Why not pork strips?

Trim fat from   1   pound boneless **PORK LOIN ROAST**
Cut into 3x½x½-inch strips. Set aside.
In mixing bowl, combine   3   Tbsp. **FLOUR**
   ⅓   cup **YELLOW CORNMEAL**
   ½   tsp. **SALT**
   1   **EGG**, beaten
   ¼   cup **MILK**
   2   Tbsp. **OIL**

Mix well. Dip pieces of pork into cornmeal mixture. Deep fry a few at a time in hot **OIL** until pork is done and no pink remains. Serve with **MUSTARD SAUCE** or **BARBEQUE SAUCE**.

CURRIED PORK CHOPS AND RICE

Mary Louder's son, Sam, called from Dallas for this one.

Cook according to directions   1   package **SEASONED WILD** and **WHITE RICE**
Mix with . . . .   ½   cup **HEAVY CREAM**
Place in slightly oiled 13x9x2-inch baking dish. Set aside. Brown 6 or 8 lean **PORK CHOPS** in small amount of **OIL** and 2 tablespoons **WORCESTERSHIRE SAUCE**. Drain. Place on top of **RICE**.
Mix   1   can **CREAM OF CHICKEN SOUP**
   ½   tsp. **CURRY POWDER**
   ¼   cup **COFFEE CREAM**

Pour over casserole. Bake uncovered for 45 minutes at 350-degrees. Uncover and bake 15 minutes longer.

VARIATION:
Substitute skinned, boneless **CHICKEN BREASTS** for the **PORK CHOPS.**

"QUICK TO FIX" PORK

GLAZED PORK CHOPS: Mix together ⅔ cup **BROWN SUGAR**, 1 teaspoon each **PAPRIKA, SAGE, DRY MUSTARD**, ½ teaspoon **SALT** and **PEPPER**. Spread over **PORK CHOPS**. Bake uncovered at 250-degrees for 45 minutes. Turn **CHOPS** over and spoon drippings over. Cook for 15 more minutes. Increase oven heat to 350-degrees and cook 15 minutes.

PORK AND APPLES: Brown 4 **BUTTERFLY PORK CHOPS** in frying pan. Layer 3 unpeeled, cored and sliced **APPLES** in greased 11x7x2-inch baking dish. Sprinkle with ⅓ cup **BROWN SUGAR** and 2 teaspoons **CINNAMON**. Dot with **BUTTER**. Arrange **CHOPS** over **APPLES** and cover. Bake at 350-degrees for 1 hour or until done. May be prepared ahead.

FRIED HAM AND RED-EYED GRAVY: Brown on both sides in heavy skillet 4 (8 to 10-inch) slices **HAM**. Remove to platter. Add to hot ham drippings, 1 cup **COFFEE**. Stir to allow to boil until gravy turns red. Pour the **RED-EYED GRAVY** over the fried ham or hot **BISCUITS. DELICIOUS!**

GLAZED HAM STEAK: Place 1 (1-inch-thick) smoked fully-cooked **HAM STEAK** (1½ to 2 pounds) on rack of shallow roasting pan. Set aside. Combine ½ cup **RUSSIAN DRESSING**, ¼ cup firmly packed **BROWN SUGAR** and 1 tablespoon prepared **MUSTARD**. Spoon half of mixture on **HAM**. Broil **HAM** 3 inches from heat for 10 minutes. Turn **HAM** and baste again. Broil an additional 10 minutes.

PINEAPPLE BAKED HAM: Place 1 (2½-inch thick) center-cut fully cooked slice of **HAM** (4 to 5 pounds) in heavy-duty aluminum foil. Seal tightly. Place in a 13x9x2-inch baking dish. Bake at 350-degrees for 1 hour. Combine 8 ounces crushed **PINEAPPLE**, undrained, ½ cup firmly packed dark **BROWN SUGAR** and ½ teaspoon **GROUND CLOVES**. Spread over **HAM**. Bake, uncovered, 1 hour. Let stand 15 minutes before slicing.

CHEDDAR CHEESE PORK CHOPS: Pour ½ cup **WATER** into 11x7x2-inch baking dish. Sprinkle 4 boneless **BUTTERFLY PORK CHOPS** with **SEASONED SALT** and **PEPPER**. (**GARLIC SALT** to taste.) Arrange in baking dish. Top with 4 thick slices of **CHEDDAR CHEESE**, 4 thick slices **ONION** and 2 cans **GOLDEN MUSHROM SOUP**. Bake at 400-degrees for 1 hour or until done. Use liquid in baking dish for **GRAVY**.

CANADIAN BACON AND POTATO CASSEROLE

This is also good for a brunch.

BUTTER a 13x9x2-inch baking dish.
Place alternate layers of . . . .   3 medium **POTATOES**, peeled
and thinly sliced
1 package **CANADIAN BACON**,
or several slices **PRECOOKED HAM**
2 Tbsp. **ONION**, minced
8 slices **AMERICAN CHEESE**
Pour over layers . . . .   1 can **MUSHROOM SOUP**,
undiluted

Bake 350-degrees for 1 hour.

FAST SAUSAGE SUPPER

How fast? 30 minutes!!

Cut in half-dollar size . . . .   1 **SMOKED SAUSAGE** link
Brown in skillet in . . . .   2 Tbsp. **SHORTENING**
Layer on **SAUSAGE** . . . .   1 **ONION**, sliced
1 **GREEN PEPPER**, sliced
3 **POTATOES**, sliced
Sprinkle with . . . .   **SALT** and **PEPPER**
Add . . . .   ¾ cup **WATER**

Cover with lid and simmer 25 minutes. Serve with **SALAD** and **CORNBREAD**.

GARLIC GRILLED CHICKEN

When the neighbors smell this, they just might come across the fence.

Bone and skin 2 whole **CHICKEN BREASTS**. Pound chicken and cut into 1-inch strips. Marinate 1 to 2 hours in following mixture.
Combine . . . .   1 cup **PICANTE SAUCE**
2 Tbsp. **OIL**
1 Tbsp. **LIME JUICE**
2 cloves **GARLIC**, minced
½ tsp. **SALT**
½ tsp. **GROUND CUMIN**
½ tsp. **OREGANO**, crushed

Drain chicken. Place on hot grill. Brush with marinate often. Cooking time will depend on thickness of chicken strips.

HAWAIIAN STACK UP

Leta Warren shared this great idea for a party. The decorations are limitless. Serve with Jill Warrens' SWEET and SOUR SAUCE, ROLLS, and APRICOT SAUCE over ORANGE or LEMON SHERBET. One great party!!!

Prepare approximately ½ **CHICKEN BREAST** per person, when planning a party. Cut up chicken while still partially frozen for easy dicing.

Marinate at least 2 hours .... 2 cups **CHICKEN**
2 Tbsp. **OIL**
1 Tbsp. **SOY SAUCE**
1 Tbsp. **HONEY**

(Optional: Add shredded **GINGER ROOT** or dash of **GINGER SPICE**.) Spray pan with non-sticking cooking spray. Add chicken and marinade sauce. Stir fry until done. Add **SALT** and **PEPPER** to taste.

Arrange on table in small condiment bowls as follows: **COOKED RICE, DRY CHINESE NOODLES, CHICKEN, DICED ONIONS, DICED TO-MATOES, DICED CELERY, PINEAPPLE TIDBITS** (or crushed), **GRATED CHEDDAR CHEESE, SLICED** or **SLIVERED ALMONDS, CO-CONUT, WATER CHESTNUTS, RAISINS, SOY SAUCE, SWEET** and **SOUR SAUCE.**

JILL'S SWEET AND SOUR SAUCE

Combine .... 1 cup **WATER**
½ cup **SUGAR**
⅓ cup **RED WINE VINEGAR**
1 Tbsp. **SOY SAUCE**
SALT
Stir over heat until **SUGAR** is dissolved. Bring to boil.
Mix together .... 2 Tbsp. **CORNSTARCH**
¼ cup **WATER**

Add to boiling mixture. Cook until it thickens. Add a few drops of **RED COLORING.**

CHICKEN PIE

This dish was served at Mary Taylor's bridge party.
It is very easy and makes an attractive dish.

CRUST:
Mix well . . . . 1½ cups **FLOUR**
                           3 tsp. **BAKING POWDER**
                          ½ tsp. **SALT**
Cut in . . . . 3 Tbsp. **SHORTENING**
Add . . . . ½ cup **MILK**
Mix and roll into a rectangle.
Sprinkle with . . . . ¾ cup grated **CHEESE**
                          2 **PIMENTOS**, diced
                          CAYENNE PEPPER

Roll like a jelly roll. Chill.

CHICKEN MIXTURE:
In saucepan sauté . . . . 4 Tbsp. **MARGARINE** or
                          BUTTER
                          1 medium **ONION**, diced
                          1 **SWEET GREEN PEPPER**, diced
Add . . . . 1 cup **FRESH MUSHROOMS**,
                          diced
Thicken above mixture with . . . . . 3 Tbsp. **FLOUR**
Stirring constantly, add . . . . 2 cups **CHICKEN BROTH**
                          1 cooked **CHICKEN**, boned and
                          diced
                      1½ cups **MILK**
                          2 hard boiled **EGGS**, chopped
Cook together until well heated. Set aside.

Remove dough from refrigerator. Slice ¼-inch thick. Lay flat like biscuits in a buttered 13x9x2-inch baking dish. Pour chicken mixture over dough slices. Cook in 350-degree oven for 30 to 45 minutes or until dough is done.

YIELD: 10 TO 12 SERVINGS.

FRYING CHICKEN LIVERS: Prick completely through several times with a fork before frying to keep grease from popping.

MICROWAVE CHICKEN KIEV

Pat Swinney's "micro quick" recipe for the working girl.
Very impressive dish for those unexpected guests.

Skin, bone and half . . . .   4 whole **CHICKEN BREASTS**
Pound flat. Set aside.
Combine and set aside . . . .   1 cup **CHEESE CRACKERS**,
                                           crushed
                                        1½ Tbsp. **TACO SEASONING
                                           MIX**, dry
Mix together . . . .   3 Tbsp. **BUTTER**
                                         3 Tbsp. **SOFT CHEDDAR
                                           CHEESE**
                                         2 tsp. **INSTANT MINCED ONION**
                                         1 tsp. **MONOSODIUM
                                           GLUTAMATE**
                                         2 Tbsp. **CHOPPED GREEN
                                           CHILIES**
                                         1 tsp. **SALT**

Divide butter mixture into 8 balls. Roll chicken breast around each
butter/cheese ball. Tuck in ends and fasten with a toothpick. Dip each
chicken piece in melted **BUTTER** and roll in cheese cracker/taco
seasoning mix. Lay in pan and cover with wax paper. Microwave on
HIGH for 10 to 12 minutes.

Have this recipe ready for guests to copy.

CHICKEN ALMOND BAKE

One of Nadine Roger's "goodies".

Blend together . . . .   1 can **CREAM OF CELERY SOUP**
                                         ½ cup **MILK**
Add . . . .   1 cup cooked **CHICKEN**, diced
                                         ½ cup **CELERY**, diced
                                         1 small **ONION**, diced
                                         ½ cup sliced **ALMONDS**
                                         ¼ tsp. **WORCESTERSHIRE
                                           SAUCE**
Have on hand . . . .   1 can (3 oz.) **CHINESE
                                           NOODLES**, dry

Cover bottom of 1-quart baking dish with ½ the noodles. Add mixture.
Cover with rest of noodles. Bake in preheated 350-degree oven for 40 to
45 minutes.

YIELD: 4 SERVINGS.

L. TKACS CHICKEN BREASTS

For "gravy lovers" use ½ cup WINE and 2 cans SOUP.

Lightly grease baking dish.
Place in dish . . . . 8 boned **CHICKEN BREASTS**
Cover with . . . . 8 slices **SWISS CHEESE**
Combine . . . . ¼ cup **WHITE WINE**
                                   1 can **CREAM OF MUSHROOM SOUP**, undiluted
Spoon over chicken.
Sprinkle on top . . . . 1 cup **PEPPERIDGE FARM STUFFING**
Drizzle with . . . . ¼ cup **BUTTER** or **MARGARINE**

Cover and bake in preheated oven 350-degrees for 40 minutes. Remove cover and bake for 15 more minutes. Serve over **RICE**.

VARIATION:
Add **SALT**, **PEPPER** and **POULTRY SEASONING** to **WINE** and **SOUP** mixture for more taste.

DARBY'S CREAMY BAKED CHICKEN

A delicious choice.

Arrange in 13x9x2-inch baking
  dish . . . . 4 **CHICKEN BREASTS**, cooked and chopped
Top with . . . . 8 slices **MONTEREY JACK CHEESE**
Combine and pour over
  chicken . . . . 1 can **CREAM OF MUSHROOM SOUP**
                                   1 can **CREAM OF CHICKEN SOUP**
                                   ½ cup **DRY WHITE WINE**
                                   1 cup **SOUR CREAM**
Sprinkle with . . . . 1 cup **HERB STUFFING MIX (PEPPERIDGE FARMS)**
Drizzle with . . . . ½ cup **MARGARINE, melted**

Bake at 350-degrees for 30 minutes.

CHICKEN BREAST ALMONDINE

In skillet sauté . . . . ½ cup sliced **ALMONDS**
                                              ¼ cup **MARGARINE**

When golden brown, remove from skillet with slotted spoon.
Add to drippings in skillet . . . . . . ½ tsp. crushed **ROSEMARY**
                                          LEAVES
Set aside.
Combine . . . . ¼ cup **FLOUR**
                                          ¼ tsp. each **SALT** and **PEPPER**
Dust with flour mixture . . . . 4 boneless **CHICKEN BREASTS**,
                                          split

Shake off excess and brown chicken in drippings in skillet. When brown
on both sides, add ½ cup **DRY WHITE WINE**, cover and cook over low
heat 5 to 10 minutes, or until done. Remove chicken to heated platter.
Heat pan juices to boiling. Stir in reserved almonds. Spoon over chicken
to serve.

ANKIE'S CHICK-ON-A-STICK

Clean and skin 1 **BONELESS CHICKEN BREAST** half for each person
you will be serving. Cut into pieces about 1½-inch in diameter. Make
marinade of the following ingredients.
Drain juice from . . . . 1 small can **PINEAPPLE**
                                          CHUNKS
Add equal amount . . . . **WHITE WINE**
Cut into chunks . . . . **RED** and **GREEN PEPPERS**
                                          ONIONS
Add to make liquid brown . . . . **TERIYAKI SAUCE** or **SOY**
                                          SAUCE

Add a little **BROWN SUGAR** according to your taste.

Marinate the chicken in sauce for 3 to 4 hours. **DO NOT MARINATE
OVERNIGHT**. Alternate on skewers the chicken chunks, red and green
pepper, onion and pineapple chunks. Cook on grill about 15 minutes.
Try to turn only once during cooking to keep chicken from becoming
dry.

STUFFED CHICKEN BREASTS
This is a favorite of Glenda Harrison

Pound between waxed paper sheets until thin	2	whole **CHICKEN BREASTS**
Combine	¼	cup **MARGARINE**
		CHOPPED CHIVES
		DASH OF OREGANO
Spread mixture on chicken. Then place on chicken breast a slice of		**MONTEREY JACK** or **SWISS CHEESE**.

Roll and secure with a toothpick. Roll chicken in flour, then dip in beaten **EGG**. Roll in **BREAD CRUMBS**. At this point you can refrigerate up to a day in advance. Bake in 375-degree oven for 15 minutes. Pour ⅔ cup **WHITE WINE** over chicken and bake 25 minutes longer.

CHICKEN HASH IN CASSEROLE

Place in bowl	1	package **STUFF AND SUCH CRUMB AND RICE** mixture with **SEASONING**
Place in saucepan	1½	cups **CHICKEN BROTH**, may use canned
	½	cup **HEAVY CREAM**
	2	Tbsp. **BUTTER** or **MARGARINE**

Stir in contents of **SEASONING** from **STUFF** and **SUCH** crumb mixture. Heat to boiling. Pour over mixture in bowl. Set aside.

Melt in skillet	4	Tbsp. **BUTTER** or **MARGARINE**
Add	1	bunch **FRESH GREEN ONIONS**, chopped, with tops
	½	cup **GREEN PEPPER**, chopped
	½	cup **FRESH MUSHROOMS**, sliced

Sauté until onions are clear. Mix with crumb mixture.

Add	4	cups cooked **CHICKEN**, diced
	1	small jar **PIMENTOS**, diced
		SALT and **PEPPER**

Place in greased casserole and bake in 350-degree oven for 45 minutes.

NOTE: This is a large recipe. May be placed in smaller dishes and frozen. (Cooked or uncooked.)

DINNER N' DASH
Just zap this one right out.

Lightly grease a 2-quart baking dish. Set aside.
In small bowl, combine . . . .   1 can **CREAM OF CHICKEN SOUP**
                                            1 can (4 oz.) diced **GREEN CHILIES**, drained
                                            1 tsp. **INSTANT MINCED ONIONS**
                                            ½ cup **WATER**
                                            ¼ tsp. **SALT**
                                            ½ tsp. **PEPPER**
Set aside.
Layer in casserole *one-half* of
   the following ingredients . . . . . .   6 ounces **CORN CHIPS**
                                            2 cans (5 ozs. each) boned **CHICKEN**, diced

Pour over chips and chicken one-half of the soup mixture. Sprinkle with grated **MILD CHEDDAR CHEESE**.

Repeat with rest of corn chips, chicken, soup mixture. Sprinkle top generously with more grated cheese. Microwave on High for 10 to 12 minutes. May heat in conventional oven at 350-degrees for 20 minutes.

YIELD: 4 SERVINGS.

CHICKEN LUSH
Beverly Haney, our "California cousin" sent us this recipe.
She says it will freeze very well.

Mix together . . . .   2 cups cooked **WHITE CHICKEN**, diced
                                                 ¼ cup **SALAD DRESSING**, not mayonnaise
                                                 ½ tsp. **CURRY**
                                                 1 can **CREAM OF MUSHROOM SOUP**, undiluted
                                                 1 cup slivered **ALMONDS**
                                                 1 can **WATER CHESTNUTS**, drain and quarter

Place in greased baking dish. Top with buttered **BREAD CRUMBS.** Bake at 350-degrees for 45 minutes.

VARIATION:
Substitute **PREPARED POULTRY MIX** for **BREAD CRUMBS**. May add cooked **RICE** or cooked **WILD RICE**.

CHICKEN GOURMET
Dorothy Woods famous recipe.

Strip bottom of a 13x9x2-inch baking dish with	5 strips **BACON**
Cover with	1 cup uncooked **LONG GRAIN RICE**
Place on **RICE**	1 cut-up **CHICKEN,** skinned **SALT** and **PEPPER**
Combine and pour over **CHICKEN**	1 can **CREAM OF MUSHROOM SOUP**
	1 soup can of **WATER**
Sprinkle with	1 tsp. **PAPRIKA**
	¼ tsp. **OREGANO**
	¼ tsp. **GARLIC POWDER**
	½ tsp. **PARSLEY LEAVES**
	1 medium **ONION**, diced

Completely wrap baking dish with foil. Bake in 300-degree oven for 2½ to 3 hours. Remove foil last 10 minutes to brown. This is a super recipe for company. Place in oven and forget until time to serve.

FRIED CHICKEN LIVERS WITH BACON

Wash in hot water, and puncture with a fork several times (keeps them from popping)	**CHICKEN LIVERS**
Wrap each with	½ slices **BACON**
Secure with a toothpick. Season with	**SALT** and **PEPPER**
Roll in	**FLOUR**

Have shortening hot. Gently drop livers in and fry to golden brown. Serve with cream gravy.

CREAM GRAVY
What would fried chicken or steak be without gravy??

Heat in a skillet	3 Tbsp. **OIL** drippings from fried foods
Add	3 Tbsp. **FLOUR** **SALT** and **PEPPER**
When slightly browned, add	3 cups **MILK**

Stir constantly until thickened to right consistency.

"QUICKIE CHICKIE" RECIPES

These recipes are so simple and so good.

ORANGE GLAZED CHICKEN: Mix equal parts **ORANGE MARMA-LADE** and **BAR-B-QUE SAUCE.** Roll **CHICKEN** in **SAUCE. SALT** lightly. Place in buttered casserole dish. Bake in preheated oven 350-degrees for 45 to 50 minutes.

CHICKEN ALOHA: Pound boneless, skinless, **CHICKEN BREAST** halves until about ½ the original thickness. (One per person.) Coat in **FLOUR.** Brown in small amount of **BUTTER.** Place on baking sheet covered with foil. Cover with slice of **HAM,** and slice of **MONTEREY JACK CHEESE.** Bake 350-degrees for 10 minutes.

ITALIAN CHICKEN: Coat boneless, skinless, **CHICKEN BREAST** halves with **MAYONNAISE.** Roll in **ITALIAN BREAD CRUMBS.** Bake in preheated 350-degree oven for 30 to 40 minutes.

CRISPY BAKED CHICKEN: Brush 2½ to 3 pound skinned **CHICKEN** with ¾ cup **SALAD DRESSING.** Coat with 1 cup **CORNFLAKE CRUMBS** combined with ½ cup grated **PARMESAN CHEESE, SALT** and **PEPPER.** Place in baking dish. Bake at 350-degrees for 1 hour or until tender.

CHARCOAL GRILLED CHICKEN: Melt 4 Tbsp. **BUTTER** with 2 Tbsp. **GARLIC SALT,** 2 Tbsp. **WORCESTERSHIRE SAUCE.** Add 1 can **BEER.** Heat, but do not boil. Place 8 to 10 **CHICKEN QUARTERS** on hot grill and cook, turning, for about 5 minutes. Baste **CHICKEN** generously with **SAUCE** during final 15 minutes of cooking, turning often and brushing with more **SAUCE.**

ROASTED CHICKEN: Brush boneless **CHICKEN BREASTS** with melted **BUTTER** or **MARGARINE.** Sprinkle with **SALT** and **PEPPER.** Place skin side up in a baking dish. Bake in 350-degree oven for 30 to 35 minutes or until tender.

SWEET AND SOUR CHICKEN: Arrange 1 cup cut up **CHICKEN** in a 2-quart baking dish. Top with mixture of 8 ounces **FRENCH DRESSING,** 8 ounces **APRICOT PRESERVES** and ⅓ cup dry **ONION SOUP** mix. Cover and bake at 350-degrees for 1 hour and 15 minutes. Uncover and bake 15 minutes. May be served over **RICE.**

SANTA FE TURKEY

Dee Jackson uses homemade mayonnaise. Industrious, no?

Thaw according to directions
   on package . . . . 14-16 pound **TURKEY**
Stuff cavity of bird with . . . . ½ **APPLE**
                    ½ **ONION**
                    CELERY LEAVES
COVER WITH LOTS OF **MAYONNAISE.**

Place turkey on flat rack in a roaster-pan. Place in 350-degree oven un-covered, about 9 P.M. Cook 1 hour. Lower oven to 200-degrees. Leave in oven overnight. Turkey will be ready to eat the next morning. If you don't mind if it isn't a real pretty bird, place in roaster, breast down. It will be a little mashed but very moist. You may want to turn oven up for a few minutes to brown if you prefer a browner turkey.

CREAMED TURKEY

A good way to use up that Thanksgiving turkey.
We borrowed this from our friend, Margaret McDougal's cookbook.
"HOMEMADELY YOURS."

In saucepan, melt . . . . 2 Tbsp. **BUTTER**
Whisk thoroughly . . . . 4 Tbsp. **FLOUR**
                    1½ cups **MILK**
Add to butter. (The large amount of flour is because the **BROTH** will thin the **WHITE SAUCE.**) Cook butter, milk, and flour until thick, stirring constantly.
Add . . . . 1 cup **BROTH** from **TURKEY**
                    1 small jar **PIMENTO**, chopped
                    and drained
                    1 tsp. **LEMON JUICE**, (opt.)
                    SALT to taste
Stir in . . . . 4 cups cooked **TURKEY**, cubed

Heat thoroughly. When ready to serve, sprinkle with **PAPRIKA.** Serve warm. If too thick add more **MILK.**
(Cooked **CHICKEN** may be substituted.)

YIELD: 8 SERVINGS.

GOOP
Our solution for leftover Turkey.

Mix together . . . . 2 cups cooked **TURKEY** or
CHICKEN, cut into desired size
2 cups cooked **NOODLES**
½ cup **CELERY**, diced
¼ cup **GREEN OLIVES**, chopped
4 fresh **GREEN ONIONS**,
chopped, tops also
½ cup **SOUR CREAM**
1 can **CREAM OF CHICKEN
SOUP**, undiluted

Pour into greased casserole dish. Bake in preheated 350-degree oven for 30 minutes. Serve with **FRENCH BREAD** and tossed **GREEN SALAD**. May sprinkle with **AMERICAN CHEESE** before baking.

SHRIMP CREOLE
Reminds you of New Orleans.

Heat over medium high heat in
heavy pan to make a roux . . . . . ⅓ cup **FRESH DRIPPINGS**
¼ cup **FLOUR**
Stir constantly until golden
brown. Then Add. . . . . ½ cup **ONION**, chopped
2 **GREEN ONIONS**, chopped
½ cup **GREEN PEPPER**, chopped
½ cup **CELERY**, diced
¼ cup minced **FRESH PARSLEY**
4 cloves **GARLIC**, minced
Cook vegetables 2 minutes.
Add . . . . 1 cup **WATER**
1 can (8 oz.) **TOMATO SAUCE**
1½ tsp. **SALT**
2 **BAY LEAVES**
½ tsp. **THYME**
⅛ tsp. **CAYENNE PEPPER**
1 slice **LEMON**

Turn heat low, cover pan tightly with lid. Simmer on low 20 minutes, stirring occasionally. Add 2 cans (4½ oz. ea.) **SHRIMP** or use 2 cups boiled shrimp. Heat and serve over **RICE**.

YIELD: 4 SERVINGS.

CREAMED SHRIMP AND CHICKEN
Having the boss for dinner? Try this recipe.

Brown in 4 Tbsp. **BUTTER** . . . . . . 8 boneless **CHICKEN BREAST HALVES**, skinned
8 ounces **FRESH MUSHROOMS**, sliced
2 cloves **GARLIC**, minced
Stir in . . . . 2 cans **CREAM OF MUSHROOM SOUP**
4 ounces **HALF** and **HALF CREAM**
¼ cup grated **PARMESAN CHEESE**

Cover and cook over low heat for 45 minutes.
Add . . . . 1 pound cooked **SHRIMP**, peeled
Cook for 15 more minutes or until chicken is done and shrimp is heated.
While chicken is cooking, prepare enough **RICE**, according to directions on package, to have 4 cups cooked rice.
Combine with . . . . ½ cup **BUTTER OR MARGARINE**, melted
¼ cup sliced **WATER CHESTNUTS**

Serve chicken and shrimp over rice mixture. Serve with layered **SALAD**, **HOT BREAD**, and a light **DESSERT**.

YIELD: 8 SERVINGS.

FILLETS OF PIKE-PERCH WITH ALMONDS
An Austrian recipe enjoyed by the Woods family.

Prepare amount needed of small whole **FISH** or fillets of larger **FISH**. Rub well with **LEMON JUICE**. Let stand 30 minutes. Season with **SALT** and **PEPPER**. Roll in **FLOUR**. Fry in hot **OIL**. Brown on both sides until golden brown. Meanwhile, roast until crisp, ½ cup sliced **ALMONDS**. Sprinkle over **FISH** before serving. Serve with **GREEN SALAD** and **PARSLEYED POTATOES**.

VARIATION:
TROUT, **WHITEFISH** or **SOLE** may also be prepared this way.

FARMERS SEAFOOD BOIL
You will need a very large pot.

Bring to a boil . . . . 1 gallon **WATER**
2 pkgs. (3-ounces ea.) **CRAB** and **SHRIMP BOIL**
¼ cup **SALT**

Add and boil 10 minutes . . . . 3 medium **POTATOES**, washed, unpared, and cut into chunks

Add and boil 5 minutes . . . . 3 ears **CORN**, cut in thirds

Add and boil 5 minutes . . . . 4 **ONIONS**, quartered
1 link **PORK** or **ITALIAN SAUSAGE**, cut into 1½-inch pieces

Add and boil 5 minutes . . . . 2 pounds shell-on headless **SHRIMP**

Drain and serve with crusty **BREAD** and a cold **BEVERAGE**.

This makes for a fun, fun party. Cover table with butcher paper and pour **SHRIMP** and **VEGGIES** in middle. Gather around with lots of **COLD DRINKS** and have a feast!!!! Lots of fun for a backyard party.

SHRIMP ON RICE
You may wish to double recipe, so everyone can have "seconds".

In large frying pan, sauté . . . . 3 Tbsp. **BUTTER** or **MARGARINE**
2 Tbsp. chopped **ONION**
1 clove **GARLIC**, minced

Blend in . . . . 3 Tbsp. **FLOUR**

Stir well and add . . . . 1 Tbsp. **WORCESTERSHIRE SAUCE**
1 tsp. **ACCENT**
½ Tbsp. **TABASCO SAUCE**
SALT to taste

Cook until thickened and bubbly.

Stir in . . . . 1 cup **HEAVY CREAM**
¼ cup **CHILI SAUCE**

Add . . . . 1 pound cooked, peeled **SHRIMP**

Heat and serve immediately over cooked **RICE**. Sauce may be prepared ahead and frozen before adding the shrimp.

YIELD 4 SERVINGS.

BROILED FISH

Good basic recipe for the "amateur cook" or "professional dieter"!

Buy 2 pounds fresh **FISH FILLETS** or **STEAKS**. Sprinkle both sides with **SALT** and **PEPPER**.
Cover broiler pan, or shallow baking dish, with aluminum foil. Slice 1 **LEMON** into ¼-inch slices and place on foil.
Place **FISH** in pan on top of the **LEMON SLICES**.
Baste with mixture of . . . .   ¼ cup **MARGARINE**, melted
Juice of 1 **LEMON**

Broil fish about 4 inches from source of heat for 8 to 15 minutes, depending on thickness of fish. Baste once during broiling, but do not turn.

YIELD: 4 TO 6 SERVINGS.

VARIATION:
To cook on grill, place foil on grill, punch holes in foil. Cook as above.

PASQUELL MENELLI

This was exchanged at bridge club.

Melt 1 cup **BUTTER** with few **PEPPERCORNS** in skillet. Add **SHRIMP** and sauté until done. Remove shrimp, place on shallow pan. Place under broiler until begins to brown. Remove to platter. Reserve butter for dipping. ENJOY!

ONION N' FISH

The combination of flavor makes this a very popular recipe.

Cut into serving size portions . . . .   2 pounds **FISH FILLETS**
Sprinkle with . . . .   **SALT**
Combine . . . .   1 cup **MAYONNAISE**
1 cup **SOUR CREAM**
1 small package **RANCH STYLE SALAD DRESSING** mix, dry
Crush . . . .   2 cans (2.8 oz. ea.) **FRENCH FRIED ONION RINGS**

Dip fish into 1 cup mayonnaise mixture. Roll in crushed onion rings. Place in a greased 13x9x2-inch baking dish. Bake at 350-degrees for 20 minutes. Serve with remaining mayonnaise mixture.

YIELD: 4 TO 6 SERVINGS.

JEAN McCORD'S ORANGE ROUGHY

Dieter's favorite.

Dip **ORANGE ROUGHY FILLETS** in **FRENCH DRESSING,** then in crushed **RITZ CHEESE CRACKERS.** Place on foil in baking dish. Bake 500-degrees for 5 to 10 minutes. (Fish is done when it is easy to flake with fork.)

TARTAR SAUCE, via KINGS INN

Chop very fine . . . . 2 small **SWEET PEPPERS**
1 small jar **PIMENTOS**
⅓ stalk **CELERY**
1 large **ONION**
ANCHOVIES, small can

Add . . . . ½ bottle **WORCESTERSHIRE SAUCE**
3 tubes **CRACKERS,** crushed
SALT and **PEPPER**

Mash and add . . . . 10 **EGGS,** hard boiled
Toss together with . . . . 1 qt. **MAYONNAISE**
1 qt. **SALAD DRESSING**
DICED JALAPENOES, to taste

Store in refrigerator.

KAREN CRISWELLS TARTAR SAUCE

A "must" with fish.

Combine . . . . 1 cup **MAYONNAISE**
1 cup **MIRACLE WHIP DRESSING**
3 Tbsp. **SWEET PICKLE RELISH**
2 Tbsp. Chopped **ONION**
2 Tbsp. chopped **OLIVES**
¼ cup **SOUR CREAM**
JUICE of ½ **LEMON**
Dash of **PEPPER**

Store in airtight container in refrigerator.

QUICK TARTAR SAUCE: Combine 1 cup mayonnaise, ½ small onion, finely chopped, 3 Tbsp. sweet relish, 2 Tbsp. lemon juice. Mix and refrigerate.

JACK'S FROZEN MARGARITAS
Try frozen STRAWBERRIES to make strawberry margaritas.

In blender, add . . . . 1 can (8 oz.) **FROZEN LIME JUICE**
Using lime juice can, add . . . . 1 can **TEQUILA**
¼ can **TRIPLE SEC** (orange liqueur)

Fill blender with **ICE** and blend into a frozen slush. Pour into **SALT-RIMMED** cocktail glasses. May add a slice of **LIME** to garnish.

HINT: If you can't drink **TEQUILA**, substitute **VODKA** to make **VODKARITAS**.

JOE'S TEQUILA DAIQUIRI
Try the variation for a change of pace.

Combine in cocktail shaker . . . . . . 1½ ounces **TEQUILA**
1½ tsp. **LIME JUICE**
1 tsp. **SUGAR**
ICE CUBES

Shake well. Pour into a cocktail glass.

YIELD: 1 SERVING.

VARIATION:
Substitute **RUM** for the **TEQUILA**. Increase **LIME JUICE** to 1 tablespoon.

KAHLUA ALEJANDRO
Smooth, cool and not too sweet.

Combine in blender . . . . 1 ounce **KAHLUA**
1 ounce **GIN**
2 Tbsp. **VANILLA ICE CREAM**
3 **ICE CUBES**

Blend well. Pour into stemmed cocktail glass.

YIELD: 1 SERVING.

BESITO
(Kiss.)

Fill a liqueur glass ½ full with **KAHLUA**. Spoon 2 tsp. **EVAPORATED MILK** on top. The **KAHLUA** will boil up into the **MILK**. Very interesting.

TIJUANA TEQUILLA DEL SOL
Tequila Sunrise.

Place in tall cocktail glass . . . . 1½ ounce **TEQUILA**
2 tsp. **LIME JUICE**
2 tsp. **GRENADINE**
¼ cup (2 oz.) **ORANGE JUICE**

Stir and add ice cubes.

YIELD: 1 SERVING.

MARGARITA
This is Mexico's traditional drink.

Rub rim of glass with **LIME JUICE** or **HONEY**. Swirl in **SALT** until rim is coated well. Set aside.
Combine in cocktail shaker . . . . . . 2 ounces **TEQUILA**
¾ ounce **TRIPLE SEC**
1 Tbsp. **LIME JUICE**

Shake vigorously, strain into **SALT-RIMMED** glass. Add ice cubes.

YIELD: 1 SERVING.

CABANA BANANA
"Ole "CUERVO" you are a friend of mine."

Combine in blender . . . . 2½ ounces **"CUERVO ESPECIAL"**
TEQUILA
8 ounces **APPLE CIDER**
1 large **BANANA**, peeled and sliced
2 ounces **HONEY**
½ cup crushed **ICE**

Mix until smooth. Pour into cocktail glass. Garnish with **CHERRY** or **BANANA** slice.

YIELD: 2 COCKTAILS.

MEXICAN HOT SAUCE
Serve this "South of the Border Treat" with tostados.

Mix together in blender	2 cans (16 oz. each) **TOMATOES**, drained
	1 can (4 oz.) **GREEN CHILIES**, chopped
	1 medium **ONION**, chopped
Add	1½ tsp. **GARLIC SALT**
	½ tsp. **PEPPER**
	½ tsp. **SALT**
	½ tsp. **SUGAR**
Optional	**JALAPENO PEPPERS**, chopped

Place in blender for just an instant. If you want it hotter, but do not want the jalapenos, cut one pepper in half and let it set in blended sauce for a few minutes. Remove.

HOT TACO DIP
Make ahead and refrigerate. Heat when ready to serve.

In large microwave-safe bowl combine	1 cup (8 oz.) **SOUR CREAM**
	1 can (10 ½ oz.) condensed **BEAN** and **BACON SOUP**
	½ cup (2 oz.) shredded **CHEDDAR** or **AMERICAN CHEESE**
	2 Tbsp. dry **TACO SEASONING MIX**
	½ tsp. **INSTANT MINCED ONION**

Mix well. Cook, uncovered, 2½ minutes or until heated through. Stir occasionally. Serve warm with **CORN CHIPS.**

VARIATION:
For hotter flavored dip, use entire package **TACO SEASONING MIX** or 1 can (4 oz.) chopped **CHILIES.**

MEXICAN PIZZA
This will serve 6 as appetizer or 2 as an entree.

Toast 2 large **TORTILLAS** until very crisp. Cover with a mixture of **MONTEREY JACK CHEESE** and **MILD CHEDDAR CHEESE**. (About 4 ounces of each.) Broil and cut like a pizza. May top with: **CHILI, CHOPPED ONION, HOT SAUCE, GAUCAMOLE, BEANS, PICO DE GALLO SAUCE, COOKED GROUND BEEF**, or **CHOPPED TOMATOES** and **LETTUCE**.

CREAMY GUACAMOLE

Don's favorite.

Mash	3	ripe **AVOCADOS**
Add and stir	1½	Tbsp. **LEMON JUICE**
Add	1	**TOMATO,** chopped
	½	**ONION,** chopped
	1	cup **LETTUCE,** chopped
	¼	cup **PICANTE**
Season to taste with		**GARLIC SALT**
		PEPPER

The avocados and seasoning may be blended in blender. Add avocado seed to prevent avocados from turning dark. Remove before serving. Serve with warm **CORN CHIPS.**

SOPA ANACHUACALLI

This is a quickie "tortilla soup, or broth" for a cold day.

Combine in large saucepan	1	quart **CHICKEN BROTH**, may use canned
	2	**GREEN ONIONS**, chopped, with tops
	1	**TOMATO**, chopped
Slowly heat until gently simmering. About 30 to 40 minutes. While broth is simmering, heat in skillet	4	Tbsp. **BUTTER** or **MARGARINE**
Cut into thin strips	5	**CORN TORTILLAS**

Brown in melted butter or margarine until brown and crispy. **DRAIN ON PAPER TOWELING.** (May want to cook rest of corn tortillas to eat with soup.) To serve, place a handful of the crisp tortilla strips in the bottom of the soup bowl. Cover with grated **MONTEREY JACK CHEESE.** (About 2 ounces per bowl.) Pour broth into bowls. Serve warm with crispy **TORTILLAS.**

YIELD: 4 SERVINGS.

VARIATION:
Add **SOUR CREAM** and **DICED AVOCADOS** to bowl before pouring on broth or it is better to serve in bowls as condiments. (Be sure to sprinkle the **AVOCADO** with **LEMON** or **LIME** juice to prevent discoloration.

SOPA DE ARROZ
Mary Villegas wonderful rice dish.

In large skillet, heat . . . .   ¼ cup **SHORTENING**
Add . . . .   ⅓ cup **WHITE RICE**
Stir until brown. Remove from heat.
Place in blender   . . . .   ½ cup **TOMATO SAUCE**
  2 cloves **GARLIC**
  1 tsp. **CUMIN (COMINO)**
  ½ cup **WATER**
Blend well. Set aside.
Add to rice mixture . . . .   2 Tbsp. **TOMATOES**, chopped
  2 Tbsp. **ONIONS**, chopped

Pour tomato mixture from blender into rice. Use a little water to rinse out the blended ingredients. Add an additional 1½ cup **WATER**. Cover skillet and let simmer until all the water is absorbed. Do not stir.

VARIATION:
Add shredded, cooked **PORK** or **BEEF.**

FRIJOLES
Texan and Mexican staple.

Sort and wash . . . .   2 pounds **DRIED PINTO BEANS**
Add enough **WATER** to be 4-inches above beans. Soak overnight. Drain.
Place beans in large saucepan.
Combine with . . . .   ½ cup **BACON DRIPPINGS** or 4
  Tbsp. **VEGETABLE OIL**
  ½ tsp. **PEPPER**
  1 Tbsp. **SUGAR**
  1 cup **KETCHUP**
  1 large **ONION**, chopped
  1 tsp. **VINEGAR**
  ½ tsp. **COMINO**, optional
  1 Tbsp. **CHILI POWDER**
  2 cloves **GARLIC**, crushed
  SALT and **PEPPER**

Add enough **WATER** to cover well. Bring to a boil. Reduce heat. Simmer 4 to 5 hours. Don't let boil dry. May add more water, but add boiling water or it will increase the cooking time.

YIELD: 8 TO 10 SERVINGS.

FRIJOLES A LA CHARRA

This soup is served in a famous restaurant in San Antonio.
Spicy, but so good.

Fry in medium saucepan . . . . 4 slices **BACON**, cut in small
pieces
Add . . . . .1½ pints **COOKED PINTO BEANS**
2-3 cups **WATER**
Bring to boil.
Reduce heat and add . . . . ½ tsp. **SALT**
½ tsp. **CHILI POWDER**
½ tsp. **GROUND CUMIN**
1 clove **GARLIC** minced

Heat thoroughly. Serve topped with a generous helping of **PICO DE
GALLO**.

PICO DE GALLO

Combine . . . . 1 **ONION** chopped
2 **TOMATOES** chopped
FRESH CILANTRO to taste
2-3 **SERRANO CHILIES**, minced
DASH of **LEMON** or **LIME
JUICE**

VARIATION:
Add one-half can **BEER** to this recipe and it becomes **FRIJOLES
BORRACHOS**.

SOUTH OF THE BORDER ESPECIAL

Flavorful dish, hot and spicy.

In 2-quart microwave-safe bowl,
mix together . . . . 1 pound lean **GROUND BEEF**
1 medium **ONION**, sliced
2 cups (16 oz.) undrained
TOMATOES
½ cup **RIPE OLIVES**, sliced
1 tsp. **CHILI POWDER**
Sprinkle with . . . . 1 package **BROWN GRAVY MIX**

Cook on high, covered, 5 minutes. Stir. Cook 5 more minutes. Place 1
cup crushed **CORN CHIPS** in serving dish. Pour mixture over chips.
Sprinkle with 1 cup crushed corn chips.

FRIJOLES BORRACHOS
This is Becky's version of "DRUNKEN BEANS".

Rinse and sort . . . . 1 pound **DRIED PINTO BEANS**
Place in a large saucepan, covered with **WATER** and simmer gently for
3 to 3½ hours. (Or until tender.) Add additional **WATER** if necessary. (Do
not let beans become dry while cooking.) When beans are tender, add ½
can **BEER**.
Place in skillet . . . . 2 Tbsp. **SHORTENING**
Melt and add . . . . 1 bunch **FRESH GREEN**
                                      ONIONS, chopped, with tops
                                    2 **TOMATOES**, cubed
                                    4 **SERRANO CHILIES**, minced
Cook gently until **ONIONS** are clear, but not brown. Remove from heat
and add to beans.
Add to cooked beans . . . . 1 bunch **CILANTRO**, chopped
                                    SALT and **PEPPER**

Heat thoroughly before serving.

YIELD: 6 TO 8 SERVINGS.

BAKED CHILES RELLENOS

Rinse well, remove seeds, and set
     aside . . . . 4 cans (4 oz. ea.) **WHOLE GREEN**
                                    CHILIES, drained
Combine . . . . 6 ounces **SWISS CHEESE**, grated
                                    6 ounces **CHEDDAR CHEESE**,
                                    grated
Stuff chilies with approximately 3 tablespoons cheese. Arrange chilies
in a lightly greased 12x8x2-inch baking dish. Sprinkle remaining cheese
on top.
Combine . . . . 6 **EGGS** beaten
                                    ¾ cup **MILK**
                                    ¼ tsp. **SALT** and **PEPPER**

Mix well. Pour over chilies. Bake 350-degrees for 30 minutes or until set.

YIELD: 6 SERVINGS.

CHILI RELLENO CASSEROLE
Quick supper dish.

Place in the bottom of a greased 8x8x2-inch casserole dish	2	small cans **WHOLE CHILI PEPPERS**
Sprinkle with	½	pound **MONTEREY JACK CHEESE,** grated
Combine and pour over mixture	6	**EGGS,** slightly beaten **WORCESTERSHIRE,** dash **SALT** and **PEPPER**

Bake in a preheated 350-degree oven until the eggs are firm, about 20 to 25 minutes. Serve hot.

YIELD: 4 SERVINGS.

ANGIE'S ARROZ
"Mexican Rice"

Place in skillet and brown	1	cup **RICE,** regular
	⅛	cup **OIL**
Add	¼	cup **ONION,** chopped
	1	**BELL PEPPER,** chopped
	2	cups **WATER**
	3	oz. **TOMATO PASTE**
		SALT and **PEPPER**

Cook slow until rice is done.

YIELD: 6 SERVINGS.

SPANISH SQUASH
For those with a garden.

Dice	3-4	**YELLOW SQUASH**
	1	**ONION,** medium
	1	can **TOMATOES** (or 2 **FRESH**)
Stir with 2 Tbsp. **MARGARINE** until thick.		
Season with		**GARLIC SALT**
		PEPPER
		SUGAR
		BUTTER SALT

Layer in greased casserole with grated **CHEESE** on top. Bake in 350-degree oven for approximately 15 minutes or until cheese melts.

YIELD: 6 SERVINGS.

MEXICAN SALAD

DRESSING:
Blend with wire whisk
and set aside............... 1 **EGG YOLK**
2 Tbsp. **WHITE VINEGAR**
2 Tbsp. **PREPARED SPICY BROWN MUSTARD**

Beating constantly slowly add ... ½ cup **LITE OIL**
Beat until thick and creamy.
Stir and blend well .... 1 can (4 oz.) **CHOPPED GREEN CHILIES**, well-drained
1 tsp. **CRUSHED DRIED RED PEPPER**
1 tsp. **CHILI POWDER**
1 tsp. **DRIED OREGANO LEAVES**, (opt.)

Blend well. Combine mixture and refrigerate until ready to serve.

VEGGIES:
In large bowl toss.............. 5 cups torn **SALAD GREENS**
1 cup **CAULIFLOWERETS**
1 **SWEET RED PEPPER**, cut in thin strips

Pour dressing over veggies and garnish with **RED ONION RINGS**.

SOUTHWEST GARDEN DISH
Crunchy veggies with that good southwest flavor.

Fry until crisp................. 4 slices **BACON**
Remove from skillet, crumble, and set aside.
Add to **BACON DRIPPINGS** ..... 2 medium **ONIONS**, chopped
Cook until tender.
Add........................ 1 cup **NEW POTATOES**, diced (Do not peel)
2 cups **ZUCCHINI**, diced
¼ cup **PICANTE SAUCE**
1 tsp. **SUGAR**
½ tsp. **CUMIN**

Cook over medium heat until vegetables are crisp, yet tender. Stir occasionally.
Stir in .... 1 cup **TOMATOES**, diced
Pour into serving dish. Sprinkle with crumbled bacon.

BECKY'S BEEF AND CHEESE ENCHILADAS
Jack just can't get enough of these!!

Brown in skillet . . . . 1 pound **EXTRA LEAN GROUND BEEF**
Drain well and set aside.
Grate . . . . 10 ounces **CHEDDAR CHEESE**
Chop . . . . 1 **ONION** (Sauté with beef if you prefer your onions cooked.)

Place 2 tablespoons meat in a **FLOUR TORTILLA**. Sprinkle with cheese and onion. Roll up tight and place in a slightly greased 13x9x2-inch baking dish, seam side down. (If you prefer **CORN TORTILLAS**, dip into ¼-inch hot grease for just a minute on each side, so that they will be more pliable.) Cover with **SAUCE**.

SAUCE:

Melt in saucepan . . . . ½ cup **MARGARINE**
Add . . . . 3 Tbsp. **FLOUR**
Gradually add . . . . 2 cups **MILK**
Cook until slightly thickened. 8 ounces **VELVEETA CHEESE**
Add . . . . 1 can **CHOPPED CHILIES**

Pour over filled tortillas. Cover with grated **AMERICAN CHEESE**. Cover with foil and bake in preheated oven at 350-degrees for 15 minutes. Make ahead of time and freeze for those drop-in guests.
HINT: Use half **FLOUR TORTILLAS** and half **CORN TORTILLAS**, this makes everyone happy.

QUICK ENCHILADA CASSEROLE

Brown together . . . . 1½ pounds **GROUND MEAT**
1 medium **ONION**, chopped
Add . . . . 1 can (29 oz.) **TOMATO SAUCE**
1 Tbsp. **CHILI POWDER**
1 tsp. **GARLIC SALT**
Grate . . . . 1 pound **CHEDDAR CHEESE**
Set aside.

Heat **SALAD OIL.** Cut in half, 1 dozen **TORTILLAS.** Drop tortillas in hot oil and cook 1 minute, turning once; drain. Spoon ⅓ meat mixture into a shallow 2-quart casserole; top with ⅓ tortillas and ⅓ cheese. Repeat layers until all ingredients are used. Bake at 325-degrees for 20 minutes or until bubbly.

YIELD: 8 TO 10 SERVINGS.

MEXICAN HAMBURGERS

These are stuffed meatballs that the Franklin's maid "Angie" cooks.

Make 2 pounds **GROUND MEAT into 8 patties.**
Place on 4 of the patties each ....   1 slice **ONION**
                                         1 slice **CHEESE**
                                         CHOPPED JALAPENO

Place remaining 4 patties on top. Seal edges **WELL**. Kind of shape into a ball. Place in skillet and brown on both sides. (Will make own oil, or juice.) Remove from skillet. Make **GRAVY**.

GRAVY:
Place in skillet ....   3 Tbsp. **OIL**
                                      1 Tbsp. **FLOUR**, heaping
Brown. Gradually add ....   2 cups **WATER**

Stir until slightly thickened. Add patties. Cook 20 to 30 minutes longer. Turn meatballs over and cook 15 more minutes. Serve with **CORN**, **SALAD**, and **ROLLS**.

AUSTIN FAJITAS

Cut into cutlet size pieces, 1½ pounds **SKIRT STEAK**, or cheap cut of **BEEF**. Pierce meat with fork to insure flavor and tenderness.
Marinate for 2 to 3 hours in the
    refrigerator with marinade
    made with the following
    ingredients ....   ¼ cup **TEQUILLA**
                                         ½ cup **LIME JUICE**
                                         4 Tbsp. **LIQUID SMOKE**
                                         1 tsp. **WORCESTERSHIRE SAUCE**
                                         ¼ tsp. **OREGANO**
                                         ½ tsp. **SALT** and **PEPPER**
                                         ¾ tsp. **PAPRIKA**

After steak has marinated for several hours, drain. (Save some of the marinade.) Grill for 8 to 10 minutes over hot charcoal fire. Before grilling the second side, toss **ONION RINGS** and **PEPPER STRIPS** with a little of the marinade in **OIL** in a hot skillet. Cook until tender-crisp. Do not overcook. Cut meat into 1-inch wide strips. Place on platter. Cover with pepper and onion mixture to serve. Heat **TORTILLAS** in a foil packet (10 to 12 at a time) in a 350-degree oven for 12 to 15 minutes. Serve with **PICO de GALLO SAUCE, GUACAMOLE** and **SOUR CREAM**.

TACO SALAD WEDGES

Prepare favorite pie crust for 1 9-inch pie. (Or buy ready-prepared crust that you buy in dairy section of store.) Bake and cool completely.
FILLING:

Brown......................	1 pound	**GROUND MEAT**

Drain well and remove from heat.

Add........................	¼ tsp.	**GARLIC POWDER**
	¼ tsp.	**SALT**
	4 ounces chopped	**GREEN CHILIES,** drained
	1 cup chopped	**TOMATO**
	¼ cup sliced	**RIPE OLIVES**

Cool; spoon into cooled pie crust.

Spread over meat mixture	6 ounce carton	**FROZEN AVOCADO DIP,** thawed
Sprinkle with	4 ounces shredded	**CHEDDAR CHEESE**
Spread over cheese	½ cup	**SOUR CREAM**
Garnish top with	½ cup shredded	**LETTUCE**
	1 medium	**TOMATO,** cut into wedges
	2 Tbsp. sliced	**GREEN ONION**
	¼ package (11 oz.)	**TORTILLA CHIPS**

Store in refrigerator. Cut into wedges and serve with **SALSA**.

YIELD: 6 SERVINGS.

CHALUPAS

Cover well with water and soak overnight about 2 pounds dried **PINTO BEANS**. Drain and rinse. Place in large saucepan.

Add to beans	4 pounds	**PORK ROAST,** trimmed and cut in chunks
	8 ounces chopped	**GREEN CHILIES**
	2 cloves	**GARLIC,** minced
	1½ tsp.	**OREGANO**
	1½ tsp.	**COMINO**
	2 Tbsp.	**CHILI POWDER**
		SALT and **PEPPER**

Add enough **WATER** to be at least 1 inch above all the ingredients. Cook slowly all day, stirring often. Meat will fall apart. Serve over broken up **CORN CHIPS**. Top with any, or all of the following ingredients: **CHOPPED ONIONS, CHOPPED TOMATOES, CHOPPED JALAPENOS, GRATED CHEESE, CHOPPED LETTUCE, CHOPPED AVOCADOS** or **COOKED RICE**

CHICKEN SPAGHETTI
With a TEX-MEX flavor. Spicy!

Boil, bone and chop into bite size	1	3-lb. **CHICKEN,** or **CHICKEN PARTS**
Reserve 1 cup of **BROTH** and set aside.		
Cook according to directions	1	12-oz. pkg. **SPAGHETTI**
Drain. Set aside.		
In 4-quart saucepan, cook until tender	1	medium **ONION,** diced
In	½	cup **MARGARINE**
Add	1	small jar **MUSHROOMS**
	1½	pounds **MEXICAN VELVEETA CHEESE,** grated
	1	can **TOMATOES** with **GREEN CHILIES**
Add		**CHICKEN**

Heat well. Add reserved liquid if too dry. To serve, place spaghetti in dish. Pour chicken mixture over top. Serve with **SALAD,** heated **FLOUR TORTILLAS,** and **DESSERT.**

VARIATION:
For milder flavor, substitute regular **VELVEETA.**

ANGIE'S CARNE ASADA
One of those make-ahead, one-dish meals.

Place into non-stick or iron skillet	3	pounds inexpensive **BEEF STEAK,** cut into cubes
	1	**SWEET BELL PEPPER,** diced
	1	small **ONION,** diced
Cook until brown. Season	¼	Tbsp. **GARLIC POWDER**
with	½	tsp. **CELERY SALT SALT** and **PEPPER**

Move mixture to one side of skillet. On empty side, place 2 Tbsp. **OIL.** Heat. Add 3 tsp. **FLOUR.** Stir until well blended. Stir into meat mixture.

Add	3	ounces **TOMATO PASTE,** blended with ½ cup **WATER**
	2	cups **WATER**

Let simmer for approximately 1 hour. Stirring occasionally. Serve over **WHITE RICE.** Serve with **FLOUR TORTILLAS, SALAD,** and **DESSERT.**

YIELD: 6 SERVINGS.

LAREDO DUMPLIN'S
Ready for a hungry family in 20 minutes.

Combine in 3-quart microwave-
safe bowl . . . . 1 pound **GROUND BEEF**
                                          1 tsp. **CHILI POWDER**
Cook on **HIGH**, 2½ minutes. Stir, cook 2 more minutes.
Stir in . . . . ½ tsp. **SALT**
                                          ¼ cup **ONION** chopped
                                          1 cup (8 oz.) **TOMATO SAUCE**
                                          with **ONION, CELERY** and
                                          GREEN PEPPER
                                          1 cup (8 oz.) undrained
                                          TOMATOES
                                          1 cup (8 oz.) drained **WHOLE**
                                          KERNEL CORN
Cook on **HIGH**, uncovered, 5 minutes or until mixture boils. Meanwhile
prepare **DUMPLINGS.**
Combine and mix well . . . . ½ cup **PANCAKE MIX**
                                          ¼ cup **YELLOW CORNMEAL**
                                          3 Tbsp. **WATER**
                                          1 **EGG** beaten

Spoon mixture on top of beef mixture. Cook on **HIGH**, uncovered 7 to 8
minutes, or until center dumpling is no longer doughy underneath. Remove from microwave, cover, and let stand for 5 minutes before serving.

SAN ANTONIO STYLE BAKED CHICKEN
*This can be prepared in the morning, refrigerated, and baked just
in time for the arrival of your guests.*

Mix . . . . 4 **EGGS**, beaten
                                          5 Tbsp. **PICANTE SAUCE**
Set aside.
Mix . . . . 2 cups dry **BREAD CRUMBS**
                                          2 Tbsp. **CHILI POWDER**
                                          1½ tsp. **CUMIN**
                                          ½ tsp. **GARLIC POWDER**
                                          1 tsp. **OREGANO**
Set aside.
Melt ⅓ cup **MARGARINE** in foil-lined baking dish.
Bone and skin . . . . 6 **CHICKEN BREAST** halves

Dip each chicken breast half in egg mixture, then in crumb mixture.
Place in melted margarine and turn to coat both sides. Repeat until all
are done. Bake, uncovered, for 25 to 30 minutes at 375-degrees. To serve,
place on bed of shredded **LETTUCE.** Serve with condiments of **SOUR
CREAM, GREEN ONIONS, CHERRY TOMATOES, LIME WEDGES** and
slices of **AVOCADO. DON'T FORGET THE PICO DE GALLO!!!!**

BABETTE'S CARNITAS
Use two forks to shred this deliciously moist, tender meat.

On a large piece of heavy-duty foil, place a 3 to 4 pound **BEEF CHUCK ROAST**.

Combine in small bowl ....
- 1 can (7 oz.) **CHOPPED GREEN CHILIES**
- 2 Tbsp. **CHILI POWDER**
- ½ tsp. **OREGANO**
- ⅓ tsp. **CUMIN**
- 1 clove **GARLIC**, minced
- **SALT**, to taste

Spread mixture on top surface of the beef roast. Wrap in foil and seal securely. Place in ovenproof dish and bake for 3½ to 4 hours at 300-degrees. Cook longer if necessary. (The meat should be so tender that it will fall apart.) For each serving spoon meat into hot **TORTILLAS**. Serve with **GUACAMOLE** and **SALSA**.

YIELD: 4 TO 6 SERVINGS.

RED SNAPPER VERACRUZ
For variety, serve the sauce over SHRIMP.

Clean and prick with a fork ......
- 3 pounds **RED SNAPPER FILLETS**

Sprinkle with **SALT** and **LIME JUICE**. Let marinate in refrigerator for 2 or 3 hours.
Meanwhile, make the **SAUCE**.

Heat in saucepan ....
- 4 Tbsp. **OIL**

Add ....
- 1 medium **ONION**, diced
- 2 cloves **GARLIC**, minced

Cook until clear. Add ....
- 6 **TOMATOES**, peeled and diced
- 1 **SWEET GREEN PEPPER**, cut in very thin slices
- 1 **BAY LEAF**
- ½ tsp. **OREGANO**
- 2 **JALAPENOS**, pickled or fresh minced
- ¼ cup dry **WHITE WINE**
- ¼ cup **RIPE OLIVES**, rinse and dice

Heat until flavors have blended. Place fish on foil-lined pan. Drizzle with melted **BUTTER**. Pour sauce over fish and bake in 350-degree oven until fish will flake with a fork. **DO NOT OVERBAKE**.

NOTE: This is good as leftover. Just as good cold as warm.

MEXICAN TACO STACK

A savory meat mixture spooned over chips, followed by any combination of toppings. What better way to serve a crowd.

In large saucepan, cook until
brown . . . . .2½ pounds **LEAN GROUND MEAT**
                       1 large **ONION**, chopped
Drain well.
Add . . . . 2 tsp. **CHILI POWDER**
                       2 tsp. **DRIED WHOLE OREGANO**
                       2 tsp. **GROUND CUMIN**
                       2 tsp. **SALT**
                       ¼ cup **SUGAR**
                       ¼ tsp. **GARLIC POWDER**
                    16 ounces **TOMATO SAUCE**
                    18 ounces **TOMATO PASTE**
                     4 cups **WATER**
Simmer for 1 hour over low heat. Stir occasionally. Pour into chafing dish to keep warm.
Crush . . . . 1 package (10-ounce) **CORN CHIPS**
Place corn chips on plates then spoon meat mixture over chips. Let your guests layer with following condiments.
Chop and serve in small bowls . . . 1 large **ONION**
                       2 **GREEN PEPPERS**
                       1 **AVOCADO**
                       1 head **LETTUCE**
                       3 **TOMATOES**
                       1 cup **RIPE** or **PIMENTO-STUFFED OLIVES**
                    8 ounces shredded **CHEDDAR CHEESE**
                       TACO SAUCE
                       PICANTE SAUCE

YIELD: 12 SERVINGS.

STICKY CHEESE: Rub grater with butter or spray with vegetable shortening to keep cheese from sticking.

177

OPEN-FACED BURRITO PIE
Good served with a dollop of SOUR CREAM on each wedge.

Combine in a medium bowl . . . . . 1 can (16 oz.) **REFRIED BEANS**
with **GREEN CHILIES, ONION,**
and **GARLIC**
1 cup **BISCUIT MIX**
¼ cup **WATER**
Mix well. Spoon mixture into a lightly greased 9-inch pie plate to form
a shell. Set aside.
Cook together . . . . 1½ pounds **GROUND MEAT**
1 **ONION**, chopped
¼ tsp. **SALT**
½ tsp. **GARLIC SALT**
½ tsp. **PEPPER**
Drain well. Spread on top of bean mixture in pie plate.
Top with . . . . ¾ cup **SALSA**
Bake at 375-degrees for 25 minutes.
Sprinkle with . . . . 1 cup **MONTEREY JACK
CHEESE**, grated

Bake 5 minutes longer. Cut into wedges. Add a **GREEN SALAD** and **TOR-
TILLA CHIPS** for a great meal.

YIELD: 6 SERVINGS.

TACO STIR FRY

Heat in wok or skillet . . . . 1 Tbsp. **OIL**
Add . . . . 1 pound **GROUND BEEF**, lean
¼ cup **ONION**, chopped
Stir-fry over medium heat until
meat is cooked. Drain and
add . . . . 2 Tbsp. **CHILI POWDER**
½ tsp. **SALT**
½ tsp. **GARLIC SALT**
¼ tsp. **OREGANO**
¼ tsp. **PEPPER**
1 can (8 oz.) **WHOLE KERNEL
CORN**
1 can (16 oz.) **STEWED
TOMATOES**
Simmer about 10 minutes in covered pan.
Stir in . . . . 1 pkg. (9½ ozs.) **CORN CHIPS**
1 cup **CHEDDAR CHEESE**, grated

Cook stirring until cheese is partially melted. Spoon over chopped
TOMATOES and shredded **LETTUCE**. Garnish with **AVOCADO** slice.

MEXICANA GOOD STUFF
Sure to please.

Cook together until meat is done
and vegetables are tender . . . . . .   1 pound **GROUND BEEF**
1 small **ONION**, chopped
½ cup **GREEN PEPPER**, chopped
1 clove **GARLIC**, minced
1 Tbsp. **CHILI POWDER**
1 tsp. **SALT**
Stir in . . . .   1 can **TOMATO SAUCE**
½ cup **MILK**
2 cups **RICE**, cooked
Heat thoroughly and fold in . . . . .   1 cup **CHEDDAR CHEESE**, cubed

Roll in warmed **FLOUR TORTILLAS** and serve with **HOT SAUCE**. Or
may serve piled on top of **CORN CHIPS**, if desired.

SOUTH TEXAS-STYLE CHICKEN BREASTS

Skin and score . . . .   4 boneless **CHICKEN BREAST
HALVES**
Rub chicken with . . . .   ¼ tsp. **CHILI POWDER**
In skillet over medium-high
heat . . . .   1 Tbsp. **OIL**
1 Tbsp. **BUTTER** or
MARGARINE
Add chicken breasts, cook 3 to 5 minutes on each side until browned
and done in the middle. Remove to plate.
To drippings in skillet add . . . .   1 Tbsp. **ORANGE MARMALADE**
1 Tbsp. **LIME JUICE**

Heat over medium heat, stirring to loosen brown bits from bottom of
skillet. Return chicken to skillet. Cook 2 to 3 minutes longer until heated
through and coated with glaze on both sides. Serve with **TORTILLA
CHIPS**, **GUACAMOLE RELISH** on **LETTUCE LEAVES**, and **DESSERT**.

GUACAMOLE RELISH

Cut 1 large ripe **AVOCADO** in half. Remove seed, slice pulp of avocado while still in skin, in criss-cross pattern, then remove with spoon and put in bowl.

Add . . . .　2 **TOMATOES**, chopped
　　　　　　　　　　　　　　　　　　1 small **ONION**, chopped
　　　　　　　　　　　　　　　　　　1 clove **GARLIC**, crushed
　　　　　　　　　　　　　　　　　　2 Tbsp. **PARSLEY**, chopped or
　　　　　　　　　　　　　　　　　　　dried
　　　　　　　　　　　　　　　　　　1 tsp. **SALT**
　　　　　　　　　　　　　　　　　　Fresh ground **PEPPER**, to taste
Sprinkle with . . . .　2 Tbsp. **LIME JUICE**

Refrigerate, covered. This is better if allowed to marinate for at least 2 hours before serving.

BEEF AND BEAN BURRITOS

Cook in large skillet until
　brown . . . .　1 pound **GROUND BEEF**
　　　　　　　　　　　　　　　　　　1 medium **ONION**, chopped
　　　　　　　　　　　　　　　　　　1 clove **GARLIC**, diced
Drain well and add . . . .　2 tsp. **CHILI POWDER**
　　　　　　　　　　　　　　　　　　1 tsp. **DRIED WHOLE OREGANO**
　　　　　　　　　　　　　　　　　　½ tsp. **GROUND CUMIN**
　　　　　　　　　　　　　　　　　　½ tsp. **SALT**
　　　　　　　　　　　　　　　　　　¼ tsp. **PEPPER**
Simmer 5 to 10 minutes.
Add . . . .　1 can (16 oz.) **REFRIED BEANS**
　　　　　　　　　　　　　　　　　　1 can (10 oz.) **ENCHILADA**
　　　　　　　　　　　　　　　　　　SAUCE, divided in half

Heat thoroughly. Wrap 6 (8-inch) **FLOUR TORTILLAS** securely in foil. Bake at 350-degrees for 10 minutes. (Or heat in microwave.) Spoon about ½ cup beef mixture on each tortilla. Roll tightly. Place seam side down on serving platter lined with shredded **LETTUCE.** Spoon remaining enchilada sauce over tortillas. Serve with favorite toppings. Some of ours are **SHREDDED CHEESE, TOMATOES, SOUR CREAM, RAISINS,** and **COCONUT.**

YIELD: 6 SERVINGS.

CHILI PIE
Forgot to thaw!!

Spread in medium casserole . . . . . 1½ cups **CORN CHIPS**
Layer with . . . . 1 large **ONION**, chopped
Heat and spread on top . . . . 1 can (19 oz.) **CHILI**
Sprinkle with . . . . 1 cup **CHEESE**, grated

Bake in 350-degree oven until hot. (About 10 to 15 minutes.) This can be adjusted to fit your crowd.

INDIAN TACOS
The base of these tacos is a fried flour tortilla. Dubbed "fry bread" by the Indians. Many versions of this crisp, golden, puffy bread is served in the trendy restaurants.

FRY BREAD:
Mix together . . . . 2 cups **FLOUR**
                        ½ cup **INSTANT NONFAT DRY MILK**
                        1 Tbsp. **BAKING POWDER**
                        ½ tsp. **SALT**
                        2 Tbsp. **SHORTENING**

Rub mixture with fingers until coarse crumbs form. Add ¾ cup **COLD WATER** and stir with a fork until dough clings together. Use floured hands, like the Indian women, or put dough on a lightly floured board. Knead until smooth, 2 to 3 minutes. Divide dough into 6 equal portions. Keep covered with plastic wrap. Shape into a ball. Roll with rolling pin, turning to keep floured, into a 6 or 7-inch round. Cover with plastic wrap and repeat to shape remaining portions. You can stack the pieces of dough with plastic wrap between each.

In a pan at least 8 or 9-inches wide and 2 inches deep, heat ¾ inch **SALAD OIL** to 375-degrees. Cook each fry bread in oil until puffy and golden brown. *TURN ONLY ONCE.* Put several layers of paper towels on cookie sheets to drain the bread well. Keep in warm oven until all are cooked. (200-degrees). If made ahead, package airtight. Next day, warm in a single layer, uncovered, on baking sheets in a 375-degree oven until hot. May also be heated in the microwave.

Continued

CHILI MIXTURE:

Sort and rinse well	1 cup dry **PINTO BEANS**, or **GREAT NORTHERN BEANS**

Put beans in a 3-quart pan with 1 quart **WATER**. Bring to boiling on high heat. Cook, uncovered, 10 minutes. Turn burner off. Cover. Let stand 1 hour. Drain beans and set aside.

Place in a skillet	1 Tbsp. **OIL**
Add	1 large **ONION**, chopped

Stir until onion is limp. Remove from skillet.

Crumble in skillet	1 pound lean **GROUND BEEF** or **PORK SAUSAGE**

Cook until well browned. Drain off fat. Add cooked beef and onions to beans in large pot.

Add	3 cups **CHICKEN BROTH**, may use canned
	1 Tbsp. **CHILI POWDER**
	2 cloves **GARLIC**, minced
	2 tsp. *each* **GROUND CUMIN**, **DRY OREGANO LEAVES**, and **DRY BASIL LEAVES**

Bring to a boil over high heat. Lower heat and simmer, covered, until beans are tender. (1½ to 2 hours). If too much liquid is left in the beans, uncover the last 20 minutes of cooking. Stir frequently during cooking. Use, or cool and refrigerate up to 3 days. To reheat, place over medium-high heat until boiling, stirring often. Makes about 4 cups.

NAVAJO TACOS:

Core and chop	2 large **TOMATOES**
Shred	¾ pound mild **CHEDDAR CHEESE**
	1 head of **LETTUCE**
Chop	2 bunches **FRESH GREEN ONIONS**, including tops

Place the hot **FRY BREAD,** cupped side up, on the plate. Spoon **CHILI MIXTURE** equally into each cup, then top with the cheese, lettuce, onions and tomatoes. Serve with **SOUR CREAM** and **SALSA.**

YIELD: 6 SERVINGS.

STRAWBERRY FRY BREAD:

Sprinkle **SUGAR** over **FRESH STRAWBERRIES** that have been washed and the stems removed. Add a small amount of **WATER**. Bring to a boil. Simmer for about 10 minutes. Make recipe of **FRY BREAD**. Divide dough into 24, or more portions: Fry 2 or 3 at a time. Serve warm with **STRAWBERRIES.**

A similar version is served at the Deckhouse restaurant in Ruidoso, New Mexico. The Franklin's favorite place for a late brunch.

TEX-MEX CHILI

We add a JALAPENO, for taste. May be too "hot" for your taste.
You may want to adjust the GREEN CHILIES, too.

Brown in large saucepan . . . . 1 pound **GROUND MEAT**, lean
Add and cook until clear . . . . 1 large **ONION**, chopped
Drain off excess juice.
Add . . . . 1 can (14 oz.) **TOMATOES**,
                             chopped
                            1 can (4 oz.) **CHOPPED GREEN CHILIES**
                            2 **SWEET BELL PEPPERS**, diced
                            1 can (15 oz.) **KIDNEY BEANS** or **PINTO BEANS**
                            4 Tbsp. **CHILI POWDER**, scant
                            1 clove **GARLIC**, minced
                            ½ tsp. **OREGANO**
                            Dash of **CUMIN** (opt.)
                            SALT and **PEPPER**

Add 1 can **BEEF BROTH** and enough **WATER** to make 6 cups liquid. (Or you may just use **WATER**. The broth makes it a little more flavorful.) May need to add a little more liquid if not juicy enough. To serve, place in bowls. Crush **TORTILLAS** on top. Also, good with grated **CHEESE** on top.

CHICKEN FLAUTAS

Warm **FLOUR TORTILLAS** one at a time by placing in a warm skillet. Turn once. Heat only until warm and pliable. Place 1 Tbsp. chopped cooked **CHICKEN** and 1 Tbsp. grated **CHEESE** in middle of tortilla. Roll up tightly. Fasten with toothpick. Heat shortening in skillet. Fry slightly. Serve over chopped **LETTUCE**. Cover with **SOUR CREAM**. Place sliced **TOMATOES** around on lettuce. Serve with **SALSA**.

CHILI TOPPINGS: Cheese, pinto beans, hot sauce, onions, chili sauce, chopped weiners. Have each in individual bowls. Let your guests "doctor" their chili to suit their taste. Great for a party.

PUERCO CON PAN

A spicy pork dish served over Aztec bread.

In a large skillet, lightly brown ... 1½ pounds boneless **PORK SHOULDER**, cut in ½-inch cubes
1 Tbsp. **OIL**
Add .... 1 cup chopped **ONION**
2 cloves **GARLIC**, minced
Cook until pork is brown and onion is transparent. Drain off fat.
Add .... 1 can (14½ oz.) **TOMATOES**, chopped
8 ounces sliced **MUSHROOMS**, drained
4 ounces chopped **GREEN CHILIES**, drained
½ tsp. dried **OREGANO**, crushed
¼ tsp. crushed **RED PEPPER**
¼ tsp. **GROUND ALLSPICE**
¼ tsp. **GROUND CUMIN**
Heat to boiling. Reduce heat, cover and simmer 45 to 60 minutes or until pork is tender.
Stir together in small bowl ...... 2 Tbsp. **CORNSTARCH**
2 Tbsp. **WATER**

Add to pork mixture. Cook and stir until thickened and bubbly. Cook and stir 2 minutes longer. Remove from heat and stir in ¼ cup sliced **PIMENTO-STUFFED GREEN OLIVES**. Serve in **PITA BREAD POCKETS** or roll in **FLOUR TORTILLAS**. When time allows, try the **AZTEC BREAD**.

AZTEC BREAD

Combine .... 1¾ cups **FLOUR**
¼ cup **YELLOW CORNMEAL**
1 tsp. **BAKING POWDER**
½ tsp. **SALT**
Cut in with pastry blender or two knives using scissor motion ... 2 Tbsp. **SHORTENING**
Add .... ¾ cup **MILK**

Stir just enough to form a ball. On lighly floured board, knead until smooth. About 3 minutes. Shape into 6 balls. Roll each ball into a 6-inch circle. Fry in 1½-inches of hot **OIL**. (375-degrees). Fry bread about 1 minute per side. Bread will puff. Drain well on paper towels. Serve immediately.

"KAHLUA" MOUSSE

Babette serves this dessert after a meal of CARNITAS and SALAD.

Heat . . . . ⅓ cup **WHIPPING CREAM**
Add . . . . 16 **MARSHMALLOWS**
Heat until softened, fluffy and smooth.
Stir in . . . . .1½ ounces **KAHLUA**
Cool.
Whip and fold into above
mixture . . . . ⅔ cup **WHIPPING CREAM**

Freeze in 6 sherbet dishes. Garnish with teaspoon of whipped cream and
CHERRY.

CHEWY PRALINES

Always finish off a Mexican fiesta party with pralines!

Combine in medium saucepan
over medium-low heat . . . . 1 cup **SUGAR**
1 cup **WHITE CORN SYRUP**
Cook until candy thermometer reaches 250-degrees. (Soft ball stage).
Remove from heat and add . . . . . . 1 cup **BUTTER** or **MARGARINE**
1 cup **HEAVY CREAM**
Return to heat and cook until candy thermometer reaches 242-degrees,
stirring constantly.
Remove from heat and add . . . . . . 4 cups **PECAN HALVES**
1 tsp. **VANILLA**

Stir well. Drop by teaspoonfuls on foil. When cool, wrap each piece,
separately, in plastic wrap.

EASY, CREAMY, PRALINES

Lightly grease a large sheet of foil. Set aside.
Mix in a large heavy saucepan . . .   1 cup **BUTTERMILK**
2 cups **SUGAR**
1 tsp. **SODA**
Stir mixture until sugar is completely dissolved before placing on burner. Cook mixture, on medium heat, to 240-degrees on candy thermometer. (Soft ball stage). Stir constantly. Remove from heat.
Add . . . .   2 cups **PECAN HALVES**
1 tsp. **VANILLA**
1 Tbsp. **BUTTER** or
MARGARINE

Beat mixture by hand until it becomes glossy and very thick. Quickly spoon onto greased foil. When pralines are cool, remove from foil. Store pralines in tightly covered container. (Place wax paper between each layer of candy.) NOTE: If mixture becomes too hard before you have it all out of the pan, return to heat for a few minutes.

If time permits, before candy sets up, turn over pecan halves.

MEXICAN BREAD PUDDING
Microwave quick!

BUTTER a round microwave safe dish.
Place in dish . . . .   5 slices **TOASTED WHITE
BREAD**, cubed
Set aside.
In 1 quart bowl, combine . . . .   2 cups **MILK**
3 ounces **CREAM CHEESE**, softened
Microwave on **HIGH** for 4 minutes. Pour milk mixture over bread cubes. Let set 10 minutes.
While mixture is setting, melt in
1 quart bowl . . . .   ¼ cup **BUTTER** or **MARGARINE**
Add . . . .   1 cup **BROWN SUGAR**
3 **EGGS**, well beaten
1 tsp. **NUTMEG**
1½ tsp. **CINNAMON**
1 tsp. **VANILLA**
Dash of **SALT**
½ cup **RAISINS**
½ cup chopped **PECANS**, (opt.)

Pour over bread mixture and stir until blended. Microwave on **HIGH** for 7 to 8 more minutes. Rotate dish every 3 minutes. Let stand 10 minutes before serving.

MEXICAN FRUIT CAKE

Beat well . . . . 2 **EGGS**
Add and beat until fluffy . . . . 2 cups **SUGAR**
Add . . . . 2 tsp. **BAKING SODA**
                                            2 cups **FLOUR**
                                            1 can (20 oz.) **CRUSHED PINEAPPLE**, do not drain
                                            1 cup **PECANS**, chopped

Mix well. Pour into a greased and floured 9x13x2-inch baking dish. Bake 30 to 35 minutes at 350-degrees. Top with **CREAM CHEESE FROSTING.**

CREAM CHEESE FROSTING:

Cream until fluffy . . . . 6 ounces **CREAM CHEESE**, softened
Add . . . . 2 cups **CONFECTIONER'S SUGAR**
                                            ¼ cup **MARGARINE**, softened
                                            1 tsp. **VANILLA**

Mix well. Frost cooled cake.

KAHLUA CREME MINTS

We give at Christmas time with a bottle of our homemade KAHLUA.

Blend together . . . . 1½ cups **CONFECTIONER'S POWDERED SUGAR**
                                            2 Tbsp. **HEAVY CREAM**
                                            2 Tbsp. **BUTTER**, melted
                                            2 tsp. **KAHLUA**
                                            1 tsp. **INSTANT COFFEE**

Shape into small balls and flatten with thumb. (Or press into small molds.) May need to add more **POWDERED SUGAR** if mixture seems too moist.

SOPAPILLAS
With honey, or cinnamon and sugar mixture, umm, good.

Sift together . . . . 　2　cups sifted **FLOUR**
　　　　　　　　　　　　　　　　1½　tsp. **BAKING POWDER**
　　　　　　　　　　　　　　　　　2　Tbsp. **SUGAR**
　　　　　　　　　　　　　　　　　1　tsp. **SALT**
Work with fingers until mixture
　resembles coarse meal . . . . .1½　Tbsp. **SHORTENING**
At this point you may add . . . .　2　**EGGS** (opt.)

Add enough **WATER** to make a soft dough. Let rest for 15 minutes. Roll out dough about ⅛-inch thick. Cut into triangles or rectangles. Fry in hot shortening, (375-degrees) until golden brown. Turn. They will puff up quite a bit.

BUNUELOS
The major difference between sopapillas and bunuelos is the shape. Bunuelos are cut round with a hole in the middle. Sopapillas are cut in triangles or rectangles.

Mix well . . . . 　4　cups **FLOUR**
　　　　　　　　　　　　　　　　　1　tsp. **BAKING POWDER**
　　　　　　　　　　　　　　　　　1　tsp. **SALT**
　　　　　　　　　　　　　　　　　2　**EGGS**
　　　　　　　　　　　　　　　　　1　cup **MILK**
　　　　　　　　　　　　　　　　　1　Tbsp. **SHORTENING**
Cut with doughnut cutter. Fry in hot **OIL** (400-degrees) until brown. Turn over and fry the other side. Turn only once. Drain on paper towels. Cover with **SAUCE** and serve with **MEXICAN COFFEE.**

SAUCE:
Combine and boil until thick . . . . 　6　tsp. **BROWN SUGAR**
　　　　　　　　　　　　　　　　¼　cup **SWEET WINE** or **FRUIT JUICE**
　　　　　　　　　　　　　　　　¾　cup **WATER**
　　　　　　　　　　　　　　　　½　cup **RAISINS**
　　　　　　　　　　　　　　　　½　tsp. **CINNAMON**

BROCCOLI WITH HORSERADISH SAUCE
One of Larry Hagood's favorites.

SAUCE:

Combine .... 2 Tbsp. **BUTTER** or
MARGARINE, melted
½ cup **MAYONNAISE**
1 Tbsp. **HORSERADISH**
1 Tbsp. grated **ONION**
¼ tsp. **SALT**
¼ tsp. **DRY MUSTARD**
Pinch of **RED PEPPER**

Refrigerate at least 3 to 4 hours.

Trim off large leaves of 1-pound bunch **BROCCOLI**. Remove tough ends of stalks. Rinse well. Cook broccoli, covered, in a small amount of boiling water 8 to 10 minutes or until crisp-tender. Arrange in a dish. Top with the horseradish sauce.

YIELD: 4 SERVINGS.

FRIED GREEN TOMATOES

Cut into ¼-inch slices .... 6 large, firm **GREEN TOMATOES**
Season with .... **SALT** and **PEPPER**
Dredge in .... 1 cup **CORNMEAL**

Heat **BACON DRIPPINGS** or **OIL** in a heavy skillet. Add tomatoes. Fry slowly until browned, turning once. Drain on paper towels.

PICKLED BEETS
As colorful as they are good.

Drain .... 2 cans **BEETS** sliced or whole
Bring to a boil .... 1 cup **SUGAR**
¾ cup **VINEGAR**

Put beets in a quart jar and pour hot mixture over them. Place in refrigerator for 24 hours with lid on. These will keep indefinitely in the refrigerator. As you use the beets just add another can of drained **BEETS** to the liquid, stir them to the bottom of jar.

COMPANY BEETS WITH PINEAPPLE

Combine in medium sauce
    pan . . . . 2 Tbsp. **BROWN SUGAR**
                                  1 Tbsp. **CORNSTARCH**
                                    ¼ tsp. **SALT**
                                    1 can (8 oz.) **PINEAPPLE TIDBITS**, with syrup
Cook stirring constantly until clear and thick.
Add . . . . 1 Tbsp. **MARGARINE**
                                    1 Tbsp. **LEMON JUICE**
Drain and add . . . . 1 can (16 oz.) **BEETS**, sliced
                                    or diced

Heat for 4 to 5 minutes. Serve.

COUNTRY FRIED OKRA

Wash, cut off tips and stem ends,
    cut into ½-inch slices . . . . 4 cups **OKRA**
Season with . . . . **SALT** and **PEPPER**
Set aside. Combine . . . . ½ cup **FLOUR**
                                    1 cup **CORNMEAL**
                                    1 tsp. **SALT**
                                    ½ tsp. **PEPPER**
Dredge in dry mixture and
    fry in . . . . ½ inch **HOT OIL**
When brown and crispy remove with slotted spoon and drain on paper towels.

YIELD: 4 TO 6 SERVINGS.

VARIATION:
Okra may be dipped in 1 beaten **EGG** and ½ cup **BUTTERMILK** mixed together before it is coated with dry mixture for a thicker crust.

HANDY POTATOES: Boil a few extras and have in re-frigerator for a quick dish. Makes a good potato salad. Slice for scalloped or grate for hash browns.

KINGS INN ONION RINGS
One of South Texas famous restaurant's recipes.

Peel and slice **ONIONS**. Separate into rings.
Combine and mix well . . . . ¼ cup evaporated **MILK**
         ¼ cup **WATER**
         2 **EGGS** well beaten
         ¾ cups **SUGAR**
Add, to thicken . . . . ⅓ to ⅔ cup **FLOUR**,

Pour over **ONION RINGS** to form a thin coating. Dredge with **FLOUR**.
Fry in hot oil until brown.

YIELD: 4 TO 5 SERVINGS.

ONION IN MUSHROOM SAUCE
Easy and delicious.

Peel and quarter . . . . 1½ pounds small **YELLOW ONIONS**
Cook 15 to 20 minutes in . . . . 1 cup **WATER**
Drain and add . . . . 1 can **CREAM OF MUSHROOM SOUP**, undiluted

Simmer 10 to 15 minutes. Garnish with **PARSLEY**.

VARIATION:
After adding onions to mushroom soup, this may be baked in 350-degree oven for 20 minutes. Sprinkle with **GRATED CHEESE**.

BAKED ONIONS
Double for a dinner party.

Butter an 8x8x2-inch baking dish.
Layer . . . . 6 medium **ONIONS**, thinly sliced
         1 cup **POTATO CHIPS**, crushed
         1 cup grated mild **CHEDDAR CHEESE**
Combine . . . . 1 can **CREAM OF MUSHROOM SOUP**
         ¼ cup **MILK**
         1½ tsp. **WORCESTERSHIRE SAUCE**

Pour mixture over layers in casserole. Sprinkle with **CAYENNE PEPPER**.
Bake at 350-degrees for 45 to 50 minutes.

STEAMED RED CABBAGE

Put in cold **WATER** . . . .   1 small head **RED CABBAGE**, shredded
Cook until crisp . . . .   4 slices **BACON**, diced
Remove bacon. Drain cabbage but don't dry. Add to drippings, cover and steam until tender-crisp. Remove from heat. Toss bacon with cabbage.
Add . . . .   2 rounded Tbsp. **MAYONNAISE**

Toss lightly. Serve.

CABBAGE SUPREME
Sue Hagood's exciting side dish.
Someone is always asking for this recipe.

Combine in large saucepan . . . . . .   ¼ cup **WATER**
   1 **BEEF-FLAVORED BOUILLON CUBE**
Bring to a boil and stir until bouillon cube is dissolved.
Add . . . .   5 cups shredded **CABBAGE**
   1 cup **CARROT**, thinly sliced
   ½ cup **ONION**, chopped
   ½ tsp. **SALT**
   ½ tsp. **PEPPER**
Stir well. Cover, reduce heat, and simmer about 5 minutes. Stir occasionally.
Melt in small saucepan . . . .   ¼ cup **BUTTER** or **MARGARINE**
Add . . . .   ⅓ cup chopped **PECANS**
   1 tsp. **PREPARED MUSTARD**

Cook over medium heat 2 minutes, stirring constantly. Pour over cabbage mixture. Stir well. Spoon into serving dish. Sprinkle with **PAPRIKA**.

YIELD: 6 TO 8 SERVINGS.

FAST SEASONING: Keep a large shaker with salt and pepper mixed. (Six parts salt and 1 part pepper.)

SWEET AND SOUR RED CABBAGE
Just a hint of German.

In large pan sauté until tender . . .	2 Tbsp. **ONION**, chopped
In	2 Tbsp. **MARGARINE**
Add	6 cups **RED CABBAGE**, shredded
	1 small tart **APPLE**, sliced thin
	¼ cup **BROWN SUGAR**, packed
	½ tsp. **SALT**
	½ cup **SUGAR**
	¼ cup **VINEGAR**

Stir to combine. Cover and simmer 45 minutes. Stir occasionally.

YIELD: 3 CUPS COOKED

GREEN BEANS PICANTE
Adds a little zing.

In saucepan melt	1 Tbsp. **MARGARINE**
Add and sauté until tender	2 small **ONIONS**, sliced and separated into rings
Add	2 cans (16 ozs.) cut **GREEN BEANS**, drained
	¼ cup **PICANTE SAUCE**
	¼ tsp. **SALT**
	¼ tsp. **PEPPER**
	¼ tsp. **LEMON JUICE**

Cover and heat thoroughly.

YIELD: 8 SERVINGS.

DOUBLING RECIPES: Taste before doubling the seasonings when doubling a recipe. Twice the seasoning is often a little too much.

GREEN BEANS WITH NEW POTATOES
Still one of our favorites.

Wash, trim ends, and remove
  strings from . . . . 1½ pounds **FRESH GREEN BEANS**
Place in Dutch oven or larger
  pan . . . . 6 small **NEW POTATOES**
                                          1 cup **WATER**
                                          1 tsp. **BEEF BOUILLON GRANULES**
                                          Dash of ground **NUTMEG**
                                          Dash of **PEPPER**

Bring to boil. Cover. Reduce heat. Simmer 25 minutes or until beans are crisp-tender and potatoes are done. **SALT** to taste.

YIELD: 6 SERVINGS.

GLORIFIED GREEN BEANS
A tasty combination.

Drain . . . . 2 cans **GREEN BEANS**
Place beans in a buttered casserole.
Mix . . . . 1 can **CREAM OF MUSHROOM SOUP**, undiluted
                                          1 tsp. **SALT**
                                          ¼ tsp. **PEPPER**
                                          ½ tsp. **WORCESTERSHIRE SAUCE**
Pour over beans.
Cover with . . . . 1 can **FRENCH FRIED ONIONS**

Bake in 350-degree oven until hot, about 30 minutes. This can be made up ahead of time, and heated just before serving.

YIELD: 8 TO 10 SERVINGS.

MICRO CORN: Leave corn on cob. Remove shucks and silks. Place corn, 1 layer deep, in a microwave safe dish or plastic bag. Cook on high for about 2 minutes per ear.

HOPPING JOHN FOR COMPANY
Ann Whitesides suggests serving with CORNBREAD STICKS.
We have. Great meal!!!!

Combine in Dutch oven . . . . 4 cups **FROZEN BLACK-EYED PEAS**
1 large **HAM HOCK**, or ½ pound cubed **HAM**
1 cup **ONION**, chopped
1 cup **CELERY**, chopped
2 to 3 tsp. **SALT**
2½ tsp. **CHILI POWDER**
¼ tsp. **DRIED BASIL LEAVES**
1 **BAY LEAF**
1 can (16 oz.) **TOMATOES**, drained cut into small pieces, reserve juice

Add enough **WATER** to slightly cover ingredients. Cook, uncovered over medium heat, stirring occasionally, 25 minutes. Stir in 1 cup uncooked **RICE**. Cover and cook 20 more minutes. Add more water if needed. Uncover last 10 minutes if too juicy.

YIELD: 8 TO 10 SERVINGS.

QUICK HOPPING JOHN
Perfect New Years good luck dish.

Mix in a medium-size sauce
pan . . . . 1 can (16 oz.) **BLACKEYED PEAS** with **SNAPS**, undrained
½ cup **ONION**, chopped
1 tsp. **BACON DRIPPINGS**
Bring to a boil; stir gently. Simmer 15 minutes in covered pan. If possible wait 1 hour.
Just before serving reheat and
add . . . . 2 cups hot cooked **RICE**
½ tsp. **TABASCO SAUCE**
CORNBREAD is a must with this.

YIELD: 4 SERVINGS.

VARIATION:
Add ½ cup or more small pieces of **HAM**.

CORN-STUFFED SWEET PEPPERS

Slice tops from . . . . 6 medium **GREEN PEPPERS**
Remove seed. Place in saucepan. Add enough boiling **WATER** to cover.
Cook, covered, for 5 minutes. Drain. Place in baking dish.
Combine . . . . 3 cups **CORN**
                                ½ tsp. **INSTANT MINCED ONION**
                                ¾ tsp. **SALT**
                                ¼ tsp. **PEPPER**
                                ⅛ tsp. **GARLIC POWDER**
                                1 tsp. **CHILI POWDER**
                                1 large **FRESH TOMATO**,
                                chopped
                                3 Tbsp. **FLOUR**
                                2 Tbsp. **BUTTER**, melted

Mix well. Spoon mixture into green peppers. Bake at 375-degrees for 35 minutes.

YIELD: 6 SERVINGS.

SKILLET CORN
Garden Fresh.

Cut fresh from cobb . . . . 3 cups **CORN**
Place in a 10-inch skillet.
Add . . . . 1 tsp. **SALT**
                                ½ tsp. **PEPPER**
                                1 Tbsp. **SUGAR**
                                ½ cup **MARGARINE**
                                ½ cup **WATER**
Cover and simmer 15 minutes over medium heat, stirring occasionally.
Combine and blend until
  smooth . . . . ¼ cup **MILK**
                                1 Tbsp. **FLOUR**

Add and cook an additional 5 minutes over low heat stirring constantly.

YIELD: 6 SERVINGS

VARIATION:
Fry until crisp 4 slices **BACON**. Crumble and add to corn. Add 2 table-spoons **BACON DRIPPINGS** for more flavor.

IMA DEE'S CORN CASSEROLE
We have been sharing recipes for many years.

Mix in large bowl . . . . 1 can (15 oz.) **WHOLE KERNEL CORN**
1 can **CREAM STYLE CORN**
½ cup **MARGARINE**, melted
1 carton (8 oz.) **SOUR CREAM**
1 pkg. (6 oz.) **JALAPENO CORNBREAD MIX,** dry

Pour into a greased 13x9x2-inch dish. Bake in 350-degree oven for 20 to 30 minutes. The minute it comes from oven, sprinkle with ½ cup grated **CHEESE.**

SUPER SQUASH CASSEROLE BY CHARLOTTE

Boil together until tender . . . . 4 to 5 lb. **SQUASH**, sliced
1 medium **ONION**, chopped
1 **BELL PEPPER**, chopped
1 can (8 oz.) **MUSHROOMS,** chopped
1 tsp. **SALT**
Drain and set aside.
Over medium heat melt . . . . 6 Tbsp. **MARGARINE**
Stir in until smooth . . . . 3 Tbsp. **FLOUR**
Remove from heat and
   gradually stir in . . . . 2 cups **HALF** and **HALF MILK**
1 can (5 oz.) **EVAPORATED MILK**
Return to heat and cook slowly until thick.
Fold in . . . . ¾ pound **VELVEETA CHEESE,** grated
Combine with squash mixture. Pour into 13x9x2-inch casserole.
Top with . . . . 1½ cups **CRACKER CRUMBS**
Sautéed in . . . . 3 Tbsp. **MARGARINE**

Bake 45 to 60 minutes at 300-degrees.

YIELD: 12 SERVINGS.

STUFFIN' TOPPED SQUASH CASSEROLE
This is the best we have eaten. Thanks Thelma!

Boil together	2 cups **SQUASH**, yellow or zucchini
	½ cup **WATER**
	1 tsp. **ONION FLAKES**
When tender drain well and add	1 **CARROT**, grated
	1 can **WATER CHESTNUTS**
	1 can **CREAM OF MUSHROOM SOUP**
Mix separately	1 pkg. **PEPPERIDGE FARM CORNBREAD STUFFING**, dry
With	½ cup **MARGARINE**

Sprinkle ½ on the bottom of lightly greased baking dish. Cover with squash mixture and sprinkle remaining crumbs. Bake at 350-degrees for 25 to 30 minutes.

SQUASH CASSEROLE
Pop into oven. Ready in a jiffy.

Mix together	4 cups **SQUASH**, cooked and drained
	1 cup **SOUR CREAM**
	1 medium **ONION**, chopped
	1 medium **GREEN PEPPER**, chopped (opt.)
	1 can **CREAM OF MUSHROOM SOUP**
	SALT and **PEPPER** to taste
Line bottom of oiled 13x9x2-inch casserole with	2 cups **BUTTERED CORNBREAD CRUMBS**

Add **SQUASH** mixture. Sprinkle with 2 more cups **BUTTERED CORNBREAD CRUMBS**. Bake in preheated 400-degree oven for 30 minutes.

DELURA'S DELICIOUS SQUASH CASSEROLE
Straight out of the "Ole SOUTH."

Use a large saucepan.
Sauté . . . .   1 pound **HAM**, chopped
  3 medium **ONIONS**, chopped
  3 **SWEET BELL PEPPERS**, chopped

Cook until **ONIONS** turn white.
Add . . . .   3 **YELLOW SQUASH**, chopped in large pieces
  3 **ZUCCHINI SQUASH**, chopped in large pieces
  1 can **ROTEL TOMATOES AND CHILLIES**, do not drain
  1 small can **TOMATOES**

Cook about 5 minutes.
Combine . . . .   ½ cup **HOT WATER**
  3 **CHICKEN BOUILLON CUBES**

Stir until dissolved.
Add . . . .   1 tsp. **SALT**
  ¼ tsp. **PEPPER**
  3 tsp. **SWEET BASIL**
  3 tsp. **OIL**
Add the hot **WATER** mixture to the **SQUASH**.

Quarter 3 **WHOLE FRESH TOMATOES**. Place on top. Steam 3 to 4 minutes.

SQUASH PATTIE CAKES
"For confirmed squash-haters."

Grate in medium bowl . . . .   2 cups **SQUASH**, uncooked
Add . . . .   2 tsp. **SUGAR**
  ¼ tsp. **PEPPER**
  ½ tsp. **SALT**
  2 tsp. grated **ONION**
Let stand for 30 minutes. Drain.
Add and mix . . . .   ¼ cup **FLOUR**
  2 tsp. **CORNMEAL**
  2 **EGGS**
Melt in large skillet . . . .   2 Tbsp. **MARGARINE**

Drop by tablespoonsfuls into skillet. Cook until golden brown over medium heat. Turn and brown on both sides.

YIELD: 6 SERVINGS.

OVEN PINTO BEAN POT
These don't have to be watched.

Soak in 3-4 cups of cold **WATER**
    for 1 hour . . . .   2 cups **PINTO BEANS,** dried
Drain and add . . . .   1 small **ONION**, chopped
                                    1½ inch square **SALT PORK**, diced
                                    1 tsp. **SALT**
                                    1 tsp. **SEASONED SALT**
                                    5 small dried **CHILI PEPPERS**
                                    1 cup **COLA BEVERAGE**

Add **WATER** to cover. Bake at 250-degrees for 8 hours. Stir 2 or 3 times, adding water if needed to keep beans covered.

YIELD: 8 SERVINGS.

VARIATION:
May substitute 3 slices of **BACON** for **SALT PORK**.

BEANS AND RICE
New Orleans Fare.

Cook according to directions on
    package . . . .   2 pounds **DRIED PINTO BEANS**
Halfway through cooking
    BEANS, fry . . . .   8 slices **BACON**, cut in pieces
Remove **BACON**. Add to
    drippings in pan . . . .   2 **SWEET GREEN PEPPERS**,
                                         chopped
                                      3 **ONIONS**, chopped
                                      3 cloves **GARLIC**, minced
                                      2 tsp. **RED PEPPER**, crushed
                                      SALT and **PEPPER** to taste

Add to partially cooked beans. Cover and simmer until beans are done. Serve over cooked rice. Sprinkle with cooked bacon.

SWEET RICE
Good way to use leftover rice. Kids love it!

Measure into saucepan . . . .   4 cups *cooked* **RICE**
Add . . . .   ½ cup **SUGAR**

Add enough **MILK** to cover the rice. Cook over low heat until thickened, stirring constantly. Add additional sugar if desired. Pour ½ cup melted **BUTTER** over top. Sprinkle with **CINNAMON**. Ladle into serving bowls.

RODEO RICE

Heat in skillet . . . . 2 Tbsp. **BACON DRIPPINGS**
Sauté . . . . ⅓ cup **ONION,** chopped
                              ¼ cup **GREEN PEPPER,** diced
                              1 cup regular **LONG GRAIN RICE,** raw
When golden brown pour into shallow 2-quart casserole.
Stir in . . . . 2 cups **BEEF BROTH**
                              1 Tbsp. **WORCESTERSHIRE SAUCE**
                              ¾ **CUMIN SEED**
To taste . . . . **SALT** and **PEPPER**

Cover tightly with lid or foil. Bake at 350-degrees for 30 minutes or until rice is tender and liquid is absorbed. Fluff with a fork.

YIELD: 6 SERVINGS.

CLARICE'S GREEN RICE

Brown . . . . 1 cup **ONIONS,** chopped
                              1 cup **CELERY,** chopped
In . . . . ½ cup **MARGARINE**
Mix with . . . . 1 can **CREAM OF CHICKEN SOUP**
                              ¼ cup **MILK**
                              2 cups **RICE,** cooked
                              1 pkg. frozen **BROCCOLI**
Mix all together and pour into 13x9x2-inch pan.
Melt and pour over the top . . . . . . 1 small jar **CHEESE WHIZ**

Bake in 350-degree oven 30 to 40 minutes.

YIELD: 12 TO 14 SERVINGS.

VARIATION:
Add 1 cup **MUSHROOMS** or ½ can **GREEN CHILIES.**

GREEN RICE
Santa Fe style.

Cook according to package
   directions .... 1 cup **REGULAR RICE**
Add .... ¾ cup fresh **PARSLEY**, chopped
                               ½ cup **ONION**, chopped
                               1 cup **SOUR CREAM**
                               ¼ cup **SALAD OIL**
                               2 **GARLIC CLOVES**, crushed
                               1 can chopped **GREEN CHILIES**, drained
                               ¼ tsp. **CHILI POWDER**
                               1 tsp. **CUMIN POWDER**
                               1 **JALAPENO PEPPER**, seeded and chopped
Grate and add .... 2 cups **SHARP CHEDDAR CHEESE**
                               1 cup **MONTEREY JACK CHEESE**, reserve ½ cup for top of casserole

Preheat oven to 275-degrees. Mix and pour into a lightly greased dish. Sprinkle remaining **CHEESE** on top. Bake uncovered for 45 minutes or until hot.

YIELD: 10 SERVINGS

PARMESAN NOODLES
This makes a good side dish.

Cook according to package
   directions .... 1 pkg. (16 oz.) **MEDIUM EGG NOODLES**
Drain well, pour over noodles ... ½ cup **MARGARINE**, melted
Add .... 1 tsp. **GARLIC SALT**
                               3 Tbsp. dried **PARSLEY FLAKES**
Toss gently and place in serving
   dish, sprinkle with .... ¼ cup grated **PARMESAN CHEESE**

Serve while hot. May be cut in half.

YIELD: 8 SERVINGS.

FETTUCCINE ALFREDO
Angelo's Italian Cuisine.

Cook according to directions on
package .... 1 box (12 oz.) **FETTUCCINE NOODLES**
Drain, rinse and set aside.
In heavy saucepan over medium
heat, combine .... 3 cups **HEAVY CREAM**
2 cups grated **ROMANO CHEESE**
2 cups grated **PARMESAN CHEESE**
2 tsp. **COARSE BLACK PEPPER**
Stir with wire whisk until smooth and cheese is melted.
Add......................... 4 **EGG YOLKS**
Continue to whisk until sauce thickens.

Add noodles and toss lightly. Divide evenly into four platters: sprinkle each with chopped **FRESH PARSLEY**. Serve immediately.

VARIATION:
Top with a bit of chopped **PROSCIUTTO HAM**.

BAKED SWEET POTATOES

Wash and dry .... **SWEET POTATOES**, uniform in size
Rub with a little .... **SHORTENING**

Bake on cookie sheet at 425-degrees for 35 to 60 minutes depending on the size. Using a potholder, press firmly to see if potatoes are tender. Split and mix **BUTTER** and **SUGAR** into potatoes.

HURRY-UP POTATOES: Let whole potatoes stand in boiling water for 15 minutes. Bake in very hot oven. (Will take half the usual time.)

YUMMY YAMS

Bake in skin .... 3 pounds **SWEET POTATOES**
Mash baked potatoes.
Add .... 5 Tbsp. **MARGARINE**
4 Tbsp. **BROWN SUGAR**
1 tsp. **CINNAMON**
Drain and add .... 1 can (14 oz.) crushed
PINEAPPLE
Bake in 1½-quart glass dish until very warm.
Add on top ....1½ cups miniature
MARSHMALLOWS

Place back in oven just a few minutes to melt marshmallows.

VARIATION:
½ cup **PECANS** may be added to mixture.

BAKED SPUDS

Melt in bottom of large
baking dish .... ½ cup **MARGARINE**
Sprinkle with .... **GARLIC SALT**
Scrub well and cut in half .... 8 small **POTATOES,** do not peel

Place in pan, cut side down. Cover tightly with foil. Bake at 400-degrees
for approximately 1 hour.

STUFFING POTATO WEDGES
An easy family favorite.

Cut lengthwise into 8 wedges .... 3 medium **POTATOES**
Combine .... ¾ cup **HERB-SEASONED**
STUFFING MIX
1 tsp. **SALT**
½ tsp. **PEPPER**
Dip wedges into .... ¼ cup **MARGARINE**, melted
Then dip into stuffing mixture.

Place on lightly greased 15x10x1-inch jellyroll pan. Bake at 425-degrees
for 30 minutes or until potatoes are tender.

YIELD: 4 TO 6 SERVINGS.

REAL MASHED POTATOES

Like mama used to make.

Peel and cut into quarters ....   6 medium **POTATOES**
Cover and boil until tender in....   **SALTED WATER**
Drain and pour into a large mixing bowl. Mash with a potato masher or on low with electric mixer.
Add.........................   4 Tbsp. **BUTTER**
Season to taste ....   **SALT** and **PEPPER**
     ½ cup **MILK**

Whip until fluffy. Can add more milk if needed to make potatoes smooth.

YIELD: 6 SERVINGS.

BAKED POTATO WEDGES

Scrub ....   3 large **POTATOES**, about
     2 pounds
Cut potatoes into 1-inch-wide wedges. Arrange in a single layer, skin side down, in a 10x15-inch pan.
In a small bowl, mix ....   4 tsp. **OIL**
     2 cloves **GARLIC**, minced
     1½ tsp. chopped **FRESH ROSEMARY LEAVES** or ¾ tsp. dry rosemary leaves

Brush cut surfaces of potato wedges with oil mixture. Bake on the lowest rack in a 350-degree oven until potatoes are golden brown. About 1 hour and 45 minutes. Add **SALT** to taste.

YIELD: 4 SERVINGS.

CHEESEY SCALLOPED POTATOES

Slice in saucepan . . . . 3 large **POTATOES**
Boil in salted **WATER** for 5 minutes, drain, put potatoes in layers in greased casserole dish.
Heat in pan . . . . ⅔ cup **MILK**
                               2 cans **CREAM OF MUSHROOM SOUP**, undiluted
Add . . . . 1 cup grated **CHEESE**
                               1 **ONION**, chopped

Pour over potatoes, top with grated **CHEESE** and sprinkle with **PAPRIKA**. Bake in a 350-degree oven for 30 to 35 minutes.

YIELD: 6 SERVINGS.

POTATO WRAP-UPS

Lay out one piece of aluminum foil for each person. Peel and cut into bite size pieces . . . . 1 **POTATO**, per person
                               3 pats of **BUTTER** or **MARGARINE**
Amount desired of . . . . **ONION**, chopped
Sprinkle **GENEROUSLY** with . . . . **WORCESTERSHIRE SAUCE**
                              SALT and **PEPPER** to taste

Wrap tightly. Bake in 350-degree oven for 1 hour.

FAVORITE "TATORS"
Of Phillip Mitchell

Lightly butter a 13x9x2-inch baking dish.
Layer with . . . . **POTATOES**, sliced
                               CANADIAN BACON, sliced
                               SMALL ONION, chopped

Repeat above ingredients. Pour 1 can (10¾ oz.) **MUSHROOM SOUP** over mixture. (Do not dilute soup.) Bake for 1 hour in preheated 350-degree oven. Check potatoes for tenderness. Top with **CHEESE**. Return to oven until cheese is melted.

SUPER-DUPER POTATOES

Makes mashed potatoes special!

Evenly spread in a lightly greased
   10x6x2-inch baking dish ...... 3 cups **MASHED POTATOES**, seasoned

Top with .... 1 carton (8 oz.) **SOUR CREAM**

Sprinkle with .... 6 slices **BACON**, cooked and crumbled

   3 small **GREEN ONIONS**, chopped

Top with .... 1 cup **CHEDDAR CHEESE**, grated

Bake potatoes at 300-degrees for 30 minutes. Serve hot.

YIELD: 6 SERVINGS.

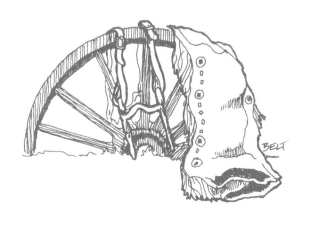

WHITE CHOCOLATE CHEESECAKE

This is an outstanding cake.

CRUST:

Combine in mixing bowl . . . . 1½ cups **GRAHAM CRACKER** crumbs
¼ cup **PECANS**, finely chopped
¼ cup + 1 Tbsp. **MARGARINE**, melted

Stir until blended. Press mixture into bottom and 1-inch up sides of a 9-inch springform pan. Bake at 375-degrees for 8 minutes.

FILLING:

Melt in top of double boiler . . . . . 1 pound **WHITE CHOCOLATE**, coarsely chopped

Cool slightly.
Mix until fluffy with mixer . . . . . . 16 ounces **CREAM CHEESE**, softened
½ cup **SOUR CREAM**
Add and beat after each . . . . 3 **EGGS**

Add, stirring just until blended, melted chocolate.
Add . . . . 1 tsp. **VANILLA**

Pour over crust. Bake at 300-degrees for 50 minutes or until cheesecake is almost set. Turn off oven and promptly open door. Leave in oven 30 minutes. Cool, then chill.

TOPPING:

Drain and reserve ½ cup of
liquid from . . . . 1 can (11 oz.) **MANDARIN ORANGES**
Combine oranges with . . . . ¼ cup **ORANGE FLAVORED LIQUEUR**

Drain oranges, reserve liqueur. Combine with reserved orange liquid in saucepan.
Add . . . . 1 Tbsp. plus 1 tsp. **CORNSTARCH**
½ cup **ORANGE JUICE**

Stir constantly for 5 minutes over medium heat until thickened. Remove outer rim of springform pan. Arrange orange sections in center and around edge of cheesecake. Spoon glaze over top of cake. May freeze.

ALMOND-AMARETTO CHEESECAKE
Forget the calories and "ENJOY!"

CRUST:

Mix together . . . . 40 **VANILLA WAFERS**, finely
crushed
¾ cup toasted **ALMONDS**,
chopped
⅓ cup **SUGAR**
¼ cup plus 2 Tbsp. **MARGARINE**,
melted
Press into bottom and 1¾-inches up side of springform pan, sprayed
with cooking spray.

FILLING:

In mixer bowl put . . . . 3 pkgs. (8 ozs. each) **CREAM
CHEESE**, softened
Cream until fluffy with . . . . 1 cup **SUGAR**
Add, one at a time, beating after
each addition . . . . 4 **EGGS**
On medium speed add . . . . ⅓ cup **WHIPPING CREAM**
¼ cup **AMARETTO LIQUEUR**
1 tsp. **VANILLA**

Beat well and pour into prepared crust. Bake in preheated 350-degree
oven for 15 minutes. Reduce heat to 325-degrees and bake for 1 hour.
Cool for 5 minutes.

TOPPING:

Mix . . . . 2 cups **SOUR CREAM**
1 Tbsp. **AMARETTO LIQUEUR**
1 tsp. **VANILLA**
1 Tbsp. **SUGAR**

Spread on cake. Cook 5 more minutes. Garnish with **ALMONDS** on top.
Cool. Cover and chill overnight or freeze.

YIELD: 16 TO 18 SERVINGS.

*SOFTENED CREAM CHEESE: Soften one 8-ounce pack-
age of cream cheese by microwaving at 30% power for 2
to 2½ minutes. One 3-ounce package of cream cheese
will soften in 1½ to 2 minutes.*

CHEESECAKE
Sweet and rich!

CRUST:
Blend well for crust and
  press into a greased
  springform pan . . . . 22 **CINNAMON CRISP,** crushed
                                        ¼ cup **MARGARINE**
Bake crust at 300-degrees for 8 to 10 minutes.
FILLING:
Blend well . . . . 24 ozs. **CREAM CHEESE**
                                        1 cup **SUGAR**
                                        1½ tsps. **VANILLA**
Pour into cooled crust.
Bake in 350-degree oven for 30 minutes.
TOPPING:
Mix together . . . . 1 carton (16 oz.) **SOUR CREAM**
                                        ½ cup **SUGAR**
                                        ½ tsp. **VANILLA**

Mix well and pour on top of **CHEESECAKE.** Bake 350-degrees for 15 minutes. Refrigerate overnight. Before serving, top with 1 can **CHERRY PIE FILLING** or your favorite topping.

ITALIAN CREAM CAKE
Everyone who bought the other cookbook wished
for this recipe, so here it is!!!

Cream . . . . ½ cup **SHORTENING**
                                        ½ cup **BUTTER** or **MARGARINE,**
                                        softened
                                        2 cups **SUGAR**
Add . . . . 5 **EGG YOLKS,** one at a time
                                        2 tsp. **VANILLA**
Sift together . . . . 1 tsp. **SODA**
                                        2 cups **FLOUR**
Add alternately with . . . . 1 cup **BUTTERMILK**
Fold in . . . . 5 **EGG WHITES,** *stiffly beaten*
                                        2 cups frozen **COCONUT,** may
                                        use **ANGEL FLAKE**
                                        1 cup chopped **PECANS**

Pour into 3 greased and floured cake pans. Bake at 350-degrees for 25 minutes. Cool in pans 10 minutes. Turn out on dish towels to cool.

FROSTING:

Cream	½ cup **BUTTER** or **MARGARINE**
	8 ounces **CREAM CHEESE,** softened
	1 pound **CONFECTIONERS' SUGAR**
	1 tsp. **VANILLA**
Stir in	1 cup **PECANS**, chopped

SYB'S RUINED CAKE

"Best ever" chocolate cake

Cream together	½ cup **SHORTENING**
	2 cups **SUGAR**
Add	½ cup **COCOA**
Add, beating after each	2 **EGGS**
Sift together	2 cups **FLOUR**
	½ tsp. **BAKING POWDER**
	½ tsp. **SALT**
Blend together	¾ cup **BUTTERMILK**
	1½ tsp. **SODA**
Add flour mixture and buttermilk to sugar mixture alternating as they are added. Then add	1 cup **HOT WATER**
	1 tsp. **VANILLA**

Mix and pour into 3 well greased and floured cake pans. Bake in pre-heated 350-degree oven for 25 to 30 minutes. Cool and top with frosting. This makes a pretty cake as well as good.

FROSTING:

Mix together	2 cups **SUGAR**
	5 Tbsp. **FLOUR**
Add	1 cup **MILK**
	1 cup **MARGARINE**
	1 tsp. **VANILLA**

Cook slowly until thick, stirring constantly (about 20 minutes.) Beat until cool and spread between layers and on sides of cake.

RED VELVET CAKE
One of the all-time favorites.

Cream together	½ cup **SHORTENING**
	1½ cups **SUGAR**
	2 **EGGS**
	1 tsp. **VANILLA**
	1 tsp. **BUTTER FLAVOR**
Mix into a paste	3 Tbsp. **COCOA**, leveled
	1 bottle (1½ oz.) **RED FOOD COLOR**

Add to first mixture.

Alternately add	2½ cups **CAKE FLOUR**, sifted
With	1 cup **BUTTERMILK**
Add	1 tsp. **SALT**
	1 Tbsp. **VINEGAR**
	1 tsp. **SODA**

Blend and pour into 3 greased and floured cake pans. Bake in preheated 350-degree oven for 20 to 25 minutes. Let cool and frost.

FROSTING:

Cook in saucepan	3 Tbsp. **FLOUR**
	½ tsp. **SALT**
	1 cup **MILK**

Cook until thick. Let cool.

Cream separately	1 cup **SHORTENING**
	1 cup **SUGAR**
Add	2 tsp. **VANILLA**
	¼ tsp. **BUTTER FLAVOR**

Combine both mixtures and beat well and frost cake.

FRESH PEACH CAKE
Talk about GOOOOD!!!

Mix together in large
mixing bowl . . . . 1½ cups **SUGAR**
¾ cups **OIL**
1⅓ cups **PEACHES**, mashed
1 tsp. **SODA**
½ tsp. **NUTMEG**
2 cups **FLOUR**
¼ tsp. **SALT**
2 **EGGS**
½ cup **PECANS**, chopped
½ cup **COCONUT**

Bake in well-greased and floured 13x9x2-inch baking dish. Bake in a 350-degree oven, 45 to 50 minutes or until done. While warm spread with icing.

ICING:
Mix in medium saucepan . . . . 6 Tbsp. **MARGARINE**
1 cup **SUGAR**
1 cup **MILK**
1 **EGG**, slightly beaten
½ tsp. **VANILLA**
½ tsp. **YELLOW FOOD COLORING**
Cook until thick.
Add . . . . ½ cup **NUTS**

CHERRY CHERRY CAKE

Mix in large mixing bowl . . . . 1 box **CHERRY SUPREME CAKE MIX,** dry
½ cup **MARGARINE**, melted
2 **EGGS**
1 can **CHERRY PIE FILLING**
1 cup **PECANS**, chopped
1 tsp. **ALMOND EXTRACT**

Mix together and pour into greased and floured bundt pan. Bake in preheated 350-degree oven for 1 hour.

215

HEAVENLY MANDARIN ORANGE CAKE
"And it is heavenly!"

Combine .... 1 box **YELLOW BUTTER RECIPE CAKE MIX,** dry
½ cup **VEGETABLE OIL**
1 can (8 oz.) **MANDARIN ORANGES** with juice
4 **EGGS**
1 tsp. **VANILLA**

Beat for 4 minutes. Pour into 3 greased and floured 8-inch pans. Bake in preheated 350-degree oven for 20 minutes.

ICING:
Mix together .... 1 box (3 oz.) instant **VANILLA PUDDING,** dry
1 can **CRUSHED PINEAPPLE,** with juice
Fold in .... 1 carton **WHIPPED TOPPING,** thawed

Spread between layers and on top of cooled cake. Refrigerate before serving. Keep refrigerated or will freeze.

CONNIE'S ALMOND JOY CAKE
Sinfully Rich!!!

Mix according to pkg.
directions .... 1 **CHOCOLATE CAKE MIX WITH PUDDING**
Bake in a greased and floured 13x9x2-inch pan.
Combine in a medium
saucepan .... 1 cup **EVAPORATED MILK**
1 cup **SUGAR**
Bring just to a boil and add ...... 24 large **MARSHMALLOWS**
Stir until melted and add .... 1 pkg. (14 oz.) **COCONUT**

Pour over cake while both are hot.

TOPPING:
Melt together .... ½ cup **EVAPORATED MILK**
¼ cup **MARGARINE**
When heated add .... 1 pkg. (12 oz.) **MILK CHOCOLATE CHIPS**
Stir until melted and add .... 1 cup toasted **ALMOND** slivers

Pour on top of warm cake. Better if made the day before serving. A little of this goes a long way.

GERMAN CHOCOLATE CAKE
Remember when Mom used to make this cake?

Combine in saucepan . . . . 4 ounces **SWEET BAKING CHOCOLATE**
½ cup **WATER**
Bring to boil, stir until melted. Cool.
Add . . . . 1 tsp. **VANILLA**
Set aside.
Cream in mixing bowl . . . . 1 cup **MARGARINE**, softened
1 cup **SUGAR**
Beat until fluffy.
Add, one at a time . . . . 4 **EGG YOLKS**
Add chocolate mixture and beat until blended.
Combine . . . . 3 cups **CAKE FLOUR**
1 tsp. **SODA**
½ tsp. **SALT**
Add to creamy mixture.
Alternating with . . . . 1 cup **BUTTERMILK**
Beat until stiff . . . . 4 **EGG WHITES**

Fold mixtures together. Pour batter into 3 greased and floured 9-inch round cake pans. Bake in preheated 350-degree oven for 30 to 35 minutes or until toothpick inserted in center comes out clean. Cool 10 minutes. Remove from pans. Let cool completely. Frost.

COCONUT-PECAN FROSTING:
Combine in saucepan . . . . 1⅓ cups **EVAPORATED MILK**
1⅓ cups **SUGAR**
4 **EGG YOLKS**, slightly beaten
⅔ cup **BUTTER**
Bring to a boil. Cook over medium heat for 12 minutes, stirring constantly. Remove from heat.
Add . . . . 1½ tsp. **VANILLA**
1⅓ cups **FLAKE COCONUT**
1⅓ cups **PECANS**, chopped

Stir until cool. Spread between layers of cake, top and sides. This will stay moist for days.

100 YEAR SOFT CHOCOLATE CAKE
One of Wood's favorites.

Cream together	2 cups **SUGAR**
	1 cup **SHORTENING**
	2 **EGGS**
Beat well. Sift together 3 times . . .	2 cups **FLOUR**
	½ cup **COCOA**
	½ tsp. **SALT**
Add and mix well	1 cup **BUTTERMILK**
	1 cup **BOILING WATER**
	2 tsp. **SODA**
	1 tsp. **VANILLA**

Spread into a greased 13x9x2-inch baking dish. Bake at 350-degrees for 30 minutes.

CHOCOLATE ICING:

Mix together in medium saucepan	2 cups **SUGAR**
	½ cup **COCOA**
	½ cup **MILK**
	½ cup **MARGARINE**
Boil 1 minute. Add	1 cup **PECANS**
	½ tsp. **VANILLA**

Leave this thin and pour over cake while syrup is hot; reheat if needed.

PINA COLADA CAKE
One bite calls for more.

Mix and bake according to package directions	1 **WHITE CAKE MIX**
Bake in 13x9x2-inch pan.	
While cake is hot, mix	1 can **CREAM OF COCONUT**
	1 can **SWEETENED CONDENSED MILK**

With a fork, punch lots of holes in cake and pour mixture over hot cake.

When cake is completely cool cover with	1 carton (8 oz.) **WHIPPED TOPPING**
Sprinkle with	1½ cups **COCONUT**

Keep refrigerated. Will keep several days.

VARIATION:
May use **PINEAPPLE SUPREME CAKE MIX**. Also 1 cup **COCONUT** added to cake batter is good. Makes it richer.

OLD FASHIONED PRUNE CAKE
From Goldie's collection of favorite recipes.

Cream together . . . . ¾ cup **MARGARINE**
1 cup **SUGAR**
Add . . . . 4 Tbsp. **BUTTERMILK**
3 **EGGS**, beaten
1 cup **PRUNES**, cooked with juice
½ tsp. **SODA**
1 tsp. **SALT**
2 tsp. **CINNAMON**
1 tsp. **ALLSPICE**
1 cup **PECANS**
1½ cups **FLOUR**

Bake in 2 greased, round cake pans for 30 minutes at 350-degrees. Cool on rack and cover with filling.

FILLING:
Cook together in saucepan . . . . 2 cups **BUTTERMILK**
2 Tbsp. **MARGARINE**
1 cup **PRUNES**, cooked
1 cup **SUGAR**
2 **EGGS**, beaten
1 tsp. **VANILLA**
1 cup **PECANS**

Cook until slightly thick. Cake iced with this filling stays moist for several days.

SLAP TOGETHER CAKE
Make this one while you're on the run.

Grease and flour a 13x9x2-inch pan.
Make layers of . . . . 1 can (20 oz.) **CHERRY PIE FILLING**
1 can (20 oz.) crushed **PINEAPPLE**, use juice.
1 box **YELLOW CAKE MIX**, dry
1 can **COCONUT**
1 cup **PECANS**, chopped
Pour in a fine stream over all . . . . ¾ cup **MARGARINE**, melted

Bake in a preheated 350-degree oven for 35 to 40 minutes until light brown.

CHOCOLATE ECLAIR CAKE
This is absolutely the "Ultimate" dessert.

This must be prepared 24 hours before serving.
Grease a 13x9x2-inch pan.
Have ready .... 1 pound whole **GRAHAM CRACKERS**

Layer ⅓ of crackers in bottom of prepared pan.
Beat together .... 1 pkg. (8 oz.) **FRENCH VANILLA INSTANT PUDDING MIX**
3 cups **MILK**
Fold in .... 1 carton (8 oz.) **FROZEN WHIPPED TOPPING**, thawed

Spread ½ over crackers. Repeat layers ending with crackers.

FROSTING:
Blend together .... 2 ounces **UNSWEETENED LIQUID CHOCOLATE**
3 Tbsp. **MARGARINE**
2 Tbsp. **MILK**
1 tsp. **VANILLA**
1½ cups **CONFECTIONERS' SUGAR**

Frost and refrigerate 24 hours. Must be prepared ahead. May be frozen.

YIELD: 24 SERVINGS.

CHERRY CHOCOLATE CAKE
Ready for the oven in 15 minutes.

Combine in a mixing bowl .... 1 box **CHOCOLATE CAKE MIX**, dry
1 can (12 oz.) **CHERRY PIE FILLING**
2 **EGGS**
3 Tbsp. **MARGARINE**, melted

Pour into greased 13x9x2-inch pan. Bake in preheated 350-degree oven for 45 minutes. While still hot punch a few holes in the cake with a toothpick then frost.

CHOCOLATE FROSTING:
Combine in a medium
saucepan .... 1 cup **SUGAR**
1 Tbsp. **MARGARINE**
⅓ cup **MILK**
Bring to a boil. Cook 3 minutes.
Add .... 1 pkg. (6 oz.) **CHOCOLATE CHIPS**.

Stir and spread on warm cake.

"TEXAS CRUDE"
Rich!! Rich!!

In large bowl mix	1 cup **MARGARINE**, melted
Add and mix	4 Tbsp. **COCOA**
Add	2 cups **SUGAR**
	1 Tbsp. **VANILLA**
Beat while adding	4 **EGGS**
Combine in another bowl	1½ cups **FLOUR**
	1 cup **COCONUT**
	1½ cups **PECANS**, chopped

Mix both together and beat 2 minutes. Pour into a greased 13x9x2-inch pan. Bake in preheated 350-degree oven for 35 to 40 minutes. Remove from oven.

While cake is hot spread with. . . . 1 jar (9 oz.) **MARSHMALLOW CREAM**

Cool before icing.

ICING:

Combine and heat until
  melted . . . . ½ cup **MARGARINE**
                                        6 Tbsp. **MILK**
                                        ½ Tbsp. **COCOA**

Remove from heat.
Add and beat well . . . . 2 to 3 cups **POWDERED SUGAR**

Spread on cooled cake. Carefully cover all of cake with icing.

VARIATION:
Sprinkle cake with ½ cup **PECANS**.

PARTY CAKES: Fill flat-bottomed ice cream cones half-full of cake batter. Place in muffin tins. Bake according to cake directions. Cool, frost, and decorate.

CHILLED COCONUT CAKE
The perfect way to cheat on a diet.

Mix according to directions ..... 1 pkg. **BUTTER CAKE MIX WITH PUDDING**

Bake in a greased and floured 13x9x2-inch baking pan. Bake according to package directions. Punch holes in top of cake with small knife.

Combine .... 1 can (14 oz.) **SWEETENED CONDENSED MILK**
1 can (8½ oz.) **CREAM OF COCONUT**

Pour over warm cake and chill.

Spread over cake .... 1 can (15¼ oz.) **CRUSHED PINEAPPLE**, drained

Top with..................... 1 carton (8 oz.) frozen **WHIPPED TOPPING**, thawed

Sprinkle with .... 1 pkg. (12 oz.) frozen **COCONUT**, thawed

Cover and chill at least 8 hours. Cut in squares to serve. Keep refrigerated.

YIELD: 15 TO 18 SQUARES.

UPSIDE DOWN CHOCOLATE CAKE
Fit for a King.

Mix together in large mixing
bowl .... 1 cup **FLOUR**
¾ cup **SUGAR**
½ tsp. **SALT**

Add and mix.................. ½ cup **MILK**
2 Tbsp. **MARGARINE**, melted
1 tsp. **VANILLA**
½ cup **PECANS**, chopped

Pour into 13x9x2-inch greased and floured pan.

Mix .... ½ cup **BROWN SUGAR**
½ cup **WHITE SUGAR**
¼ cup **COCOA**
1¼ **BOILING WATER**

Pour over batter. Bake in preheated 350-degree oven for 45 minutes.

RUTH'S DATE CAKE
This makes a small cake.

In a medium mixing bowl
pour .... 1 cup **BOILING WATER**
Over .... 1 pkg. (8 oz.) pitted **DATES,**
chopped
Add......................... 1 cup **SUGAR**
2 Tbsp. **MARGARINE**, melted
1 cup **FLOUR**
1 tsp. **SODA**
1 tsp. **VANILLA**
¼ tsp. **SALT**
1 cup **PECANS**, chopped

Mix well and spread into greased and floured 9x9x2-inch pan. Bake at
350-degrees for 25 minutes or until done. Serve in squares with 1 tablespoon of **WHIPPED CREAM.**

AMARETTO BUNDT CAKE
Yummy Yummy!!!!

Grease and flour bundt pan.
Lightly brown .... ½ cup **ALMONDS**, sliced
In .... 1 Tbsp. **MARGARINE**
Sprinkle over bottom of prepared pan. Set aside.
Mix in large mixing bowl .... 1 box **YELLOW BUTTER RECIPE
CAKE MIX**
4 **EGGS**
½ cup **AMARETTO**
½ cup **WATER**
½ cup **VEGETABLE OIL**
Beat well for 2 minutes. Pour batter over nuts. Bake in preheated 350-
degree oven for 45 minutes.

GLAZE:
Mix in saucepan............... 1 cup **SUGAR**
½ cup **MARGARINE**
¼ cup **AMARETTO**
¼ cup **WATER**

Boil 3 minutes. Pour over hot cake while still in pan. Remove from pan
after 1 hour.

NUT POUND CAKE
Texans use a lot of their native fruit, PECANS.

Cream together . . . . 2 cups **SUGAR**
1 cup **MARGARINE**
Add one at a time beating well
after each . . . . 5 **EGGS**
Add . . . . 1¾ cups **FLOUR**
1 Tbsp. **VANILLA**
1 tsp. **ALMOND EXTRACT**
Mix together . . . . ¼ cup **FLOUR**
2 cups **PECANS**, chopped

Fold together. Bake in a greased and floured tube pan. Cook in a pre-heated 325-degree oven for 1 hour and 15 minutes.

COCONUT POUND CAKE
Super Moist

Cream together . . . . 1½ cups **BUTTER**
2½ cups **SUGAR**
Add one at a time and beat well
after each . . . . 5 **EGGS**
Add . . . . 2 tsp. **COCONUT FLAVORING**
Sift together . . . . ½ tsp. **SALT**
1 tsp. **BAKING POWDER**
3 cups **FLOUR**
Add, alternating with flour
mixture . . . . 1 cup **MILK**
Add . . . . 1⅓ cups flaked **COCONUT**
Pour into a greased and floured tube pan. Place in cold oven. Heat oven to 350-degrees. Bake 1 hour 20 minutes. May take longer.

GLAZE:
Mix in saucepan . . . . 2 cups **SUGAR**
1 cup **WATER**
¼ cup **LIGHT CORN SYRUP**
3 Tbsp. **BUTTER**
Bring to a boil and cook 5 minutes.
Add . . . . 2 Tbsp. **COCONUT FLAVORING**

Cool slightly and pour over hot cake in pan. Let stand in pan until completely cold. Run spatula around pan sides and tube to remove. Cake must be cold before removing from pan or it will fall apart.

LUCKY ALMOND CAKE

A New Year's tradition of our families.
The one that finds the whole ALMOND is blessed with
"extra" good luck.

Grease and flour a Bundt pan.
Sprinkle with . . . . 1 package (2½ oz.) **SLIVERED ALMONDS**, chopped
Set aside. Cream. . . . . ⅓ cup **MARGARINE**, softened
⅓ cup **SHORTENING**
1¼ cups **SUGAR**
Beat until fluffy. Add . . . . 3 **EGG YOLKS**
2 Tbsp. **LEMON JUICE**
1 tsp. grated **LEMON RIND**
1 tsp. **VANILLA**
1 tsp. **ALMOND EXTRACT**
Sift together separately . . . . 2⅓ cups **FLOUR**
2 tsp. **BAKING POWDER**
¼ tsp. **SODA**
¾ tsp. **SALT**
Add to creamed mixture,
  alternating with . . . . ¾ cup **MILK**
Set aside. Beat separately . . . . 3 **EGG WHITES**
½ tsp. **CREAM OF TARTAR**
¼ cup **SUGAR**

Beat until stiff peaks form. Fold into cake batter, then pour into prepared pan. *Press just below the surface of the batter, 1 WHOLE ALMOND.* Bake in preheated 300-degree oven for 1 hour and 20 minutes or until cake tests done. Let cool 10 minutes. Invert on cake plate. Cool and glaze with mixture of 1/2 cup **APRICOT PRESERVES** and 2 tsp. **ORANGE JUICE**.

APRICOT RING

Mix in medium bowl . . . . 2 cups **FLOUR**
2 cups **SUGAR**
1 tsp. **SODA**
1 cup **OIL**
3 **EGGS**
1 junior size **APRICOT** baby food
1 tsp. **CINNAMON**
1 tsp. **NUTMEG**
Stir until smooth.
Fold in . . . . 1 cup **COCONUT**

Bake in greased and floured bundt pan. Bake in preheated 350-degree oven for 1 hour.

THELMA SCOTT'S FRUIT CAKE

She shares this with her pastors at Christmas.

Beat together . . . . 1 pound **BROWN SUGAR**
1 pound **REAL BUTTER**,
not margarine
Add one at a time. . . . . 6 **EGGS**
1 oz. pure **LEMON EXTRACT**
1 oz. pure **RUM**
3 cups **FLOUR**
Beat a long time, the longer the better.
Fold in . . . . ½ pound **CANDIED CHERRIES**
½ pound **CANDIED PINEAPPLE**
1 pound **PECANS**

Bake in large tube pan at 300-degrees for 2 hours. Turn out immediately.

BLACK RUSSIAN CAKE

Always gets great reviews

Mix together in large bowl . . . . 1 **DEVILS FOOD CAKE MIX**,
without pudding, dry
1 pkg. (3½ oz.) instant
CHOCOLATE PUDDING MIX
½ cup **OIL**
4 **EGGS**
Blend together and add . . . . ½ cup **HOT WATER**
3 tsp. instant **COFFEE
GRANULES**
Add . . . . ½ cup **KAHLUA**
¼ cup **VODKA**
¼ cup **CREME DE COCOA**

Blend together and bake in greased and floured bundt pan. Bake in pre-heated 350-degree oven for 50 minutes or until toothpick inserted comes out clean. Remove from oven and leave in pan.

GLAZE:
Combine . . . . 1 cup **CONFECTIONER'S
SUGAR**
2 Tbsp. **STRONG COFFEE**
2 Tbsp. **KAHLUA**
2 Tbsp. **CREME DE COCOA**

Pour over hot cake and let set 15 minutes before removing from pan.

TROPICAL CAKE

Cream together	2 cups **SUGAR**
	3 **EGGS**
	1½ cups **OIL**
Mix together and add	3 cups **FLOUR**
	1 tsp. **BAKING SODA**
	1 tsp. **CINNAMON**
	1 tsp. **SALT**
Add	2 cups **RIPE MASHED BANANAS**, (approximately 4 large **BANANAS**)
	1 can (15 oz.) **CRUSHED PINEAPPLE**, drained
	1 cup **PECANS**, chopped
	1 Tbsp. **VANILLA**

Pour into a greased and floured bundt pan. Bake in preheated 350-degree oven for 1 hour and 15 minutes.

PRESERVE SPICE CAKE

We substitute at Christmas time for fruitcake.

Combine in large bowl	¾ cup **MARGARINE**
	2 cups **SUGAR**
	1 cup **BUTTERMILK**
	¾ tsp. **SODA**
	4 **EGGS**
	3 cups **FLOUR**
	1 tsp. **VANILLA**
	½ tsp. **ALLSPICE**
	½ tsp. **CINNAMON**
	½ tsp. **NUTMEG**
	¾ cup **APRICOT PRESERVES**
	¾ cup **CHERRY PRESERVES**
	¾ cup **PINEAPPLE PRESERVES**
	1 cup **PECANS**, chopped
	¼ tsp. **SALT**

Mix well. Bake in a tube pan at 325-degrees for 1½ hours. Stays moist indefinitely.

POPPY SEED CAKE

Especially designed for the "I hate to cook" person.

In medium mixing bowl mix
together . . . . 1 **BUTTER CAKE MIX**, dry
 4 **EGGS**
 ½ cup **SUGAR**
 ¼ cup **POPPY SEED**
 ¾ cup **OIL**
 1 cup **SOUR CREAM**

Pour mixture into a greased and floured bundt pan. Bake at 350-degrees for 45 to 60 minutes until it tests done with a toothpick. This stays fresh for days. (If it lasts that long.)

ANKIE'S APRICOT CAKE

Mix together . . . . 1 **YELLOW CAKE MIX**, dry
 ¾ cup **OIL**
 ¾ cup **APRICOT NECTAR**
 2 Tbsp. **LEMON EXTRACT**
Add, one at a time . . . . 4 **EGGS**
Beat and pour into a greased and floured bundt pan. Bake in preheated 350-degree oven for 1 hour or until toothpick inserted in center comes out clean.
While hot, mix . . . . 1 cup **POWDERED SUGAR**
Juice of . . . . 2 **LEMONS**

Punch holes in hot cake and pour glaze over it.

BLUEBERRY CAKE

Mix together . . . . 1 box **YELLOW CAKE MIX**, dry
 1 box instant **VANILLA PUDDING** and **PIE FILLING**, dry
 1 pkg. (8 oz.) **CREAM CHEESE**
 ½ cup **OIL**
 4 **EGGS**
 2 tsp. **VANILLA**
When mixed well, add . . . . 1 can (16 oz.) **BLUEBERRIES**, well drained
 1 cup **PECANS**, chopped

Bake in well greased and floured bundt pan. Bake in preheated 325-degree oven for 1 hour. Remove from pan and dust with **POWDERED SUGAR**.

BEST-EVER ORANGE CAKE

Preheat oven to 350-degrees.
In large mixing bowl beat until
   foamy . . . . 6 **EGG WHITES**, have at room
                         temperature
Gradually add and beat until soft
   peaks form . . . . ½ cup **SUGAR**
Set aside.
Beat until thick (3 min.) . . . . 6 **EGG YOLKS**
Add another . . . . 1 cup **SUGAR**
At low speed add alternately
   with **EGG YOLKS** . . . . 1¾ cup **FLOUR**, sifted
                         6 Tbsp. fresh **ORANGE JUICE**
Add . . . . 1 Tbsp. grated **ORANGE PEEL**

Gently fold both mixtures together with a rubber spatula. Bake in tube
pan for 35 to 40 minutes at 350-degrees. Remove from oven, turn out on
a plate and sprinkle with **CONFECTIONER'S SUGAR**. This cake will
fall slightly but it is very good.

MILK CHOCOLATE POUND CAKE
Susanne Darby gave us this one across the bridge table.
Soooo Good!!

Cream together until light
   and fluffy . . . . 1 cup **MARGARINE**, softened
                         1½ cups **SUGAR**
Add one at a time and beat well
   after each . . . . 4 **EGGS**
Add . . . . 9 **HERSHEY CANDY BARS**,
                         melted (no nuts)
                        1 cup **BUTTERMILK**
Mix well.
Mix separately . . . . 2½ cups **FLOUR**
                         ⅛ tsp. **SALT**
                         ¼ tsp. **SODA**
Add and stir into first mixture.
Add . . . . 1 can (5½ oz.) **CHOCOLATE**
                         SYRUP
                         2 tsps. **VANILLA**
                         1 cup **PECANS**

Blend well and pour into a greased and floured tube pan. Bake in preheated 325-degree oven for 1 hour and 15 minutes.

MOM'S PIE CRUST

This "fool-proof" recipe is a repeat from our first cookbook.
Just in case you don't have the first one.

Mix . . . . 3 cups **FLOUR**
                                              1 tsp. **SALT**
                                              1 Tbsp. **SUGAR**
Cut in with pastry blender or two
   knives, using scissor motion . . . 1 cup **SHORTENING**
Add . . . . ⅓ cup **WATER**
                                              1 **EGG**, well beaten
                                              1 tsp. **VINEGAR**

Mix with a fork until mixture forms a ball. Roll into 2 9-inch pie crusts.
UNFILLED CRUSTS: Generously prick with fork. Bake 350-degrees for
9 to 11 minutes. **FILLED CRUST:** Do not prick. Fill and cook according
to directions on recipe. (This dough will keep several days if put into a
plastic bag, sealed and refrigerated. Let warm to room temperature before rolling.)

SOUTHERN STYLE PIE CRUST

Place in a mixing bowl and cream
   with your hands . . . . 1 cup **BUTTER**, softened
                                           2⅔ cups **FLOUR**
                                              SALT to taste
                                              1 tsp. **SUGAR**

When mixed well, break 1 **EGG** into a measuring cup and fill to the half-
full mark with **COLD WATER**. Stir well and add to the flour mixture.
Blend well. Roll thin for a crisp crust, thicker for a soft crust. When recipe calls for prebaked pastry, cook in a preheated oven 10 minutes at
375-degrees.

YIELD: 1 PASTRY SHELL.

COCONUT CRUST
A good addition to cream pie.

Spread evenly into a 9-inch
pie pan . . . .   2 Tbsp. **MARGARINE,** softened
Sprinkle into the pan and pat
evenly into butter . . . . .1½ cups **COCONUT**

Bake in preheated 350-degree oven for 10 to 12 minutes, until crisp and golden brown. Cool and fill with your favorite filling.

BAKED (FRIED) PIE CRUST

Mix together . . . .   2 cups **FLOUR**
                                                 ¼ tsp. **SALT**
                                                 1 cup **MARGARINE**
                                                 1 pkg. (8 oz.) **CREAM CHEESE**

Roll out and cut in rounds the size of saucer. Fill with dried cooked **APRICOTS** or **FRUIT PIE** filling. Fold over and crimp edges together. Beat 1 **EGG** and brush crust and sprinkle with a little **SUGAR**. Bake in 450-degree oven until golden brown.

SELDOM WEEP MERINGUE
You know better, don't you??

Separate in glass or metal
bowl and have at room
temperature . . . .   4 **EGG WHITES**
Add . . . . ½ tsp. **CREAM OF TARTAR**
Beat at high speed; after one
minute add gradually one
tablespoon at a time . . . . ¼ cup plus 2 tablespoons **SUGAR**
Beat until stiff peaks form and sugar is dissolved.
Beat in . . . . ½ tsp. **VANILLA**

Spread meringue over hot pie filling. Make sure to seal to edge. Bake in preheated 350-degrees for 12 to 15 minutes or until brown. Cool, away from drafts. Let cool completely before cutting.

VARIATION:
3 **EGG WHITES** may be used.

PEACHES 'N' CREAM PIE

This is a favorite for summertime.

Slice into unbaked **PASTRY**
    SHELL .... 7 or 8 **PEACHES**, peeled
Make mixture of .... 1 cup **SUGAR**
                           ¼ cup **FLOUR**
                           ¼ tsp. **SALT**
                           ½ tsp. **CINNAMON**
Add and mix .... 1 cup **WHIPPING CREAM**

Pour over fruit and bake in a 400-degree oven for 45 minutes. Keep refrigerated.

YIELD: 6 SERVINGS.

VARIATIONS:
May use 1 can (1 pound, 13 oz.) **PEACHES**, drained, or **BERRIES** of your choice, 4 cups fresh.

"SLICES OF LEMON" PIE

Right! It really has slices of lemon. Try it, you'll like it!

Prepare your favorite recipe for 2 pie crusts. (Or buy the ready pie crusts in dairy section of store.) Use a 9-inch pie pan.
Combine in large bowl .... 2 cups **SUGAR**
                           ⅓ cup **FLOUR**
                           ¼ tsp. **SALT**
                           ⅔ cup **WATER**
                           2 Tbsp. **BUTTER** or
                           MARGARINE, softened
                           3 **EGGS**, slightly beaten
                           3 tsp. grated **ORANGE PEEL**
Beat until well blended.
Stir in .... 2 medium **LEMONS**, peeled, sliced ⅛-inch thick

Pour mixture into pie crust-lined pan. Top with second crust and flute. Cut slits in several places. Bake at 400-degrees for 35 to 45 minutes or until golden brown. Cool before serving. Garnish with **WHIPPED TOP-PING** and **LEMON TWISTS**.

"COMPANY'S COMING" SOUR CREAM PIE
This will impress your guests.

Mix in medium saucepan .... | 1 can (8 oz.) **CRUSHED PINEAPPLE**, undrained
1 Tbsp. **SUGAR**
1 cup **MILK**
1 pkg. (4¾ oz.) **VANILLA PUDDING & PIE FILLING MIX**, not instant

Cook over medium heat until it comes to a boil.
Add small amount to .... | 1 carton (8 oz.) **SOUR CREAM**
Then add to above mixture.
Stir in .... | 1 cup **COCONUT**
Allow to cool.
Slice in baked **PASTRY SHELL** .... | 1 **BANANA**
Spoon pie mixture over bananas.
Spread with.................. | 1 carton (4½ oz.) frozen **WHIPPED TOPPING**, thawed
Sprinkle with .... | ½ cup **COCONUT**

Chill several hours.

YIELD: ONE 9-INCH PIE

SOUR CREAM-LEMON PIE
Light, summer dessert.

Combine in microwave safe bowl .... | 1 cup **SUGAR**
3½ Tbsp. **CORNSTARCH**
1 Tbsp. grated **LEMON RIND**
3 **EGG YOLKS**, slightly beaten
½ cup fresh **LEMON JUICE**
1 cup **MILK**

Cook for 4 minutes. Stir. Cook at 1 minute intervals, stirring after each addition, until thick.
Add .... | ¼ cup **BUTTER**
Stir well and cool.
Stir in .... | 1 cup **SOUR CREAM**

Pour into a *baked* 9-inch **PIE CRUST**. Store in refrigerator. To serve, put a dollop of **WHIPPED TOPPING** on each slice. Sprinkle crushed **LEMON DROP CANDY** on topping.

233

THE BROWN BEAR

It's cool, it's refreshing, and best of all,
it has chocolate, almonds and whipped cream.

CRUST:

Blend with mixer at low speed . . .	1	cup **FLOUR**
	6	Tbsp. **BUTTER** or **MARGARINE**, room temperature
	3	Tbsp. **CONFECTIONER'S SUGAR**
	¼	cup **TOASTED ALMONDS**, finely chopped
	¼	tsp. **VANILLA**

Mix well and press on bottom and side of a 9-inch pie pan. Bake at 400 degrees for 8 to 10 minutes. Completely cool.

FILLING:

Beat with mixer until light and fluffy	1	cup **SUGAR**
	¾	cup **BUTTER** or **MARGARINE**, room temperature
Add	2	squares (1-ounce ea.) unsweetened **CHOCOLATE**, melted and cooled
	½	tsp. **ALMOND FLAVORING** or 3 Tbsp. **ALMOND-FLAVORED LIQUEUR**
Beat until well mixed.		
Add, one at a time	3	**EGGS**, *beat 2 minutes after each addition*

Spoon filling into cooled crust. Refrigerate until firm. Garnish with **WHIPPED CREAM** or **TOPPING** and sliced toasted **ALMONDS**. Keep refrigerated.

SOGGY CRUST? Brush uncooked pie shell with beaten egg white. Bake at 425 degrees for 5 to 10 minutes. Then fill with egg custard or quiches.

GIRDLE-BUSTER PIE
The title should tell you something.

Combine .... 20 **OREO COOKIES**, crushed
With .... ¼ cup **MARGARINE**, melted
Pat into 9-inch pie pan to make crust. Freeze.
Spoon into frozen crust .... 1 quart **VANILLA ICE CREAM**,
      slightly softened
Return to freezer.
In saucepan combine .... 1 can (5⅓ oz.) **EVAPORATED MILK**
      2 Tbsp. **MARGARINE**
      ½ cup **SUGAR**
      2 squares **UNSWEETENED CHOCOLATE**
      ½ tsp. **VANILLA**

Cook over low heat until sauce is dark chocolate color and smooth, stirring constantly. Keep refrigerated. When ready to serve, warm slightly. Spoon over pie slices and top with 2 tablespoons of **WHIPPED CREAM**.

FRENCH LEMON PIE
One of Dorothy's specialties.

In medium bowl, beat .... 4 **EGGS**
Add .... 1 cup **LIGHT CORN SYRUP**
      1 tsp. **LEMON PEEL**, grated
      ⅓ cup **LEMON JUICE**
      2 Tbsp. **MARGARINE**, melted
Combine .... ½ cup **SUGAR**
      2 Tbsp. **FLOUR**
Stir into egg mixture.

Pour into unbaked **PASTRY SHELL**. Bake in preheated oven at 350-degrees for 50 minutes. Chill. To serve whip ½ cup **WHIPPING CREAM** and spoon onto pie.

BROWN AND GLOSSY PIE CRUST: Brush with milk before baking.

AMARETTO MOUSSE PIE
"Quick, easy and yummy"

Prepare according to package
   directions .... 2 envelopes (1.5 oz. ea.)
   WHIPPED TOPPING
Add .... 1½ cups **MILK**
   2 pkgs. (4⅛ oz. ea.) **INSTANT
   CHOCOLATE PUDDING MIX**
   ¼ cup **AMARETTO**

Beat 2 minutes at high speed of electric mixer. Spoon into a baked 9-inch
PASTRY SHELL.
Top with .... 1 container (8 oz.) **WHIPPED
   TOPPING**
Grate and sprinkle top with ...... **CHOCOLATE SHAVINGS**

Chill several hours.

YIELD: ONE 9-INCH OR TWO 8-INCH PIES.

TEXAS CREAM PIE
Delightfully refreshing!

Heat in double boiler .... 2 cups **MILK**
In separate bowl mix .... ½ cup **SUGAR**
   3 Tbsp. **FLOUR**
   3 Tbsp. **CORNSTARCH**
Mix in .... ⅛ cup **MILK**
Add and stir well .... 2 **EGG YOLKS**, beaten
Pour into hot milk. Stir until thick over medium heat, remove from heat.
Set aside.
Beat until stiff .... 2 **EGG WHITES**
Add slowly .... 4 Tbsp. **SUGAR**

Fold the two mixtures together gently. Pour into a pre-baked **PASTRY
SHELL**. Cool and top with **WHIPPED CREAM** and grate **CHOCOLATE**
with fine grater. Chill at least two hours or longer.

CALORIE PIE

Rumored to be the pie that helped start weight watchers.

Mix together . . . . 2 cans **SWEETENED CONDENSED MILK**
16 ounces **CREAM CHEESE**
1 can (15¼ oz.) crushed **PINEAPPLE**, drained
2 tsp. **VANILLA**
1 cup **COCONUT**

Spread over **GRAHAM CRACKER CRUST** in 13x9x2-inch pan.
Then top with . . . . 2 cans (20 oz. each) **CHERRY PIE FILLING**

GRAHAM CRACKER CRUST:
Combine . . . . 1⅔ cups **GRAHAM CRACKERS**, crushed
¼ cup **SUGAR**
¼ cup plus 2 Tbsp. **MARGARINE**, melted

Mix well and press into 13x9x2-inch pan. Freeze to make crust flakier.

VARIATION:
BLUEBERRY, **PEACH** or **APRICOT** pie filling may be substituted.

STRAWBERRY PIE

Picture perfect.

Combine . . . . 3 ounces **CREAM CHEESE**
1 Tbsp. **MILK**

Beat until smooth on medium speed of electric mixer. Spread on bottom of precooked **PASTRY SHELL**.
Wash and stem . . . . 4 cups **FRESH STRAWBERRIES**
Arrange over creamy mixture, stem end down, to cover bottom of pastry shell. Set aside.
Mash remaining strawberries in small saucepan.
Add . . . . ¾ cup **SUGAR**
3 Tbsp. **CORNSTARCH**

Cook over medium heat, stirring constantly, boil 1 minute. Remove from heat. Cool. Spoon over strawberries. Cover pie and chill. Serve with **WHIPPED TOPPING**.

APRICOT TORTE
A refreshing treat in hot weather.

MERINGUE:

Beat until soft peaks form	3	**EGG WHITES**
Gradually add	¾ cup	**SUGAR**
	½ tsp.	**VINEGAR**
	½ tsp.	**VANILLA**

Beat until stiff peaks form. Set aside.

Combine	½ cup	**GRAHAM CRACKER CRUMBS**
	½ cup shredded	**COCONUT**
	1 cup chopped	**PECANS**

Fold into the egg white mixture. Lightly oil bottom and sides of 9-inch pie plate. Spoon meringue onto pie plate, gently sloping around edges to form shell. Bake at 300-degrees for 30 minutes. Turn off oven and leave torte in oven to cool and dry.

FILLING:

Add **SUGAR**, to taste, to 2 cups drained **STEWED APRICOTS**. Whip lightly with a fork. Spread over torte. Top with **WHIPPED CREAM** sweetened with 1 Tbsp. of **SUGAR**. (May use prepared **WHIPPED TOPPING**.) *Refrigerate for 2 to 3 hours before serving. Very rich!*

DELUXE STRAWBERRY GLACÉ CREAM PIE
Strawberries make a delectable dessert.

Prepare	1 (8-inch)	**GRAHAM CRACKER CRUST**
Cream together	1 cup	**SOUR CREAM**
	1 cup	**MILK**
	1 pkg. (3 oz.)	**VANILLA INSTANT PUDDING MIX**

Spread in crust.

Wash and slice	1 pint	**FRESH STRAWBERRIES**

Put all but ½ cup over sour cream mixture. Prepare **GLACÉ**:

In a small saucepan, mix	½ cup	**STRAWBERRIES**
	¼ cup	**WATER**

Simmer about 3 minutes.

Stir together	½ cup	**SUGAR**
	1½ Tbsp.	**CORNSTARCH**
Stir in	¼ cup	**WATER**

Add to hot strawberry mixture. Cook over medium heat until mixture thickens and boils. Boil 1 minute. Cool. Spoon over strawberries in pie. Chill about 2 hours or until firm.

YIELD: 8 SERVINGS.

BLUEBERRY BANANA PIE
Pretty as a picture!!

Prepare and bake 1 **PASTRY SHELL** until slightly brown. Cool.
Place in bottom of prepared
    pastry shell . . . . 2 **BANANAS**, sliced
Cover with . . . . 1 can **BLUEBERRY PIE FILLING**
Top with . . . . 2 cups **WHIPPED TOPPING**

Chill thoroughly and serve.

VARIATION:
May use **PEACH**, **APRICOT**, **CHERRY** or **STRAWBERRY** pie filling.

YIELD: 8 SERVINGS.

CHERRY ALMOND PIE
Large. Great for family reunion or church picnic.

Combine and mix well . . . . ½ cup **MARGARINE**
                                1 cup **FLOUR**
                                Dash of **SALT**
Pour into a 13x9x2-inch baking dish. Pat in bottom to form crust.
Sprinkle with ½ cup **ALMONDS** and bake for 15 minutes at 400-degrees.
Cool and set aside.
Combine . . . . 1 can **SWEETENED CONDENSED
                                MILK**
                                ⅓ cup **LEMON JUICE**
                                ½ tsp. **ALMOND FLAVORING**
                                1 tsp. **VANILLA FLAVORING**
Stir until thick.
Whip . . . . 1 cup **HEAVY CREAM**

Fold into condensed milk mixture. Put on baked crust and top with 1
can **CHERRY PIE FILLING**.

NOTE: May substitute 2 cups prepared **WHIPPED** topping for whipped
heavy cream. Try using 2 cans **CHERRY PIE FILLING**. We like lots of
cherries.

*TOAST COCONUT IN THE MICROWAVE: Watch
closely as it browns quickly once it begins to brown.
Spread ½ cup coconut in a pie plate and cook for 3-4
minutes, stirring every 30 seconds after 2 minutes.*

OLD FASHIONED EGG CUSTARD PIE
This was one of my beloved Aunt Nora's goodies.

Beat by hand until blended . . . . . .   5 **EGGS**
Gradually add . . . .   1 cup **SUGAR**
In another bowl mix . . . .   2 cups **MILK**
                                             1 Tbsp. **VANILLA**
                                             2 Tbsp. **MARGARINE**
                                             ¼ tsp. **SALT**

Pour both mixtures together. Pour into unbaked **PASTRY SHELL,** sprinkle top with **NUTMEG.** Bake in a preheated oven at 475-degrees for 7 minutes then turn oven to 350-degrees. Bake 20 to 30 minutes or until firm and crust is nice and brown.

HINT: When making **EGG CUSTARD PIES**, place unbaked **PIE CRUST** in oven just long enough to get hot before pouring filling in, the crust won't rise to the top, in the middle of your pie.

OLD TIMEY VINEGAR PIE
Our Mothers made these during the Depression years.

Combine . . . .   ½ cup **MARGARINE**, melted
                                             and cooled
                                         1½ cups **SUGAR**
                                             2 Tbsp. **FLOUR**
                                             1 tsp. **VANILLA**
                                             3 Tbsp. **CIDER VINEGAR**
                                             3 **EGGS**

Pour into unbaked **PASTRY SHELL**. Bake in a preheated 300-degree oven for 45 minutes or until set.

JANET HARRIS' WONDER RECIPE
This is so simple and good, you will discard that old favorite,
"like Grandma used to make" recipe. Promise!

USE FOR PUDDING OR PIE FILLING.
(Use a large bowl to prevent mixture from boiling over in microwave.)
Microwave on **HIGH** until
warm ....1½ cups **MILK**
Mix together and add to milk ....1½ cups **SUGAR**
4 Tbsp. **FLOUR**
Microwave 5 minutes.
Blend together .... 2 **EGG YOLKS**, well beaten
½ cup **MILK**
Mix well and pour into milk mixture. Cook for 1 minute intervals until
mixture is thick, stirring between each minute of cooking.
Stir in .... 1 tsp. **VANILLA**

Cool. For pie, pour into baked **PASTRY SHELL** and top with
MERINGUE.

VARIATIONS:
CHOCOLATE PIE: Add 3 Tbsp. **COCOA** to sugar-flour mixture.
BANANA PIE: Pour over sliced Bananas in pastry shell. For **BANANA
PUDDING**, layer custard with **BANANAS** and **VANILLA WAFERS**.
COCONUT PIE: Stir 1 can ANGEL FLAKE COCONUT into the custard
mixture.
PINEAPPLE PIE: Stir *well-drained* **PINEAPPLE** into custard mixture.

CRUSTLESS COCONUT PIE
This really works!

Mix .... 2 cups **MILK**
⅔ cup **SUGAR**
½ cup **BISQUICK**
2 **EGGS**
¼ cup **MARGARINE**, melted
1½ tsp. **VANILLA**

Blend for 3 minutes. Pour into a glass pie pan. Let set 5 minutes. Sprinkle
with 1 cup **COCONUT**. Bake in preheated oven at 350-degrees for 40
minutes.

LAYERED PINEAPPLE-CHEESE PIE

Combine in microwave safe
bowl .... 1 can (8 ounces) crushed
PINEAPPLE, with juice
1 Tbsp. **CORNSTARCH**
⅓ cup **SUGAR**
Cook for 2 minutes in microwave. Stir. Cook at 1 minute intervals until
thick. Stir each time. Cool. Set aside.
Blend in mixer .... 8 ounces **CREAM CHEESE**,
softened
½ cup **SUGAR**
1 tsp. **SALT**
Add, one at a time .... 2 **EGGS**, beat 1 minute after
each addition
Blend in .... ½ cup **MILK**
1 tsp. **VANILLA**
(Mixture may separate but will be smooth after baking.)

Spread cooled pineapple layer over bottom of *unbaked* **PIE SHELL.** Pour
cream cheese mixture over pineapple. Sprinkle with ½ cup chopped
PECANS. Bake at 400-degrees for 10 minutes. Reduce heat to 325-degrees and bake for 50 minutes. Cool.

VARIATION:
For a real pineapple lover, use the 15½ ounce size and increase the cornstarch to 2 Tbsp.

NONA'S PECAN PIE

*Nona Pirtle thinks this recipe is better than the one she gave us for
our first cookbook, CALF FRIES TO CAVIAR. We give them both
BLUE RIBBONS*

Preheat oven to 450-degrees. Prepare favorite **PIE CRUST** for 10-inch
pie. Spread unbaked pie shell with 1 cup **PECANS**. Set aside.
Beat just until blended but not
frothy .... 4 **EGGS**
Add.......................... 1 cup **SUGAR**
¾ cup **DARK CORN SYRUP**
¾ cup **LIGHT CORN SYRUP**
⅛ tsp. **SALT**
Melt 2 Tbsp. plus 1 tsp. **BUTTER**. Let cool. Blend into syrup/sugar
mixture.
Add.......................... 1 tsp. **VANILLA**

Mix just enough to blend. Pour filling over pecans in pie shell. Place pie
in oven. **REDUCE HEAT TO 350-DEGREES,** at once. Bake 50 to 60
minutes.

OLD FAITHFUL PECAN PIE

Beat until frothy . . . .   3 **EGGS**
Add . . . .   1 cup **SUGAR**
                                        1 cup light **CORN SYRUP**
                                        ½ tsp. **SALT**
                                        1¼ tsp. **VANILLA**
                                        3 Tbsp. **MARGARINE**, melted
Mix well and add . . . . .1¼ cups **PECANS**, chopped

Pour into an unbaked **PASTRY SHELL.** Bake at 325-degrees for 1 hour or until set in middle.

CHOCOLATE CHIP PECAN PIE
Plan to go on a diet after this one.

Mix together . . . .   1 stick **MARGARINE**, softened
                                        4 **EGGS**
                                        1 cup **SUGAR**
                                        1 cup **LIGHT CORN SYRUP**
                                        1 Tbsp. **BOURBON**
                                        1 cup **CHOCOLATE CHIPS**
                                        1 cup **PECANS**, chopped

Combine and pour into 1 large or 2 small unbaked **PASTRY SHELLS.** Bake at 350-degrees for 45 to 50 minutes. (Can be frozen after cooking.) Extra good served warmed with **WHIPPED CREAM.**

YIELD: 8 SERVINGS.

PECAN PUMPKIN PIE
This has just a hint of pumpkin flavor.

Mix together . . . .   3 **EGGS**
                                        1 cup **SUGAR**
                                        ½ tsp. **SALT**
                                        2 Tbsp. **MARGARINE**
                                        ½ cup dark **CORN SYRUP**
                                        ½ cup **WHIPPING CREAM**
                                        ¼ cup **BRANDY**
                                        1 cup canned **PUMPKIN**
Stir and add . . . .   1 cup **PECANS**, chopped

Pour into unbaked **PASTRY SHELL** and bake at 375-degrees for 45 to 50 minutes until set.

GERMAN SWEET CHOCOLATE PIE
Rich, rich, but oh so good!

Melt over low heat	1	pkg. (4 oz.) **GERMAN SWEET CHOCOLATE**
	¼	cup **BUTTER**

Stir until blended. Remove from heat.
Gradually blend in and set
aside . . . . 1 can (14½ oz.) **EVAPORATED MILK**

Mix together in medium
mixing bowl . . . . 1½ cups **SUGAR**
3 Tbsp. **CORNSTARCH**
⅛ tsp. **SALT**
Beat in . . . . 2 **EGGS**
1 tsp. **VANILLA**
Gradually blend in chocolate mixture. Pour into an unbaked **PASTRY SHELL**.
Mix together . . . . 1⅓ cups **ANGEL FLAKE COCONUT**
½ cup chopped **PECANS**

Sprinkle over filling. Bake in a preheated 375-degree oven for 45 minutes or until top is puffed. Filling will be soft, but will set when cool. Cool at least 4 hours before serving.

SAWDUST PIE
Jannel Nelson's intriguing pie.

Combine in large bowl . . . . 1¼ cups **SUGAR**
1½ cups **PECANS**, chopped
1½ cups **VANILLA WAFER**, crumbs
1½ cups flaked **COCONUT**
½ tsp. **CINNAMON**
½ tsp. **NUTMEG**
7 **EGG WHITES**, unbeaten
Stir until just blended.
Pour into . . . . 1 9-inch **PASTRY SHELL**, unbaked

Bake at 375-degrees for 35 minutes or until filling is set. Serve warm or at room temperature. Top each slice with a dollop of **WHIPPED CREAM** and a slice of **BANANA**.

VARIATION:
May substitute **CRAHAM CRACKER CRUMBS**, if you prefer. May also substitute **BROWN SUGAR** for **WHITE SUGAR**.

STRAWBERRY FREEZE
A layered dessert that tastes as good as it looks!

Mix together .... 1¼ cups **FLOUR**
                                 ½ cup **BROWN SUGAR**
                                 ½ cup **MARGARINE**, melted
                                 ½ cup **NUTS**, chopped
Press into a 13x9x2-inch baking dish. Bake 20 minutes at 350-degrees.
Set aside to cool.
Beat until frothy .... 2 **EGG WHITES**
Gradually add and beat until
   stiff .... ½ cup **SUGAR**
Add .... 2 (10 oz. ea.) pkgs. frozen
                                 STRAWBERRIES
                                 2 Tbsp. **LEMON JUICE**

Continue beating for 10 minutes.
Fold in .... 1 carton (8 oz.) **WHIPPED
                                 TOPPING**

Pour over crust, cover and freeze. Cut into squares as needed and serve frozen. A good make-ahead dish.

THREE LAYERED PRETZEL DESSERT
A sensational taste treat.

CRUST:
Coarsely crush .... 2 cups **PRETZELS**
Mix with .... 3 Tbsp. **SUGAR**
                               ¾ cup **MARGARINE**
Pat into 13x9x2-inch baking dish. Bake 8 to 10 minutes at 400-degrees.
Cool.
Mix together .... 1 pkg. (8 oz.) **CREAM CHEESE**
                               1 cup **SUGAR**
Fold in .... 1 carton (10 oz.) **WHIPPED
                               TOPPING**

Spread over crust.
Dissolve .... 1 box (6 oz.) **STRAWBERRY
                               JELLO**
In .... 2 cups **HOT WATER**
Add and stir to melt .... 2 pkgs. (10 oz. each)
                               STRAWBERRIES, frozen

When dissolved and cool, spread on top of last layer. Chill well. Cut into squares. For salad, serve on **LETTUCE LEAVES**. For dessert, top with **WHIPPED TOPPING** and a **STRAWBERRY**. Will keep for days.

APPLE PIZZA
A good way to get your "Apple-A-Day"!

To dry **PIE CRUST** mix, *for two pies*, add ¾ cup grated **CHEDDAR CHEESE** and **ICE WATER** to form crust. Roll on floured board and place in pizza pan. Make a high fluted edge.

Combine .... ½ cup **BROWN SUGAR**, firmly packed
½ cup **WHITE SUGAR**
½ cup **COFFEE MATE**, dry
⅓ cup **FLOUR**
¼ tsp. **NUTMEG**
1 tsp. **CINNAMON**

Divide in half. Sprinkle ½ mixture over crust.

Arrange in pattern .... 3 or 4 cups **APPLES**, that have been cut into ½-inch slices

Cut into remaining sugar
mixture .... ¼ cup **BUTTER** or **MARGARINE**, softened

Sprinkle over apples. Bake at 350-degrees until apples are done. (30 to 40 minutes. Time varies with different types of apples.)

ENGLISH TRIFLE
Fit for a king.

Place in clear glass bowl, bite
sizes of .... **ANGEL FOOD CAKE**
If desired sprinkle with .... **SHERRY, RUM** or **BRANDY**
Prepare your favorite .... **VANILLA CUSTARD RECIPE** (or **VANILLA PUDDING** and **PIE FILLING**)

Spoon ⅓ over cake. Add layers
(your choice) of .... **FRESH FRUIT**, sliced
Alternate two additional layers of cake, pudding and fruit.
Top with.................... **WHIPPED CREAM**, sweetened

Suggestions for fruit are, **STRAWBERRIES, SEEDLESS GRAPES, KIWI, BANANAS, PEACHES** and **APRICOTS**. This is beautiful and a real Summertime treat.

YIELD: 8 TO 10 SERVINGS.

CHOCOLATE WAFFLES WITH STRAWBERRY CREAM

Waffles don't have to be just for breakfast.

Combine in large bowl . . . . ¾ cup plus 2 Tbsp. **FLOUR**
                           ¼ tsp. **SALT**
                           ½ tsp. **SODA**
                           ¼ cup plus 2 Tbsp. **SUGAR**
                           3 Tbsp. **COCOA**
Combine, then add to flour
  mixture . . . . 1 **EGG YOLK**
                           1 cup **BUTTERMILK**
                           2 Tbsp. **MARGARINE**, melted
Beat until stiff peaks form . . . . 1 **EGG WHITE**

Fold egg whites into batter. Bake in preheated, oiled, waffle iron. Cut waffles to make eight 4-inch squares. Serve with **STRAWBERRY CREAM**.

YIELD: 8 SERVINGS.

STRAWBERRY CREAM:
Beat until foamy . . . . ¾ cup **WHIPPING CREAM**
Add and beat until soft
  peaks form . . . . ⅓ cup **POWDERED SUGAR**
Fold in . . . . 2 cups **STRAWBERRIES**
Serve over waffles.

YIELD: 2 CUPS.

SOFTEN BUTTER OR MARGARINE: One stick of butter or margarine will soften in 1 minute when microwaved at 20% power. Butter will melt faster than margarine. Oil heats slowly so should be heated on conventional stove.

POOR MAN'S PUDDING
Try the Whiskey Sauce. M-M-M GOOD!

In a medium mixing bowl, beat
  until fluffy . . . .   4 **EGGS**
Add . . . .   ½ cup **SUGAR**
Blend in . . . .   ½ tsp. **SALT**
                              1 tsp. **CINNAMON**
                              1 tsp. **NUTMEG**
                              1 tsp. **VANILLA**
                              ½ cup **RAISINS**, optional
                              4 cups **BREAD CRUMBS**
                              2 cups **MILK**, lukewarm

Mix well. Pour into a buttered 9x5x3-inch casserole. Bake in a preheated 375-degree oven for 45 to 50 minutes. Serve with **WHISKEY SAUCE**.

YIELD: 6 SERVINGS.

WHISKEY SAUCE:
Cook on medium heat until
  dissolved . . . .   ½ cup **SUGAR**
                              ½ cup **WATER**
                              2 Tbsp. **BUTTER** or
                              MARGARINE
Remove from heat and add . . . . . .   1 to 2 jiggers **WHISKEY**

Serve over **BREAD PUDDING**. Best served warm.

YIELD: 6 SERVINGS.

RAISIN BREAD PUDDING

Place in a greased 8-inch square
  pan or baking dish . . . .   ½ loaf **RAISIN BREAD**, cubed
Combine in a small bowl . . . .   2 **EGGS**
                              ¼ cup **SUGAR**
                              2 cups **MILK**
                              1 tsp. **VANILLA**

Pour over cubed bread and dot with 2 Tbsp. **MARGARINE**. Bake at 350 degrees for 55 minutes, or until knife inserted in center comes out clean. Serve warm or cold.

APRICOT PASTRIES

A pretty addition to any party. Approximately 64 pastries.

FILLING:

Combine in medium saucepan . . .	2 cups **DRIED APRICOTS**
Cover with	**WATER**

Simmer uncovered for about 15 minutes or until very tender. Mash and drain well.

Add	½ cup **SUGAR**

Mix well and set aside.

PASTRY:

Combine in medium mixing bowl	3 cups **FLOUR**
	1 Tbsp. **SUGAR**
	½ tsp. **SALT**
Cut in with pastry blender or two knives using scissor motion . . .	1 cup **SHORTENING**
Dissolve	1 pkg. **DRY YEAST**
In	½ cup warm **MILK**
Stir in, mix well	1 **EGG**, slightly beaten
	½ tsp. **VANILLA**

Add to dry ingredients, stir until blended. Divide dough into fourths; cover and chill at least 1 hour. Work with 1 portion of dough at a time. Keep remaining chilled. Roll into 10-inch square on surface covered with **POWDERED SUGAR**. Cut into 2½-inch squares; place ¾ teaspoon of apricots in center of each square. Overlap opposite corners. Place on greased cookie sheet, seam side up. Bake in preheated 350-degree oven 10 to 12 minutes. Remove immediately and dust with powdered sugar.

VARIATION:
STRAWBERRY PASTRIES. Substitute ¾ cup **STRAWBERRY JAM** in pastries.

PUMPKIN MOUSSE

A light and airy dessert.

Mix	1 can (16 oz.) **PUMPKIN**
	⅔ cup **BROWN SUGAR**, firmly packed
	1 tsp. **CINNAMON**
	¼ tsp. **NUTMEG**
Fold into	1½ cups **WHIPPING CREAM**, whipped

Pour into sherbet dishes and garnish with **WHIPPED CREAM**.

EASY JELLYROLL

Grease a 25x10x1-inch jellyroll pan, and line with waxed paper: Grease and flour waxed paper. Set aside.

Combine .... 4 **EGGS**
                             ¾ tsp. **BAKING POWDER**
                             ¼ tsp. **SALT**

Beat at high speed until foamy.
Gradually add................ ¾ cup **SUGAR**
Beat until thick and lemon colored.
Fold in .... ¾ cup **FLOUR**
Add .... 1 tsp. **LEMON EXTRACT**

Spread in prepared pan. Bake at 400-degrees for 10 to 12 minutes. Sift **POWDERED SUGAR** onto a linen towel. When cake is done, immediately loosen from sides of pan and turn out on sugar. Peel waxed paper off. Starting at narrow end, roll up cake and towel together; cool for 10 minutes. Unroll cake and spread with **JELLY** then reroll without the towel. Place on serving plate, seam side down. Garnish with **WHIPPED CREAM** and **STRAWBERRIES**. Sounds difficult, but it isn't.

YIELD: 8 SERVINGS.

PEACH COBBLER SUPREME
What would summers be without fresh fruit cobblers.

Combine .... 8 cups fresh **PEACHES**, sliced
                             2 cups **SUGAR**
                             3 Tbsp. **FLOUR**
                             ½ tsp. **NUTMEG**

Set aside until juice forms.

Bring to a boil, cook over low heat, 15 minutes until tender.
Remove from heat and add ...... 1 tsp. **ALMOND EXTRACT**,
                               optional
                             ½ cup **MARGARINE**, melted
Prepare...................... **PASTRY** for double crust pie

Roll out half of pastry to ⅛-inch thickness. Cut into strips. Spoon half of peaches into an 8-inch square pan, lightly buttered. Top with pastry. Spoon remaining peaches into pan, cut the rest of the pastry into strips and arrange in lattice design over peaches. Bake in 350-degree oven until crust is golden brown.

YIELD: 8 TO 10 SERVINGS.

CHERRY CRUNCH

Make this one when unexpected guests arrive.

Spread in a 13x9x2-inch greased
baking dish .... 1 can (20 oz.) **CHERRY PIE
FILLING**
Top with..................... 1 can (20 oz.) **CRUSHED
PINEAPPLE**, with juice
Sprinkle with .... ¾ cup **SUGAR**
Smooth on top .... 1 box **YELLOW CAKE MIX**, dry
Pour on top .... 1 cup **MARGARINE**, melted
Sprinkle with .... 1 cup **PECANS**, chopped

Bake in preheated 350-degree oven for 45 minutes until golden brown.
Serve in bowls with a scoop of ice cream for a heavenly dessert.

APPLE DUMPLINGS

Inez makes these for her "Dumplin" D. R. Miller.

Combine .... 2 cups **FLOUR**
2 tsp. **BAKING POWDER**
1 tsp. **SALT**
With pastry blender cut in .... ¾ cup **SHORTENING**
Stir in with fork .... ½ cup **MILK**
Chill. Meanwhile, pare
and core .... 6 **APPLES**, the cooking variety

Divide dough into 6 portions. Roll each large enough to cover 1 apple.
Try to keep dough square. Place an apple on each square, sprinkle each
with 1 Tbsp. **SUGAR** and **BUTTER**. Sprinkle with **CINNAMON**. Pull
dough to top of apple and seal. Place an inch or more apart in baking
dish. Pour **SUGAR SYRUP** over the dumplings and bake at 450-degrees
for 20 minutes or until brown.

SUGAR SYRUP:
Heat until melted............... 2 cups **SUGAR**
2 cups **WATER**
¼ Tbsp. **CINNAMON**
¼ Tbsp. **NUTMEG**
¼ cup **BUTTER**

MINI-PHYLLO CHEESECAKES
These are fun to do.

Melt . . . . ½ cup **MARGARINE**
Place on damp towel . . . . 1 sheet commercial frozen
PHYLLO PASTRY, thawed
(keep remainder covered with
damp cloth.)

Brush phyllo with butter. Place another sheet on top of first sheet. Repeat with margarine. Do this 4 times. Cut all 4 layers at once into 3-inch squares using kitchen scissors. Repeat with another stack of four sheets. Place one square of layered phyllo into each cup of buttered miniature muffin tins. Press gently in center to form a pastry shell. Bake at 350-degrees for 8 to 10 minutes until golden brown. Remove very carefully and let cool on wire rack. Fill with cream cheese mixture.

FILLING:
Combine . . . . 3 pkgs. (3 oz. ea.) **CREAM
CHEESE**
½ cup **POWDERED SUGAR**
1 Tbsp. **ORANGE JUICE**
1 tsp. **ORANGE RIND**, grated
Beat at high speed until smooth. Place 1½ teaspoons cream cheese mixture into each shell.
Combine . . . . ½ cup **MARMALADE**
2 tsp. **ORANGE JUICE**

Top each cheesecake with ½ teaspoon marmalade mixture. Chill until ready to serve. They are very delicate.

YIELD: 40 PASTRIES

EASY PHYLLO: Spray sheets with butter flavored cooking spray.

FRUIT CAROUSEL
A delightful party dessert!

Make this mixture first and have ready to cover fruit as soon as it is arranged to prevent darkening. Have chilled.

Mix . . . .   ¾ cup **SUGAR**
                            ¾ cup **WATER**
                            1 cup **ORANGE JUICE**
                            ¼ cup **LEMON JUICE**
                            4 Tbsp. **CORNSTARCH**
                            ⅛ tsp. **SALT**

Cook until thick and clear. Spread over fruit. You will probably have some left over. This makes a large amount.

Slice thin and press on
pizza pan . . . .   1 pkg. **REFRIGERATOR SUGAR COOKIE DOUGH**

Bake according to directions on package. Let cool.

Cream together . . . .   1 pkg. (8 oz.) **CREAM CHEESE**
                            ½ cup **SUGAR**
                            1 tsp. **VANILLA**

Spread on crust. Chill.

Slice and arrange in circles
completely around the pan . . . .   **STRAWBERRIES**, halved
                            BANANAS, sliced
                            2 cups **MANDARIN ORANGES**, well-drained
                            GRAPES, halved
                            2 **PEACHES**, sliced
                            1 can (8 oz.) **CHUNK PINEAPPLE**, well-drained

Cover with sauce.

YIELD: 8 SERVINGS.

VARIATION:
Make this to suit your own taste. Use any kind of fruits you like. A dollop of **WHIPPED TOPPING** is also good.

EASY CHOPPING: Place dried fruit in the freezer for 2 hours before chopping. Frequently dip knife or kitchen shears in hot water to prevent sticking.

LAS VEGAS RICE PUDDING

We have a contest going. "Which hotel has the best rice pudding?"

In a large saucepan combine . . . . . 2 cups **MILK**
2 cups **WATER**
½ cup **RICE**, uncooked
¼ tsp. **SALT**

Cover and simmer until liquid is absorbed and rice is tender. About 25 minutes.

Mix together . . . . 3 **EGGS**, beaten
1 cup **SUGAR**
¼ tsp. **VANILLA**
½ cup **RAISINS** (optional)

Pour into rice mixture. Combine and cook uncovered on low heat for 5 minutes. Pour into casserole and sprinkle with **CINNAMON**. Bake for 5 minutes at 300-degrees.

LEMON LUSH

And it is luscious.

CRUST:
Blend with a pastry blender . . . . . ½ cup **MARGARINE**
1 cup **FLOUR**
½ cup **NUTS**, finely chopped

Press into an ungreased 13x9x2-inch pan. Bake at 350-degrees for 20 minutes.

1st LAYER:
Blend . . . . 1 pkg. (8 oz.) **CREAM CHEESE**, softened
With . . . . 1 cup **CONFECTIONER'S SUGAR**
1 cup **WHIPPED TOPPING**

Spread on cooled crust.

2nd LAYER:
Combine . . . . 2 pkgs. (3¾ oz. ea.) **LEMON INSTANT PUDDING MIX**
2½ cups cold **MILK**

Beat well and spread over last layer.

3rd LAYER:
Top with. . . . . 1 cup **WHIPPED TOPPING**
Sprinkle with . . . . ½ cup **PECANS**, chopped

Cut in squares to serve. Top each with thin slice of **LEMON.**

CHERRY MASH

Melt in large bowl in
   microwave for 1½ minutes
   on HIGH power   1   pkg. (12 oz.) **SEMI-SWEET
      CHOCOLATE CHIPS**
       ¾   cup **CRUNCHY PEANUT
      BUTTER**
Stir in   1   cup **NUTS**, chopped
Spread half mixture in a 13x9x2-inch pan.
Combine   1   can (16 ozs.) prepared **CHERRY
      FROSTING**
       1   jar (7 ozs.) **MARSHMALLOW
      CREAM**

Spread on top of first mixture. Top with remaining chocolate mixture.
Chill several hours until firm. Cut into 1½-inch squares.

VARIATION:
May be made in paper miniature baking cups.

SHIRLEY'S DESSERT
A delicious choice.

CRUST:
Make crust of   2   cups **GRAHAM CRACKER**
      crumbs
       ½   cup **SUGAR**
       ½   cup **MARGARINE**, melted
Press into a 13x9x2-inch dish.

FILLING:
Mix together   1   carton (8 oz.) **WHIPPED
      TOPPING**, thawed
       1   can **SWEETENED CONDENSED
      MILK**
       1   can (15½ oz.) **PINEAPPLE**,
      drained
       1   carton (10 oz.)
      STRAWBERRIES, thawed
       1   cup **COCONUT**
       1   cup **PECANS**
       2   Tbsp. **LEMON JUICE**

Spread on top of crust and chill. Cut into squares to serve.

GINGERSNAP PUDDING

Dorothy Woods is noted for being a wonderful cook.

CRUST:

Crush . . . . ⅓ pound **GINGERSNAPS**
Mix together with . . . . 4 Tbsp. **MARGARINE**, melted
Spread and pat into a 13x9x2-inch baking dish.
Place in refrigerator.

FILLING:

Cream together . . . . 2 cups **POWDERED SUGAR**
                                      1 8 ounce pkg. **CREAM CHEESE**
Add one at a time . . . . 3 **EGGS**
Beat until fluffy.
Spread on crumb mixture.
Place in refrigerator.
Dice . . . . 3 **BANANAS**
Add . . . . 1 can (15¼ oz.) **PINEAPPLE TIDBITS**, drained
Whip and fold in . . . . 1 cup **WHIPPING CREAM**
                                        ½ cup **PECANS**, chopped

Spread over other mixtures. Then sprinkle with extra **GINGERSNAP CRUMBS**. Chill for at least 2 hours. Cut and serve. GREAT!!

YIELD: 15 SERVINGS.

CHERRY BERRY TORTE

Clarice brings this treat to the Balch family reunion.

Combine . . . . 4 cups **GRAHAM CRACKER CRUMBS**
                                        ½ cup **MARGARINE**
Press into 13x9x2-inch pan. Bake at 375-degrees until lightly browned. Cool.
Then spread with . . . . 1 can **BLUEBERRY PIE FILLING**
Blend in bowl . . . . 1 pkg. (8 oz.) **CREAM CHEESE**, softened
                                        1 cup **POWDERED SUGAR**
Mix with enough **MILK** to make spreadable on **BLUEBERRY** layer.
Layer with . . . . 1 can **CHERRY PIE FILLING**
Whip by directions . . . . 2 pkgs. **DREAM WHIP**
Spread over cherries and
   sprinkle with . . . . 1 cup **PECANS**, chopped

Keep refrigerated. Good and pretty as well.

JEWEL SYKES STRAWBERRY VELVET DESSERT
This was a family tradition of the Sykes.

CRUST:

Melt in a heavy skillet	½ cup	**MARGARINE**
Add all at once	1 cup	**FLOUR**
	¼ cup	**SUGAR**
	1 cup	**PECANS**, finely chopped

Stir and cook over medium heat 3 to 4 minutes, until lightly browned and crumbly. Reserve ⅔ cup for topping. Press remainder of crumbs into 8-inch square pan with fork. Refrigerate until cool.

STRAWBERRY FILLING:

Dissolve	1 pkg. (3 ozs.)	**STRAWBERRY JELLO**
	½ cup	**SUGAR**
In	1 cup	**WATER**, boiling
Mix in	1 cup	**SOUR CREAM**
Use rotary beater until thick but not set.		
Fold in	1 pkg. (10 ozs.)	**FROZEN STRAWBERRIES**, sliced with liquid

Pour over crust, sprinkle with remaining crumbs and refrigerate until set, or overnight. Cut in squares and serve with **WHIPPED TOPPING** and a whole **STRAWBERRY** if available..

ICE CREAM
Rich and Smooth

Whip........................	2 cartons	**WHIPPING CREAM**
Add	1½ cups	**SUGAR**
Add one at a time.............	5	**EGGS**
	1 can	**SWEETENED CONDENSED MILK**
	1½ tsp.	**VANILLA**

Beat well. If desired add **STRAWBERRIES, PEACHES,** or your choice of fruit. If needed add **HALF** and **HALF CREAM** or **MILK** to fill freezer can. Follow ice cream freezer instructions.

CHICKEN FRIED ICE CREAM

Texans will "chicken fry" almost anything.
This is a repeat for company or special family meals.

Combine in medium saucepan . . .   1 cup **WATER**
   ½ cup **BUTTER** or **MARGARINE**
Bring mixture to a boil. Reduce heat to low.
Add . . . . .1½ cups **FLOUR**
STIR VIGOROUSLY until mixture leaves sides of pan and forms a smooth ball. Remove saucepan from the heat, and allow mixture to cool slightly.
Add, one at a time . . . .   5 **EGGS**

Beat with a wooden spoon after each addition. Beat until batter is smooth. Drop batter by scant one-third cupfuls about 3 inches apart on lightly greased baking sheets. Bake at 350-degrees for 40 minutes or until golden brown and puffed. Cool puffs on wire racks away from drafts. Cut off top of each puff. Pull out and discard most of the soft dough inside. Fill bottom halves with **VANILLA ICE CREAM**. Cover with top halves. Wrap in aluminum foil and freeze. Just before serving, remove puffs from foil and deep-fry in hot **OIL** (350-degrees) until they are golden brown.

NO EGG ICE CREAM

Ann Whiteside's recipe for people who need to omit eggs from their diet.

Stir together by hand in large
   mixing bowl . . . .   2 pkgs. **SALADA ICE CREAM MIX**
   1 cup **NONFAT DRY MILK**
   ½ cup **SUGAR**
Then slowly add and mix until
   fairly smooth . . . .   1 quart **HALF and HALF MILK**
   1 can **SWEETENED CONDENSED MILK**
   1 cup **WHITE KARO**
   1 tsp. **VANILLA**
Pour mixture into freezer can.
Add . . . .   1 quart **HALF and HALF MILK**
Add to within 1½ inches of top of
   freezer can . . . .   **HOMOGENIZED MILK**

Freeze according to manufacturer's instruction.

VARIATION:
SALADA ICE CREAM MIX comes in four flavors: **VANILLA, STRAW-BERRY, PEACH** and **DUTCH CHOCOLATE**. Add fruit accordingly.

11 MORE FLAVORS OF ICE CREAM
THE JAN-SU WAY

Still our favorite basic recipe, but we keep "churning" out new flavors. Soon we will have as many as the famous Baskin Robbins.

Beat well . . . . 6 **EGGS**
Gradually add . . . . 2 cups **SUGAR**
Beat at least 5 minutes.
Add . . . . 1 can **SWEETENED CONDENSED MILK**
1 cup **HEAVY CREAM**
1 can (5 oz.) **EVAPORATED MILK**
2 tsp. **VANILLA**

Beat well. Pour into freezer can. Finish filling with **MILK**. Freeze according to manufacturer's manual.

All the following flavors will make 1 gallon of **ICE CREAM**.

CHERRY CHOCOLATE:
Add ¼ cup **CHOCOLATE SYRUP** and 1 jar (10 oz.) **MARASCHINO CHERRIES** including juice.

CANDY-MAN:
Add 1½ cups candy-coated **MILK CHOCOLATE** pieces.

COFFEE N' CREAM:
Dissolve 1 Tbsp. **INSTANT COFFEE GRANULES** in ½ cup **HOT WATER**. Mix with ½ cup **CHOCOLATE SYRUP**.

HAWAIIAN LUAU:
Add 1 can (6 oz.) undiluted frozen **ORANGE JUICE** and 1 can (15 oz.) **CRUSHED PINEAPPLE**.

TOFFEE:
Add 6 ounces crushed **TOFFEE-FLAVORED** candy.

LEMON OR LIME:
Add 6 ounces frozen **LEMONADE** or **LIMEADE CONCENTRATE**.

TUTTI FRUITTI:
Add 3 mashed **BANANAS**, 1 cup sliced **STRAWBERRIES**, 1 cup **PEACHES**.

continued

BLUEBERRY HILL:
Add 2 cups fresh or frozen **BLUEBERRIES**.

CHERRY-CHOCOLATE FREEZE:
Add ½ cup **CHOCOLATE SYRUP** and 1 can drained **BING CHERRIES**. (16½ oz.).

PEANUTS IN CHOCOLATE:
Add ½ cup **CHOCOLATE SYRUP** and 2 cups **CHOCOLATE-COVERED PEANUTS**.

COOKIE MONSTER:
Add 18 **OREO COOKIES**, broken into small pieces.

STREUSEL BARS
Chocolate lover's delight.

In large bowl, combine . . . . 1¾ cups **FLOUR**
1½ cups **CONFECTIONERS SUGAR**
½ cup unsweetened **COCOA**

Mix, cut in with pastry blender or two knives using scissor motion . . . . 1 cup cold **MARGARINE**

Mixture will be crumbly.

Reserve 2 cups crumb mixture, press remainder in bottom of 13x9x2-inch baking pan. Bake 15 minutes in preheated 350-degree oven.
In mixing bowl beat until fluffy . . . . 1 pkg. (8 oz.) **CREAM CHEESE**, softened

Gradually beat in . . . . 1 can (14 oz.) **SWEETENED CONDENSED MILK**

Add . . . . 1 **EGG**
2 tsp. **VANILLA**

Pour over prepared crust.
Combine with reserved crumbs . . . . ½ cup **PECANS**, chopped

Sprinkle evenly over cheese mixture. Bake 25 minutes or until bubbly. Chill. Cut into bars. Store in refrigerator.

CHERRY DREAM BARS

CRUST:

In large bowl combine . . . .   1 box **WHITE CAKE MIX,** dry
6 Tbsp. **MARGARINE**, softened
1 cup **OATS**

Mix until crumbly. *Reserve 1 cup.*
To the remainder, add . . . .   1 **EGG**
Mix well and press into a greased 13x9x2-inch baking dish.

FILLING:

Spread over crust . . . .   1 can (21 oz.) **CHERRY PIE
FILLING**

TOPPING:

To reserved crumbs; add . . . .   ¼ cup **OATS**
2 Tbsp. **BUTTER** or
MARGARINE
¼ cup **BROWN SUGAR**, firmly
packed
½ cup **NUTS**, chopped

Beat until thoroughly mixed. Spread over cherry mixture. Bake in 350-degree oven for 30 to 40 minutes until golden brown. Serve with **WHIPPED TOPPING** or **ICE CREAM**.

YIELD: 12 SERVINGS.

BARBARA'S CHESS CAKE BARS
Quick, easy and tasty!!

Mix together . . . .   1 box **YELLOW CAKE MIX**, dry
½ cup **MARGARINE**, melted
1 **EGG**

Pour into a 13x9x2-inch pan. (It will be more like a dough.) Set aside.
Mix in medium bowl . . . .   1 pound **POWDERED SUGAR**
3 **EGGS**
1 pkg. (8 oz.) **CREAM CHEESE**,
room temperature

Pour over cake mixture. Bake at 350-degrees for 40 minutes or until golden brown. Let cool before cutting. This will fall, it is supposed to.

CHERRY CHEESE BARS
These sound complicated, but are really easy.

Grease bottom of 13x9x2-inch pan. Chop ½ cup **WALNUTS** coarsely for topping to be used later. Set aside.

CRUST:
Combine .... 1¼ cups **FLOUR**
                             ½ cup **BROWN SUGAR**, firmly
                             packed
Using knives or pastry blender, cut in ½ cup **SHORTENING**, until mixture resembles cornmeal.
Add .... ½ cup **FLAKE COCONUT**
                             ½ cup **WALNUTS**, finely chopped
Mix well. Remove ½ cup crust mixture to use later. Press in bottom of greased pan. Bake for 12 to 15 minutes at 350 degrees, until edges are slightly browned.

FILLING:
Beat until smooth .... 8 ounces **CREAM CHEESE**,
                             softened
                             ⅓ cup **SUGAR**
                             1 **EGG**
                             1 tsp. **VANILLA**
                             ¼ tsp. **ALMOND FLAVORING**
                             (opt.)
Spread over hot baked crust. Return to oven. Bake 10 minutes longer.
Spread over cheese layer .... 1 can (21 oz.) **CHERRY PIE**
                             FILLING

Combine the reserved nuts and crumb mixture. Sprinkle over cherries. Return to oven. Bake 15 minutes longer. Cool. Cut into the size bars you wish. Remember these are very rich, so keep bars small.

REESE CUPS
A rich and delicious treat!!

Mix thoroughly .... ½ cup **GRAHAM CRACKERS**,
                             crushed
                             1 cup **MARGARINE**
                             1 cup **PEANUT BUTTER**
                             1 box (1 lb.) **POWDERED SUGAR**
Press into a buttered cake pañ, or muffin tins, lined with paper muffin cups.
Melt in microwave .... 1 bag (12 oz.) **MILK CHOCOLATE**
                             CHIPS

Spread over peanut butter. Cool in the refrigerator.

GERMAN CHOCOLATE SQUARES
Quick and easy, but rich.

Preheat oven to 350-degrees.
Combine in mixing bowl	1 box **GERMAN CHOCOLATE CAKE MIX**, dry
½ cup **MARGARINE**, softened
2 **EGGS**
½ cup **NUTS**, chopped

Mix and spread in well-greased 13x9x2-inch pan. Mixture will be very thick.
Mix together until smooth	8 ounces **CREAM CHEESE**
2 **EGGS**, beaten
1 tsp. **VANILLA**
1 box (1 lb.) **POWDERED SUGAR**

Spread on top of other mixture. Bake 35 minutes **ONLY**. Cool and cut in small squares.

CHOCOLATE MOUND BARS
The Franklin children's grandmother, Mussy, had these waiting on cold days for an after school treat.

Cream	1 cup **BUTTER** or **MARGARINE**, softened
2 cups **SUGAR**
Add	4 **EGGS**, slightly beaten
1½ cups **FLOUR**
⅓ cup **COCOA**
1 cup **PECANS**, chopped

Mix and spread in a 13x9x2-inch baking dish. Bake 30 minutes at 350 degrees. Remove from oven.
Mix	1 can **SWEETENED CONDENSED MILK**
1 cup **COCONUT**
1 tsp. **VANILLA**

Spread over first mixture and bake for 10 more minutes.
Sprinkle with **CHOCOLATE CHIPS**. Return to oven just until chips are melted.

CHEWY PECAN BARS
Wonderful with a cup of coffee!

Beat with an electric mixer until
  foamy . . . . 2 **EGGS**
Add and beat until creamy . . . . . . 2 cups **LIGHT BROWN SUGAR**,
  firmly packed
  ½ cup **BUTTER FLAVORED**
  SHORTENING or **MARGARINE**
  1 tsp. **VANILLA**
Mix together and add . . . . 1½ cups **FLOUR**
  2 tsp. **BAKING POWDER**
  ½ tsp. **SALT**
  1 cup **PECANS**, chopped

This mixture will be stiff. Spread in greased and floured 13x9x2-inch pan. Bake in preheated 350-degree oven for 25 to 30 minutes or until top is light brown. Cool slightly. Cut into bars. They will be very chewy.

YIELD: 24 BARS.

CHOCOLATE GOLD BARS
These are so rich, but, oh, so good!!

Place in mixing bowl . . . . 1 box **YELLOW CAKE MIX**, dry
  ½ cup **BUTTER** or **MARGARINE**,
  softened
Mix together and add . . . . 2 **EGGS**, slightly beaten
Press ⅔ cake mixture into a greased 13x9x2-inch baking dish.
Cook over medium heat until
  melted . . . . 1 cup **CHOCOLATE CHIPS**
  1 can **SWEETENED CONDENSED**
  MILK
  2 Tbsp. **MARGARINE**
  1 package **COCONUT PECAN**
  FROSTING mix

Pour filling on top of cake mixture. Crumble remaining ⅓ cake mixture on top. Bake at 350-degrees 25 to 30 minutes. Serve hot or cold.

YIELD: 24 BARS.

PAT IN PAN COOKIES

In a large saucepan stir
   together .... 1 cup **KARO SYRUP**, light or
                                  dark
                                  1 cup **SUGAR**
                                  1 cup **PEANUT BUTTER**, creamy
                                  or chunky
Stir constantly, bring to a boil.
   Remove from heat and add .... 6 cups **RICE KRISPIES CEREAL**

Toss to coat well. Press into greased 13x9x2-inch pan. Cut into bars.

YIELD: 15 BARS.

GUESS AGAIN BARS

Combine .... 1¼ cups **FLOUR**
                                  1 cup **BROWN SUGAR**, packed
                                  ½ tsp. **BAKING SODA**
                                  ½ tsp. **SALT**
                                  ½ cup **MARGARINE**, softened
                                  1 tsp. **VANILLA**
                                  1 **EGG**
Mix well with electric mixer on medium speed.
Stir in .... 1 cup **QUICK-COOKING OATS**,
                                  uncooked
                                  ½ cup **COCONUT**
Press into lightly greased 13x9x2-inch pan.
Sprinkle with .... ½ cup **SEMI-SWEET**
                                  CHOCOLATE MORSELS
                                  ½ cup **PECANS**, chopped

Bake at 375-degrees for 15 to 20 minutes. Cool and cut into bars.

YIELD: 18 BARS.

ATTRACTIVE DROPPED COOKIES: Press top with a fork dipped in confectioners sugar. For waffle pattern, press again in opposite direction.

PLAIN OLE BROWNIES
It's hard to improve on a good "old stand-by" recipe.

Cream until fluffy .... ½ cup **SHORTENING**
                                 1 cup **SUGAR**
Add and mix well .... 2 **EGGS**
Add .... 1 square **CHOCOLATE**, melted
Add alternately .... ½ cup **FLOUR**
                                 ¼ cup **MILK**
Then add .... 1½ tsp. **VANILLA**
                                 1 cup **PECANS**, chopped

Cook in greased 9-inch square pan in preheated 350-degree oven for about 20 minutes. **DO NOT OVERCOOK.**

BRENDA'S BANANA COOKIES
Colby, Kipper & Cam's hands are always in the cookie jar.

Cream together .... ¾ cup **SHORTENING**
                                 ¾ cup **SUGAR**
                                 1 **EGG**
                                 ½ tsp. **VANILLA**
                                 2 **BANANAS**, mashed
Beat well and add .... 1 tsp. **SALT**
                                 1 tsp. **SODA**
                                 2 cups **FLOUR**

Drop by teaspoonfuls on a **GREASED** cookie sheet. Bake in preheated oven at 350-degrees for 8 to 10 minutes. Cookies will be soft and puffy. After they are cool, spread with icing.

ICING:
Bring to a boil .... 6 tsp. **BROWN SUGAR**, firmly
                                 packed
                                 4 tsp. **MILK**
                                 4 tsp. **MARGARINE**
Remove from heat and add ...... ½ tsp. **VANILLA**

Add **POWDERED SUGAR** to make into spreading consistency.

"NUTTER" PEANUT BUTTER COOKIES

Cream together in large bowl .... 1 cup **MARGARINE**, melted
1 cup **BROWN SUGAR**, firmly packed
1 cup **WHITE SUGAR**
Add .... 2 cups **PEANUT BUTTER**
2 **EGGS**
2 tsps. **VANILLA**
In another bowl, sift together .... 3 cups **FLOUR**
1 tsp. **SODA**
1 tsp. **BAKING POWDER**

Slowly add flour mixture to dough mixture. Blend well. Pinch into 1-inch balls. Place on lightly greased cookie sheets. Press down with fork. Bake in preheated 350-degree oven for 10 minutes or until lightly browned.

CINNAMON JUMBLES
Brenda makes these for her three boys.

Mix together .... ½ cup **SHORTENING** or **MARGARINE**
1 cup **SUGAR**
1 **EGG**
Then add .... ¾ cup **BUTTERMILK**
1 tsp. **VANILLA**
Blend together and add .... 2 cups **FLOUR**
½ tsp. **SODA**
½ tsp. **SALT**
½ tsp. **CINNAMON**

Chill dough. Using a teaspoon, drop dough on cookie sheet. Bake at 400 degrees for 8 to 10 minutes. **DO NOT BAKE UNTIL BROWN**. These should stay soft for several days. While cookies are hot, sprinkle with mixture of 1 teaspoon **CINNAMON** and ½ cup **SUGAR**.

Store in covered container.

CHOCOLATE TURTLE COOKIES

The cookies really resemble "turtles" and the kids love them.
(They kinda bring out the kid in all of us!)

Have on hand . . . . 8 dozen **PECAN HALVES**
Melt in microwave . . . . ½ cup **SEMI-SWEET CHOCOLATE CHIPS**
⅓ cup **BUTTER** or **MARGARINE**
Stir until smooth. Add . . . . ½ cup **SUGAR**
1 **EGG**
Beat with wooden spoon.
Combine and add . . . . ¾ cup **FLOUR**
½ tsp. **BAKING POWDER**
¼ tsp. **SALT**

Mix well. For each cookie, place 3 pecan halves (with ends touching at center) on cookie sheet. Drop rounded teaspoonfuls batter in center of pecans. Bake 350-degrees for 8-9 minutes. Cool completely and glaze with ¼ teaspoon melted **SEMI-SWEET CHOCOLATE CHIPS**. (About ½ cup).

YIELD: 2½ DOZEN.

DATE SWIRL COOKIES

These were eaten many times in the Gene Eades
home at Christmas time.

Combine . . . . 1 pound **DATES**, chopped
½ cup **SUGAR**
½ cup **WATER**
1 cup **PECANS**, chopped
Cook until thick. Cool.
Cream together . . . . 1 cup **SHORTENING**, do not use oil
1 cup **SUGAR**
1 cup **BROWN SUGAR**, firmly packed
Add . . . . 3 **EGGS**, slightly beaten
4 cups **FLOUR**
1 tsp. **SODA**
1 tsp. **SALT**
1 tsp. **VANILLA**

Chill dough. Divide into 3 or 4 portions. Roll on floured board to about ½-inch thickness. Spread with filling. Roll as jelly roll. Roll in foil or wax paper and store in refrigerator. To bake; slice, and place on ungreased cookie sheet. Bake 350-degrees for 12 to 15 minutes. May cook only 1 roll at a time. Store remainder of dough in refrigerator. Will keep several days.

BUTTER COOKIES
The "melt in your mouth" kind.

Cream well ....   1 cup **MARGARINE**
                         ½ cup **SUGAR**
Add........................   1 **EGG**
                         ½ tsp. **ALMOND FLAVORING**
                         2¼ cups **FLOUR**

Use a cookie press or drop by teaspoonfuls onto an ungreased cookie sheet. Bake in a preheated oven at 350-degrees for 8 to 10 minutes.

YIELD: 4 DOZEN.

PECAN DROP COOKIES

Mix together and set aside ....   1 cup **FLOUR**
                         ⅛ tsp. **CREAM OF TARTAR**
                         ¼ tsp. **SALT**
Cream together ....   ½ cup **MARGARINE**
                         ⅔ cup **LIGHT BROWN SUGAR**, firmly packed
                         1 **EGG YOLK**
Blend both mixtures and add .... ½ cup **PECANS**, chopped

Mix well. Drop by teaspoonfuls on ungreased cookie sheet. Bake at 325 degrees for 12 to 15 minutes.

YIELD: 2 DOZEN.

SKILLET COOKIES

Combine in skillet ....   1 cup **DATES**
                         1 cup **SUGAR**
                         2 Tbsp. **MARGARINE**
                         1 **EGG**
Cook slowly until dates are dissolved, about 10 minutes. Stir constantly with a wooden spoon.
Turn off heat and add .... 1 tsp. **VANILLA**
Fold in ....2½ cups **RICE KRISPIES**
                         1 cup **PECANS**, chopped
While still warm form into balls and roll in .... 1 cup **COCONUT**

Store in covered container.

OLD TIMEY TEA CAKES

*These are good "Grandmaw" cookies. They aren't too sweet
and the little ones can help cut them out in different shapes.*

Cream together	1 cup **MARGARINE** or **SHORTENING**
	1 cup **SUGAR**
	2 **EGGS**
Sift together and add	4 cups **FLOUR**
	1 tsp. **SALT**
	1 tsp. **SODA**
	2 tsp. **CREAM OF TARTAR**
Alternate with	¼ cup **MILK**
Add	1 tsp. **VANILLA**

Mix well and knead on a floured board. Roll as thin as you like. A little
flour may be added to make rolling easier. Traditionally, tea cakes are cut
round but may be cut with any cookie cutter. Place on ungreased cookie
sheet. Bake until light brown at 350-degrees, about 12 to 14 minutes.

VARIATION:
Omit **VANILLA** and add 2 teaspoons **ALMOND EXTRACT**.

NIEMAN-MARCUS COOKIES

The Chocoholic's cookie.

Blend to a fine powder and set aside	2½ cups **OATMEAL**
Cream together	1 cup **MARGARINE**
	1 cup **SUGAR**
	1 cup **BROWN SUGAR,** firmly packed
Add	2 **EGGS**
	2 tsp. **VANILLA**
Mix together and add to creamed mixture	2 cups **FLOUR**
	½ tsp. **SALT**
	1 tsp. **BAKING SODA**
	1 tsp. **BAKING POWDER**
Add	1 pkg. (12 oz.) **CHOCOLATE CHIPS**
	1 (4 oz.) **HERSHEY BAR**, grated
	2 cups **PECANS**, chopped

Roll into balls and place two inches apart on a cookie sheet. Bake 10 to
12 minutes at 375-degrees.

UNDERCOVER KISSES

In electric mixer, cream . . . .   1 cup **MARGARINE**, softened
                                ½ cup **SUGAR**
                                  1 tsp **VANILLA**
                                  1¾ cup **FLOUR**
                                  1 cup **PECANS**, finely chopped

Chill dough for 1 hour. Mold 1 Tbsp. dough around an unwrapped **CANDY KISS**. Roll to make a ball. Cover candy completely with dough. Place on cookie sheet. Bake 12 to 15 minutes 350-degrees or until cookies are set but not brown. When slightly cool, roll in **CONFEC-TIONERS' SUGAR**. Store in tightly covered container. (You may want to roll in sugar the second time before storing). NOTE: Cook while dough is still cold and they will keep shape better.

YIELD: 36 COOKIES.

COCONUT THUMBPRINT COOKIES
Lickin' good!!!!

In large mixing bowl cream . . . . . .   ½ cup **MARGARINE**
                                  ½ cup **SUGAR**
Add and beat . . . .   1 **EGG YOLK**
                                  1 tsp. **VANILLA**
Combine and add . . . .   ¾ cup **FLOUR**
                                  ¼ tsp. **SALT**
                                  ¼ tsp. **BAKING POWDER**
Blend well. Form into 1-inch balls.
Dip balls into . . . .   1 **EGG WHITE,** beaten until frothy
Then roll in . . . .   ⅔ cup **COCONUT**

Place on greased baking sheet. Make shallow depression in center of each cookie with thumb. Spoon ½ tsp. **STRAWBERRY PRESERVES** into each. Bake at 375-degrees in preheated oven for 8 to 9 minutes or until coconut begins to brown.

YIELD: 24 COOKIES.

VARIATION:
May use any flavor **PRESERVES**, **JAM** or **JELLY**.

PECAN CRISPIE COOKIES
Nell keeps the cookie jar full for Brad, Wade and Kyle.

Cream together . . . . ½ cup **SHORTENING**
½ cup **MARGARINE**
2½ cups **BROWN SUGAR**,
firmly packed
Add . . . . 2 **EGGS**, well beaten
Sift together and add . . . . 2½ cups **FLOUR**
¼ tsp. **SALT**
½ tsp. **SODA**
Fold in . . . . 1 cup **PECANS**

Drop by teaspoonfuls about 2 inches apart on greased cookie sheet. Bake at 350-degrees for 12 to 15 minutes.

PEANUT BUTTER MOGUL TREATS
Becky says this is an energy booster for that long day on the slopes.

Boil 30 seconds . . . . 1 cup **KARO**
1 cup **SUGAR**
Add . . . . 1 cup **PEANUT BUTTER**
Stir in . . . . 4 cups **PLAIN CAPTAIN CRUNCH CEREAL**

Drop onto waxed paper in small mounds. Let cool. Store in air-tight container. You may use microwave for this one.

LOUISE'S CRACKER CREATIONS

Spread . . . . 20 **BETTER CHEDDAR CRACKERS**
Lightly with . . . . **PEANUT BUTTER**
Top with another . . . . 20 **BETTER CHEDDAR CRACKERS**
Melt . . . . 8 oz. **ALMOND BARK**

Dip crackers in almond bark. Shake off excess. Lay on wax paper and chill.

NOTE:
Use the miniature cheese crackers for parties.

PUPPY CHOW
A reunion delight by Gay Kimmel.

Melt together in microwave or
   double boiler................ ½ cup **MARGARINE**
                      1 cup **PEANUT BUTTER**
                      1 pkg. (12 oz.) **CHOCOLATE CHIPS**
Stir to mix. Pour over .... 1 box (17 oz.) **CRISPEX CEREAL**
Measure into a large plastic
   bag........................ 3 cups **POWDERED SUGAR**

Add coated cereal mixture. Gently work plastic bag back and forth several times until cereal separates and is coated well. This keeps well and will freeze.

MICROWAVE PEANUT BRITTLE
Ruth makes this often.

Combine in 2-quart glass bowl ... 1 cup **SUGAR**
                      ½ cup light **CORN SYRUP**
Mix well. Microwave on high 4 minutes.
Stir in .... 1½ cups **PEANUTS**, salted
Microwave 4 more minutes.
Add .... 1 tsp. **MARGARINE**
                      1 tsp. **VANILLA**
Add, and stir until foamy........ ¼ tsp. **SODA**
Microwave 2 minutes.

Pour into a buttered cookie sheet and spread very thin. Cool for half an hour. Store in airtight container.

CHOCOLATE MINT CREMES

Melt in microwave .... 2 cups **MILK CHOCOLATE CHIPS**
Stir until smooth. Add .... ¼ cup **SOUR CREAM**
                      2½ Tbsp. **MINT FLAVORED LIQUEUR**

Chill until thick. (About 30 minutes.) Fill pastry bag with decorative tip. Pipe 1-inch candies onto foil-lined cookie sheets. Chill until ready to serve. Optional: drop by teaspoonfuls and roll in finely chopped nuts.

YIELD: 3½ DOZEN.

CHOCOLATE SPIDERS
Try this for a Halloween party.

Melt in microwave ....1½ cups **SEMISWEET CHOCOLATE CHIPS**
Stir in .... 1 can (5 oz.) **CHOW MEIN NOODLES**
1 cup **SALTED PEANUTS**

Stir well and drop on greased baking sheets. Refrigerate several hours.

YIELD: 3 DOZEN.

MOTHER'S SAND TARTS
"More, more, the cookie jar is empty."

Cream together .... 1 cup **MARGARINE**
5 Tbsp. **POWDERED SUGAR**
Add .... 2 cups **FLOUR**
2 tsp. **VANILLA**
1 cup **PECANS**, chopped

Mix, roll out and cut in half moon shape or round. Bake at 300-degrees until brown. While still hot, roll in powdered sugar.

YIELD: 5 DOZEN COOKIES.

DOOLIE'S GRECIAN ISLAND CHRISTMAS GOODIES
Much creamier than Pralines.

Place in a heavy skillet and
   brown lightly .... ¼ cup **MARGARINE**
1 cup **NUTS**
In medium saucepan cook
   together for 4 minutes........ ½ cup **WHITE KARO**
2½ cups **SUGAR**
½ cup **MILK**

Add browned **NUTS**, 1 tsp. **VANILLA**, 2 drops **ALMOND FLAVORING** and beat until creamy. Drop by teaspoonfuls onto greased waxed paper and allow to cool. Candy can be wrapped in separate pieces in plastic wrap and store in can or jar. Keeps well.

TIGER BUTTER
Kids love it!!

Combine in microwave proof
    bowl .... 1 pound **WHITE CHOCOLATE**
                        1 jar (12 oz.) **CHUNKY PEANUT
                                 BUTTER**
Heat just until melted. Mix well. Spread mixture onto a waxed paper-
lined jellyroll pan.
Melt in microwave .... 1 pound **SEMI-SWEET
                                 CHOCOLATE**

Pour over peanut butter mixture to resemble tiger. Swirl through with a
knife to look like stripes. Chill until firm. Cut into 1½x1-inch pieces.
Store in refrigerator.

VARIATION:
White **ALMOND BARK** may be substituted for white chocolate.

PECAN CLUSTERS

Melt in 15x10x1-inch pan .... 3 Tbsp. **MARGARINE**
Spread evenly in pan .... 3 cups **PECAN PIECES**
Bake at 300-degrees for 30 minutes, stirring every 10 minutes.
Melt in top of double boiler or
    microwave.................. ¾ lb. **CHOCOLATE** or **ALMOND
                                 BARK**

Add pecans, stir until well coated. Drop by teaspoonfuls onto waxed
paper. Cool.

YIELD: 3½ DOZEN.

*QUICKIE TREATS: Melt almond bark or chocolate for
dipping candies. One pound will take about 2 minutes,
stirring twice. If it hardens while dipping, microwave a
few seconds more.*

CREAM CHEESE CANDY

Roast 2 cups **PECANS** in 3 Tbsp. **MARGARINE** for 15 minutes in a 350-degree oven. Cool.

Cream together . . . .   8 ounces **CREAM CHEESE**
                                   1 pound **CONFECTIONERS' SUGAR**

Add pecans and mix well. Pat into pan. Let set for 1 hour. Slice.

HONEY-NUT FUDGE
This is Charlie's favorite. (Mary Louder's "Honey.")

Combine in saucepan . . . .   2 cups **SUGAR**
                                   1 cup **MILK**
                                 1 square **CHOCOLATE**

Boil to soft ball stage. (235-degrees on candy thermometer.) Remove from heat.

Add . . . . ¼ cup **HONEY**

Return to heat and cook to soft ball stage again.
Remove from heat and beat until slightly cool.

Add . . . .   2 Tbsp. **BUTTER** or **MARGARINE**
                                   1 tsp. **VANILLA**
                                   1 cup **NUTS**, chopped

Mix well and pour into a buttered dish. Cool and cut into squares.

SURPRISE! SURPRISE!

Keep **TOFFEE CANDY BARS** in the freezer with **ICE CREAM**. When unexpected guests arrive, or you want a quick dessert for the family spoon alternate layers of **ICE CREAM** and **TOFFEE CANDY** (frozen and crushed), into parfait glasses. Top with 1 to 2 Tbsp. **KAHLUA** or other **COFFEE-FLAVORED LIQUEUR**.

HEAVENLY CHOCOLATE SAUCE

This makes ice cream even more special.

Melt together in saucepan . . . .   ½ cup **MARGARINE**
4 (1 oz. each) **UNSWEETENED SQUARES CHOCOLATE**
3 cups **SUGAR**
½ tsp. **SALT**
1 can (13 oz.) **EVAPORATED MILK**

When sugar is melted, place in jars and refrigerate. May be heated in microwave to serve hot. Will keep for weeks.

YIELD: 4 CUPS.

LETA'S APRICOT SAUCE

Serve over LEMON or ORANGE SHERBET.

Melt in microwave safe dish or
  double boiler . . . .   2 Tbsp. **BUTTER**
Add and stir until smooth . . . .   1 Tbsp. **CORNSTARCH**
¼ cup **SUGAR**
1 Tbsp. **LEMON JUICE**
Gradually add . . . .   1 can (12 oz.) **APRICOT NECTAR**

Microwave on **HIGH** until thickened. Stir every 1 to 2 minutes. Remove cover and let stand for 5 minutes. (Optional: May add ½ of a small can of **APRICOTS** that have been pureed in blender.)

JEZEBEL SAUCE
Bertha Brewer gives this as gifts.

Mix well . . . . 1 jar (16 oz.) **PINEAPPLE PRESERVES**
1 jar (16 oz.) **APPLE JELLY**
½ small can (1 oz.) **DRY MUSTARD**
1 small jar **HORSERADISH**
1 Tbsp. **BLACK PEPPER**

Pour into small jars and refrigerate. Delicious served with **PORK, ROAST BEEF**, or **TURKEY.**

GOLDIE'S BAKED APPLES
These have been prepared for Henry many times.

Wash, dry and core
(do not peel) . . . . 6 **SOUR APPLES**
Place in buttered square pan. Place them so they will stand up straight.
Mix . . . . 1 cup **SUGAR**
½ cup **MARGARINE**

Fill apple holes with mixture. Spread left over mixture on top of apples. Pour ½ cup **WATER** in bottom of pan. Bake at 350-degrees until apples are tender but do not cook apart. (Note: Sour apples must be used in order for the juice to congeal.)

THELMA'S STRAWBERRY PRESERVES
Delicious!!

Bring to a boil in large
saucepan . . . . 2 cups **SUGAR**
5 Tbsp. **WATER**
Add . . . . 2 cups **STRAWBERRIES**, crushed
Boil for 10 minutes.
Add . . . . 2 cups **SUGAR**
2 cups **STRAWBERRIES**, whole
1 Tbsp. **VINEGAR**

Boil 10 minutes more. Pour in hot sterilized jars. Skim off foam and seal.

FRUIT BUTTER
Ann Whiteside shared this with us.

Beat together . . . . ½ cup **MARGARINE**, softened
1 jar (18 oz.) **MARMALADE**

Mix well and store in refrigerator in a sealed container. Very good on toast, biscuits, pancakes or waffles. Keeps indefinitely.

VARIATION:
May use **STRAWBERRY** or **APRICOT PRESERVES** or add 1 cup **RASPBERRY PRESERVES** to the **MARMALADE**.

NUT'N CRACKERS
Great for snacks.

Mix together . . . . ¾ cup **OIL**
1 pkg. **ORIGINAL HIDDEN VALLEY SALAD DRESSING MIX**, dry
¼ tsp. **LEMON PEPPER**
½ tsp. **DILL WEED**
¼ tsp. **GARLIC POWDER**
Pour over . . . . 2 pkg. (20 oz. ea.) **OYSTER CRACKERS**
1 jar (8 oz.) **DRY ROASTED PEANUTS**

Stir to coat crackers. Microwave on high for 3 minutes stirring after 1½ minutes, or may warm in 250-degree oven for 15 minutes. Store in covered container.

TONI'S CINNAMON CHEX
A healthy snack for after school.

Mix together . . . . 2 cups **CORN CHEX CEREAL**
2 cups **BRAND CHEX CEREAL**
2 cups **WHEAT CHEX CEREAL**
2 cups **LIFE CEREAL**
2 cups **PEANUTS** or **PECANS**
Mix together and pour
over cereal . . . . ½ cup **MARGARINE**, melted
1 tsp. cinnamon

Stir and spread on cookie sheet. Bake at 200-degrees for 45 minutes. Stir every 15 minutes. Store in covered container.

VARIATIONS:
May substitute other cereals.

PARTY POPPIN' CORN QUICKIES
Nutritious snacking

SOUTH-OF-THE-BORDER POPCORN

Have ready	10	cups **POPPED CORN**
In sauce pan melt..............	4	ounces **MARGARINE**
Add and stir until smooth	1	cup **MONTEREY JACK CHEESE**, grated
	1	cup **COLBY CHEESE**
Stir in	2	tsp. **TACO SEASONING MIX**.

Toss to mix. A tasty addition to any party.

NACHO POPCORN:
Melt in microwave oven ¼ cup **MARGARINE** mixed with 1 Tablespoon **TACO SEASONING MIX**. Drizzle over 10 cups **POPCORN** then add ½ cup **CHEDDAR CHEESE**, grated. Microwave on **HIGH** 30 to 60 seconds until cheese begins to melt.

RANCH POPCORN:
Melt ¼ cup **MARGARINE** with 1 Tablespoon **RANCH-TYPE PARTY DIP**. Drizzle over 10 cups **POPPED CORN**. Toss with 2 Tablespoons **PARMESAN CHEESE**.

PIZZA-POPCORN:
Combine in a bowl, 2 tablespoons grated **PARMESAN CHEESE**, 1 teaspoon **GARLIC SALT**, 1 teaspoon **ITALIAN HERB SEASONING** and 1 teaspoon **PAPRIKA**. Sprinkle over 10 cups **POPCORN**, toss to coat evenly. Store in air-tight container.

POPCORN NIBBLES:
Mix with 10 cups **POPCORN**; ¾ cup **SUNFLOWER SEED** and ½ cup **SLIVERED ALMONDS**. Combine and melt together ¼ cup **HONEY**, ¼ cup **BROWN SUGAR** and ¼ cup **MARGARINE**. Pour over popcorn and stir. Microwave on **HIGH** uncovered 4 to 5 minutes until lightly toasted, stirring 4 to 5 times. Turn onto a baking sheet and allow to cool. Store in covered container.

CINNAMON POPCORN:
Melt ⅓ cup **MARGARINE** drizzle over 10 cups **POPPED CORN**. Mix ¼ cup **SUGAR** with 2 teaspoons **CINNAMON**. Sprinkle popcorn. Bake in preheated 350-degree oven for 3 to 5 minutes to set coating.

FRUIT FLAVORED POPCORN:
Toss 10 cups **POPCORN** with one 3 ounce package **FRUIT FLAVORED GELATIN** or ¼ favorite flavor powdered **SUGAR FREE SOFT-DRINK MIX**. Bake in 350-degree oven for 3 to 5 minutes to set coating. Or it may be microwaved on 80% power for 1½ minutes.

continued

MICROWAVE CARMEL CORN:
Combine ½ cup packed **BROWN SUGAR**, ¼ cup **MARGARINE**, 2 Tablespoons **LIGHT CORN SYRUP** and ¼ tsp. **SALT**. Microwave in large glass bowl on **HIGH** 1½ minutes, or until mixture boils, stirring once. Stir and continue to microwave on **HIGH** 2½ minutes. Stir in ⅛ tsp. **SODA**. Pour syrup over 10 cups **POPPED CORN** and stir. Microwave on 30% power uncovered for 6 to 7 minutes or until lightly toasted. Stir every 2 minutes to prevent scorching.

POPCORN CRUNCH

Mix together in large bowl . . . .   3 quarts popped **POPCORN**
                                          1 cup **NUTS**, your choice
Mix and heat until well blended
  (may use microwave) . . . .   ½ cup **MARGARINE**
                                          ½ cup **HONEY**

Pour over popcorn mixture. Mix well. Spread over cookie sheet in thin layer. Bake in preheated 350-degree oven for 10 to 15 minutes or until crisp.

SAMPLERS TEA MIX
The sugar-free ingredients make it more appealing.

Mix in large bowl . . . .   1 cup **INSTANT TEA**
                                               1½ cups **SUGAR-FREE TANG**
                                               1½ cups **SUGAR SUBSTITUTE**
                                               ½ cup **SUGAR-FREE LEMONADE MIX**
                                               ¼ cup **SUGAR**
                                               ½ tsp. **CINNAMON**
                                               ¼ tsp. **GROUND CLOVES**

Store in an air-tight container in a dry place. To serve, place 2 heaping teaspoonfuls in each cup. Fill with very hot **WATER**.

BESS BIELER'S "SHAKE, RATTLE, AND ROLL" KAHLUA
Liquers with your own kitchen label.
What a keen Christmas gift.

Boil 10 minutes .... 4 cups **SUGAR**
4 cups **WATER**
Cool and add.................. ¾ cup **INSTANT COFFEE**
1 **VANILLA BEAN** crushed
1 fifth **VODKA** or 1½ pints
GRAIN ALCOHOL

Pour into bottles. Let stand 3 weeks. *SHAKE, RATTLE, and ROLL, DAILY.*

VARIATION:
To make **CREME DE COCOA**, substitute 2 ounces **COCOA** for the coffee.

"SHAKE, RATTLE, AND ROLL" AMARETTO
Use a drop or two of red, blue, and yellow coloring
if you wish the liquer to be brown.

Combine in saucepan .... 4 cups **SUGAR**
3 cups **WATER**
Stir over high heat until **SUGAR** dissolves and reaches boiling point.
Reduce heat and *simmer* for 1 hour. Remove from heat.
Stir in .... 2½ cups **VODKA**
1½ ounces **ALMOND FLAVORING**

Cool and bottle. *SHAKE, RATTLE, and ROLL* daily for three weeks.

Note: Both recipes can be made for about one-third the cost of purchased liquors.

SPICED PECANS

Combine and cook to soft ball
   stage, stirring constantly ...... 1 cup **SUGAR**
1 tsp. **SALT**
½ tsp. **NUTMEG**
½ tsp. **CLOVES**
2 tsp. **CINNAMON**
½ cup **WATER**

Remove from heat. Add ½ pound **PECANS**. Stir until pecans are evenly coated. Pour out onto waxed paper. Cool and separate.

HOT PECANS

Melt in a shallow pan . . . . ¼ cup **BUTTER**
Spread evenly in pan . . . . 2 cups **PECAN HALVES**
Bake 30 minutes at 300 degrees.
Combine and toss with pecans . . . 4 tsp. **SOY SAUCE**
                                     1 tsp. **SALT**
                                 12 drops **TABASCO**

Drain on paper towels. Let cool and serve.

BROWNED PECANS
Another recipe using our native fruit, PECANS.

SALT . . . . 4 cups **PECAN HALVES**
Drizzle over **PECANS** . . . . 6 Tbsp. **BUTTER**, melted
                                   Do not subsititute.

Single layer pecans on a cookie sheet and bake at 450-degrees for 5 to 6 minutes. Cool and serve.

WINE-LIME JELLY
Add zest to turkey or ham.

Mix in saucepan. . . . . 1 box **SURE JELL**
                                   1½ cups **WHITE WINE**
                                   6 ounces **WATER**
                                   ½ cup **LIME JUICE**
                                   2 drops **GREEN FOOD COLORING**
Cook on high heat until bubbly
   around edge. Add and stir
   well . . . . .3¾ cups **SUGAR**

Continue cooking until bubbly around edge again. Remove from heat. Skim foam off top. Pour into sterilized jars.

YIELD: 6 MEDIUM JELLY JARS

VARIATION:
For Christmas gifts, pour jelly into brandy snifters. Cover with Saran wrap. Tie with ribbon.

JOYCE'S PICKLED OKRA
These are pretty as a picture.

Select young tender pods of . . . . .   **OKRA**
Pack in sterilized jars and add to   1 clove **GARLIC**
each pint . . . .   1 **HOT PEPPER**
  ½ tsp. **DILL SEED**
Make a solution of . . . .   4 cups **VINEGAR**
  1 cup **WATER**
  ½ cup **SALT**

Bring vinegar mixture to a boil and pour over the okra. Seal and let set several weeks before opening.

VARIATION:
May use small **GREEN TOMATOES** instead of the **OKRA**.

TEXAS JALAPENO JELLY

In food processor or blender,
grind . . . .   1 pound **GREEN BELL PEPERS**
  ¼ pound **FRESH JALAPENO PEPPERS**
Place in saucepan and add . . . . . . 5½ cups **SUGAR**
  1¼ cups **WHITE VINEGAR**
Bring to boil, cook for 5 minutes,
stirring constantly. Add . . . .   ⅓ cup **LEMON JUICE**
Return to boil. Add . . . .   1 bottle (6 oz.) **CERTO**
Boil for 1 minute.

Pour into four 6-ounce sterile jelly jars. Store approximately two weeks before using. This jelly complements almost any kind of meat, and can be served with cream cheese for breakfast or for hors d'oeuvres.

METRIC SYSTEM

Measuring cups will most likely show both ounces and grams or cups (and their fractions) and milliliters:

1 cup	=	*250 milliliters (ml)*
1/4 cup	=	*62 1/2 ml*
1 teaspoon	=	*5 ml*
1 tablespoon	=	*15 ml*
1 pint	=	*0.47 liter (1)*
1 quart	=	*0.95 l*
1 gallon	=	*3.8 l*
1 liter	=	*2.1 pint*
1 liter	=	*1.06 quart*
1 liter	=	*0.26 gallon*

Index

Jan-Su Publications
1012 North 9th
Lamesa, Texas 79331
Phone 806-872-8667

Please send me _____ copies of
   MORE CALF FRIES TO CAVIAR @ $16.95 each   _____
Please send me _____ copies of
   CALF FRIES TO CAVIAR @ $16.95 each   _____
Postage and Handling @ $3.00 (per book)   _____
Please send me _____ copies of
   'CROSS THE BORDER @ $8.95 each   _____
Postage and Handling @ $2.00 per book   _____
Texas residents add appropriate tax   _____
Gift Wrap @ $2.50 per book   _____

                                                 TOTAL _____

Name: _____

Address: _____

City: _____ State: _____ Zip: _____

No C.O.D.'s   Make check payable to Jan Su
                      *Prices subject to change

- -

Jan-Su Publications
1012 North 9th
Lamesa, Texas 79331
Phone 806-872-8667

Please send me _____ copies of
   MORE CALF FRIES TO CAVIAR @ $16.95 each   _____
Please send me _____ copies of
   CALF FRIES TO CAVIAR @ $16.95 each   _____
Postage and Handling @ $3.00 (per book)   _____
Please send me _____ copies of
   'CROSS THE BORDER @ $8.95 each   _____
Postage and Handling @ $2.00 per book   _____
Texas residents add appropriate tax   _____
Gift Wrap @ $2.50 per book   _____

                                                 TOTAL _____

Name: _____

Address: _____

City: _____ State: _____ Zip: _____

No C.O.D.'s   Make check payable to Jan Su
                      *Prices subject to change

Reorder Additional Copies